IN GOOD COMPANY

In Good Company
Paul du Feu

A Story in Black & White

Kay Mann,
Craigpark,
Ardrie Rd,
Caldercruix,
by Airdrie

MAINSTREAM
PUBLISHING
EDINBURGH AND LONDON

First published in Great Britain 1991 by
MAINSTREAM PUBLISHING COMPANY (EDINBURGH) LTD
7 Albany Street
Edinburgh EH1 3UG

ISBN 1 85158 384 X

A catalogue record for this book is available from the British Library

Typeset in 10/11½ Times
Reproduced from disc by Polyprint, 48 Pleasance, Edinburgh, EH8 9TJ
Printed and bound in Great Britain by Billing & Sons Ltd, Worcester

In fond memory of Vivian Baxter,
a good companion.

CONTENTS

CHAPTER ONE

LONDON: SUMMER 1972

As we strolled down Sloane Street on the first date passers-by stared at us with open curiosity. I started to apologise for my fellow citizens' bad manners but Maya just laughed. 'You can't blame them for looking twice. We're an interesting looking couple. Let's move on to more fascinating topics, tell me all about yourself.'

I hesitated. As she turned to watch me her eyes were dancing with mischievous amusement. 'I talked to Sonia Orwell today . . . she knows all about you. She says you're rather notorious but "not exactly top drawer".'

'I'm not sure what particular part of what particular item of household furniture I am, but my notoriety came and went. Just a couple of days of newspaper trivia.'

'That wasn't quite Sonia's version . . . are you still married to Germaine Greer?'

'Legally.'

'Are you friends?'

'Hard to say exactly. We run into each other once in a while and crack a joke or two.'

'Nothing more than that?'

'We don't go to bed. If that's what you're asking.'

Maya chuckled. 'Nothing was further from my mind.' Her voice dripped histrionic insincerity.

We turned west down King's Road. 'Tell me more. What do you do?'

9

'Spring till the first frosts I usually do construction work.'

'And then what . . . skiing in Switzerland?' She was grinning.

'No. Usually I go to southern Spain or North Africa and do my year's quota of hack writing. Short, cold days are miserable for the building trades.'

'What do you write?'

'Mostly comic strip adventures, a few short stories, articles. Whatever anyone will pay me to write.'

She looked pointedly at my denim work jacket. 'Have you been building today?'

'No, I'm not working right now. Well, I'm supposed to be writing a book but it's not due till next summer.'

'So what did you do today?'

'Let me see. I woke early, read the newspapers, thought about writing my book. I find the morning is the best time to think about writing. Then it was almost eleven so I dressed and caught the train to Fleet Street and spent a long lunchtime in the pubs talking with journalist friends who were thinking about writing their copy. When the pubs closed I visited an old friend in from New York, a rock and roll journalist who's thinking about writing an updated edition of a pop music encyclopaedia she wrote a few years back. Then it was time to go home and think about getting dressed for our dinner date.'

She laughed and looked pointedly at my jacket again. 'Did it take long? Thinking about what to wear?'

'Quite a time. One has to weigh the pros and cons. First impressions on a first date are all important.'

'I'll let that pass.'

Once we were settled in the restaurant Maya started to look around at the variegated attire of the other diners. 'People really do dress every which way in Chelsea.'

'There's a long tradition of tolerance. They even let people in wearing suits and ties. Anything goes.'

As I picked up the menu I noticed her eyes focus on the bleached-out, threadbare cuffs of my jacket. She seemed about to say something but changed her mind.

'I talked about *you* today with Lillian Roxon. She's the rock and roll journalist. She said that your autobiography was destined to be an American classic and that you were "riveting on television". She also said you had been a club singer at one time and she *thought* you had made a record a few years back, "Calypso/Blues style. School of Belafonte".'

Maya nodded. 'Close enough. Anything else?'

'You've written some songs, "average music, better than average lyrics" . . . oh, and she told me you're Black.'

She chuckled. 'Are you close friends with her?'

'Not close but we meet up when she's in town. She showed me round the town when I was in New York. Took me to a Jackson Five concert. Amazing. Five kids like stair steps. That must be an interesting household. Anyway, Lillian and I got friendly after Germaine Greer stormed out of our ten-minute marriage. She and Germaine don't get along. Germaine once called her a fat cow . . . constructive criticism in the spirit of Sisterhood, of course, but Lillian bears some animus nonetheless.'

She smiled. 'I wonder why . . . Sonia described you as a working-class hero type. Is that a political stance?'

'No. That's just drinking too much and losing fights in bars. Politically I'm hard line.'

'Hard-line what?'

'Hard-line apathy.'

'Really? What exactly do hard-line apathetics do?'

'We're a major political force. We make our absence felt.'

'I've never heard of you.'

'Exactly. I'll tell you a story to illustrate my point. When there's a general election here the TV news programmes stay on all night. They keep updating the voting count as the returns come in. Rather dull, but to fill in the time they get some political pundits in to analyse the trends, predict the future of the Common Market, etc. Rather dull too. Well, last election a friend of mine who produces a news programme invited me to join the pundits as a spokesperson for apathy. He was trying to push a few easy quid my way but I already had my beer money for the week so I stuck to my principles. I declined his invitation but suggested that he set out an empty chair in the studio and explain to the viewers that it was reserved for the Apathy spokesperson who had not bothered to show up.'

'Did he do it?'

I stared at her with blank incomprehension. '*I* don't know, I didn't bother to watch the programme.'

'That, I believe, is what's known as a shaggy dog story.' She was focusing on my frayed cuffs again.

11

I felt I owed her an explanation. 'There's a story about this jacket.'

'A hundred by the look of it. Is this another shaggy dog?'

'No, this is a human interest story. I bought it in a flea market for five pounds.'

'That much?'

'It was a bargain. It's imported. There's nowhere in England you can buy denim half as heavy as this.'

'Honey, if you're doing twenty-five to life in San Quentin the State of California will *give* you a *brand new* jacket like that . . . free.'

I shook my head. '*Free* is okay but *new* doesn't get it. Too stiff, too blue. It takes a hundred washes in a heavy-handed laundry to get this colour and texture.'

'Is that the story?'

'No. The first time I wore it I was having a drink in a wine bar about a long stone's throw from where we are now. An elegantly-dressed woman at the bar kept looking over at me. After a while she came over to my table.'

'You were alone?'

'No, I was with another chap.'

'Go on.'

'She said . . . exact words . . . "You are wearing the hottest jacket in town".'

'Is this a fantasy story?'

'God's honest truth.'

'Go on.'

'She offered to buy it off my back for forty pounds.'

'Off your back! Her words?' I nodded. 'Well you obviously turned down her offer. Let me guess what happened next.' Maya fluttered her eyelids and did a fair imitation of a seductive Englishwoman. 'She said, "Call me if you change your mind" and then she gave you her phone number.'

'No.'

'No?'

'She gave me her business card. She was a buyer for Escalade.'

'That chrome and neon clothes store on Knightsbridge?' I nodded. 'She was hitting on you honey. You don't know?'

'It crossed my mind.'

'Have you called her?'

'I think I will tomorrow.' I helped myself to a generous slug of red wine and waited for her full attention. 'I'll find out if she still wants to buy it. No reasonable offer refused. I have no further use for it since it obviously does not meet with your approval.'

She smiled. 'Prettily said, sir, but let me give you fresh perspective. Black Americans have been wearing nothing but worn-out work clothes for too long out of necessity to enjoy wearing them from choice. We like to dress up, get a little pizzazz going when we hit the streets.'

I glanced at the full-length mink coat draped over the back of her chair. 'So I see. But there's another perspective too. I'm not a Black American . . .'

We lingered over dinner and a couple of bottles of wine, then several after-dinner drinks. As we turned back up Sloane Street I was rolling like a matelot first day ashore after sailing half round the world aboard a four-master. Maya was as rigid as an iron beam with legs, and goblins were hovering around her. A few drinks more than I need stir up the bats in my belfry too. When we got back to her apartment our moods were turning stormy.

Neither then nor later have I been able to reconstruct or recall the events and words that led up to what happened but Maya hit me with a roundhouse right that made my ears ring. It cleared my head a little. We stared at each other.

'Shall I call you again?'

She nodded, murmured 'Goodnight' and closed the door in my face.

I walked west, back along King's Road until I was ready to cross the river. That was my point of decision, my last chance to get a taxi ride. Once I was on the other side of the Thames, the shabby streets of South London would be empty. It was a clear, starry night and I decided to walk the rest of the way. I turned south and struck out towards the Albert Bridge. As I threaded my way south and west towards Wandsworth Common I recognised landmarks of my childhood and the street names had a familiar ring . . . but it was more than twenty years since they had been my familiar streets. Pleasant reverie made the miles slip by unnoticed.

The house was quiet. I let myself in noiselessly and went down to the kitchen/dining-room in the basement to brew a pot of tea. I was pensive at the big dining-table when Mary ambled into the room. Mary was a Fleet Street journalist but she had grown up on a ranch in Western Australia and had never lost her cowgirl swagger.

'Evening, sweetie, haven't seen you for a couple of days. What have you been up to?'

'Not too much. Hope I didn't wake you?'

She shook her head. 'I was upstairs working. Any tea left in the pot?' I nodded. She poured herself a cup and joined me at the table.

'You know, Maar, I used to play cricket against an elm tree right across the road, fifty yards from where we're sitting.' She nodded. 'In 1944 a V2 rocket dug a crater in the far corner of the green, right where the little alley starts. It didn't explode. I watched the bomb disposal squad.' She nodded. 'I've been living in your house here for a year and this is the first time I've thought about that. Best part of thirty years and here I am right in the same place.' She nodded.

'If this is going to be a "meaning of life" discussion I'm going to get us a bottle of wine.' She brought wine and tumblers to the table.

'This isn't a "meaning of life" discussion.'

'No? Well, let's drink the wine, anyway. Let me see; you're suffering from profound thoughts although you're not noticeably drunk. You're fairly recently shaved, you're wearing your best jacket, and your shoes are polished. I also happen to know that Alison was out with her husband tonight. Individually, none of these facts would be significant but . . . put them all together and the conclusion is inescapable: you've met a new lady.' I nodded. 'Tell me about her. I like her already. Anyone's got to be a vast improvement on Awful Alison.'

For several months I had been having a desultory affair with another Australian journalist whom Mary heartily detested.

'Is she Australian?'

'American.'

'Really? Does this mean your Australian period is over?'

'Maybe so.'

'Well no one can say you didn't give the sheilas a fair do. What's the tally? One wife, two . . . three girlfriends. We had our chances at you. Does she live here?' I shook my head. 'Is she married?'

'I don't know.'

'How old is she?'

'I don't know.'

'What's her name?'

'Maya Angelou.'

'Angelo . . . Italian descent?'

'No. She's Black.'

'Oh my God! Don't bring her to this house! . . . Derek will fall hopelessly in love and my marriage will be down the drain. What does she do?'

'She's a writer.'

'Another one. You just don't know how to quit, do you? Is she published here?'

'No. In America.'

'What's she written?'

'An autobiographical memoir about growing up in the rural South.'

'What's the title?'

'I don't know.'

'How do you spell her name?'

'I don't know.'

'How do you spell *your* name? . . . Hullo! . . . that was a trick question. It's a good thing you don't have to earn your living as a journalist. You'd be even worse than Awful Alison . . . although better looking, of course. Do you remember by any chance where you *met* her?'

'Just like it was yesterday. We met at Anthony Sheil's wine and cheese bash.'

'That *was* yesterday. And you took her out tonight. That's the way. Pursue her. It works every time. How did the date go?'

'Pretty well for a while but it got stormy at the end.'

'Better stormy than boring.'

'She belted me round the chops.'

'Good for her. Sounds like a sheila after my own heart.'

'It sort of leaves the future in doubt.'

'Nonsense. Take her to lunch. Take her flowers. Hang tough. Faint heart never won fair lady. Or dark lady in your case.'

Derek shuffled in blinking himself awake. He was wearing an ornately patterned silk dressing-gown that made him look like a clean-shaven Abe Lincoln playing in a Noel Coward farce. 'Oo roo, mate. Thought I heard voices.' He glanced at the diminished contents of the wine bottle and brought another one to the table. 'Yes, what was I saying? Oh yes, sorry I couldn't make the literary bash yesterday. Last-minute job. Waste of bloody time as it turned out. Yes. Did you go?'

'He met a new lady there.'

'Oh, great.' He yawned.

'So that's the end of Awful Alison,' said Mary.

'Not necessarily.' He yawned again. 'Anyway, who is she etc?'

'She's an American writer, that's about all he knows. I've already interviewed him.'

'Better looking than Alison?'

'Of course she is, lamby bear. Alison is just good make-up and expensive clothes.'

'Get real, Maar. Alison is fucking gorgeous. Not the best journo in the world, but one of the best looking.'

I cut in before the marital sparring turned into a fifteen-round title fight. 'She's very beautiful, in a different way.'

'The lady's Black,' said Mary.

'Really? Tall? Short? Thin? Buxom?'

'Six foot tall, long legs, strong, athletic build.'

'He knows about strong. He got out of line and she cleaned his clock for him.'

Derek scrutinised my face. 'No marks. But you always could take a punch.' He filled our glasses and started to chuckle. 'Remember that demonstration up in Notting Hill when the young cop belted you?' I nodded. 'And you stood there and laughed in his face?' I nodded. 'This was before your time, Maar. Paul laughs at this copper and says, "If you can't hit harder than that, sonny Jim, you better turn in your stick and try interior decorating". The kid blushed to the roots of his hair and all the other coppers started laughing at him. It took the steam out of a good demonstration. What were we demonstrating about that day? Do you remember?'

'Squatters' rights, I think.'

Mary yawned. 'If this is going to be a "those were the good old revolutionary days" evening, I'm going to bed.'

'Bliss were it in that Dawn to be alive, but to be young was very heaven.'

Mary removed my tumbler of wine from the table. 'That's it! No more drink for Paul. Once he starts quoting eighteenth-century poets he's gone.'

'*Prelude* was turn of the century. Very much so.'

'Pedant. Alright, you get your drink back but one more quotation and the bar is closed.'

'Invite her over for dinner tonight,' said Derek. Behind his back Mary shrugged, grimaced to express hopeless resignation and mimed pulling off her wedding ring and tossing it over her shoulder. 'What does she like to eat?' asked Derek.

'He doesn't *know*.'

Derek was already prowling the kitchen bookshelves. 'I picked up a review copy of a book on Cajun cooking. It reads interestingly. Cajun is Black and French, Louisiana, right mate?'

16

'He doesn't know.'

'She's seriously allergic to fish. She was very specific about that. Her throat swells up and she can't breathe.'

'That more or less takes care of Cajun cuisine. All the best dishes were fish one way or another. Pity. Let's think regional then. Where's she from in America?'

'I know that. Arkansas.'

While he searched the bookshelves Mary poured me more wine. 'And that'll do it. You're right. I'm about to call it a night.'

'Hold on a moment, mate. Here we are . . . Stuttgart, Arkansas, is the wild rice capital of the world. Wild rice and wild duck. I think we're on to something here. Does she have any other allergies?'

'*He* doesn't know.'

'She may be allergic to me. Why don't you hold up on the dinner plans until I've conducted some more tests?' I bid them goodnight.

Maya and I were shy together on the phone and shy together at the start of lunch but after half an hour we decided we liked each other.

For the next two weeks we were together every day. We became lovers and, as lovers do, told each other stories to reveal obliquely our personal histories and delineate cultural differences. Neither of us was in the first bloom of youth so both of us had our fair share of stories and our daylight hours scuttered by in the telling of them.

We spent most evenings at Derek and Mary's house where a steady flow of company became her adoring audience. World-weary journalists and Cockney wise-guys of both sexes fell for her like skittles in a bowling alley and I accepted congratulations like a proud impresario with a hit show on my hands. Nights together we tremulously explored each other's sexual territories and played the games that lovers play.

Then one morning Maya sat bolt upright in bed, staring straight ahead. 'I think you'd better leave me alone. I have to go to work. I have a fucking book to write and it's not getting written.'

I could sympathise. My own deadline was nine months away and a lot of typing ahead. I wished her good writing and let myself out of her apartment. Somewhere along on the ten-minute taxi ride to Victoria Station I grasped the disturbing certainty that I was going to follow Maya when she went back to America. The die was cast. A glorious summer love affair had suddenly became a hairpin bend on my life's road.

As the train bisected South London streets I looked out at the ramshackle backsides of terrace houses that bordered the railway lines

17

and wondered what sort of landscape I would find myself in six months from then.

I let myself into the house and went upstairs to my typewriter, rolled in a sheet of paper, numbered the page, typed CHAPTER TWO, and underlined it. Then I went down to the kitchen to make a pot of tea. While the kettle was boiling I browsed through the bookshelves and found a paperback copy of *The Fire Next Time*. On the back cover was a quote from a review in *Harper's* magazine: 'Mr Baldwin explains what it means to be a Negro in America.'

Since my future plans probably involved spending a great deal of time with Negroes in America I decided to reread it. I brewed the tea and settled at the dining-table to read, comprehend and inwardly digest like the diligent undergraduate I once, occasionally, was.

I remembered it pretty well from my first reading. In 1963 the universality of his theme and the technical sureness with which Baldwin had blended anecdote, childhood memories, global history and polemic into a cohesive essay had made the Angry Young British Writers I was used to reading seem parochial and timid by comparison. That day at the dining-table I kept rereading, looking for the cogs and springs that made the clock keep true time. Just when I thought I had the puzzle solved another reading turned up another surprise. The reviewer had missed the point by a country mile. Mr Baldwin tells us *all* more about ourselves than is comfortable for us to admit.

I was still at the table when Derek came in from work. He stowed his camera gear and brought beers from the fridge. 'Where's Maya?'

'At her place, working.'

'Everything alright with you two?'

'Fine. Just a change of rhythm. Work calls.'

'That's good. Phone her and see if she wants dinner. Nothing fancy; steaks, cauliflower cheese, baked potatoes and a salad. We'll eat about eight when Mary gets in.'

'It's been a shitty day,' said Maya. 'Can you come and get me?' I borrowed Derek's car and settled into the cross-town traffic.

She was dressed in a shapeless sweater and baggy jeans half unzipped. She was barefoot and bareheaded and her short natural haircut was twisted and teased out of shape. Manuscript sheets were spread all around the living-room carpet. Her complexion had an unhealthy grey tinge and there were fine stress lines around her beautiful mouth.

'Bad day in the cottonfields, huh?'

'Pour us a drink and tell me you loves me. No matter what.' I came back with the drinks and told her I loved her no matter what.

'You mean that?' She sounded serious but I had learned that her dramatic fireworks could build up to a sudden comic twist. Maya enjoyed using her actor's tools; voice, gesture, facial expression. My role was to feed her lines and enjoy the show.

'No matter what,' I said.

'Why the hell does anyone write books?' She sounded frazzled to shreds.

'That's a hard question, like "What's it all about, Alfie?".'

For a while we sipped our drinks without a word. 'You don't really know who I am in America, do you?'

'Not really. I've read the biographical notes on the book jackets.'

'I'm, quote, A Great Black Sister, unquote. I go on national television and make profound pronouncements of pontifical pomposity . . .'

'What's wrong, Maya?'

'Fucking White folks won't let us just be people. Blacks have to be Martin Luther Kings or thugs in the street. Superhuman or subhuman.'

'What's wrong, Maya?'

'This book is kicking my arse. That's what's wrong.' She started to outline the book in progress. It continued her life story from where *Caged Bird* left off. She was a teenager with a new-born son and no prospects beyond dead-end, low-wage jobs. She sees show business as her only way to escape ungenteel poverty. She begs and borrows, scrimps her pennies for dance lessons. Taking advantage of her long-legged figure and off-beat beauty she finds work as an exotic dancer in a club on San Francisco's North Beach.

'What exactly,' I asked, 'is an exotic dancer?'

'As near naked as the San Francisco Police Department and the City Fathers would allow. And that was very naked. Oh, but man, I *danced*. I danced as if I was in the Bolshoi Ballet.'

'It's a great story so far. I already know that further down life's road you toured Europe as a Première Danseuse. It sounds like the American Dream . . . from San Francisco skin joint to the Paris Opera House. The ever-upward path . . .'

'The problem is that I turned off the path a few times. I got side-tracked. The problem in this book is . . .' I waited. 'You see I was a prostitute for a while.'

19

I was impressed. 'You were a call girl?'

'Nothing so fancy. I was a whore turning tricks. Also a B-girl and a madame for a hot minute.'

'What's a B-girl?'

'A bar girl. You flirt with lonely men in clubs and get them to buy you over-priced, watered-down drink to boost the bar receipts.'

'We call them nightclub hostesses. Same job, different title. That's what you're writing about now? Your time as a prostitute?'

'I've been trying to wriggle out of it. I had this idea that there could be two women in the story. They start off from the same place at the same time, they've been friends from childhood. One becomes a dancer, the other becomes a prostitute . . .'

'You're writing a first person narrative? Autobiography?'

'Dammit, you sound like my editor in New York. I told him I'd find *my* way to tell the story and caught the next plane here to be miserable in London, and I've been sweating it out in this under-heated, over-priced shoebox of an apartment ever since. Just because White writers choose to follow European literary conventions and march to Euro-centric drummers doesn't mean I have to. Black people put our own twist on everything we do. We have Black style! We wear our clothes a little differently, we put our style on the music we play, the way we walk, the food we cook, the way we talk. A Black preacher's sermon is a tone poem, on pitch and in time . . .' She stopped and stared at me with miserable eyes. 'This book is kicking my butt, honey.'

'What about writing the truth?' I went and refilled our drinks. 'A few years back I owned and operated a bawdy house in Paddington for a couple of years.'

'A boarding house.'

'No. A *maison de passe,* a house of convenience, a place where whores could ply their trade.'

'You were a pimp?'

'No. I wasn't a pimp. I couldn't handle the pimp dress code.' Maya smiled. It was the first time I had seen her smile that afternoon. 'I just rented out the rooms and served the breakfasts and kept the local constabulary happy. American servicemen from the nearby air-bases kept the rooms full and I got to know a lot of whores on a social footing. They were like Chaucer's Canterbury Pilgrims . . . "God's plenty". Everything from case-hardened street girls with "born to lose" tattooed on their buttocks to Little Miss Muffets taking a short walk on

20

the wild side. Dental nurses picking up pin money on the weekend and party girls drinking themselves silly. I'm rambling, but my point is that whoring is in the warp and woof of all our lives. So why not tell the truth? It's not an inevitable slippery slope to perdition. You're living proof of that. But I knew that long before I ever met you.'

Maya tilted her head and surveyed me with amused eyes.

'. . . and from a practical point of view there must be quite a few people around in San Francisco who remember that you were a whore back then. Better to take the bull by the horns and tell the truth now than get exposed later . . . the, quote, Great Black Liar, unquote.'

'Smartarse,' said Maya.

'Us London Cockneys have a traditional song that celebrates the positive aspects of whoring.'

'Tell it to me . . . better, sing it to me.'

To the tune of *John Brown's Body* I sang out in the best light tenor I could muster:

> *Me sister is a dilly on the game in Piccadilly*
> *And me muvver is anuvver i' the Strand,*
> *Me favver sells his arsehole dahn ve Elephanant an' Castle,*
> *We're the 'ardest workin' family in ve lan'.*
> *I' ve lan', I' ve lan',*
> *We're ve 'ardest workin' family i' ve lan'.*

Maya whooped with delight and applauded. 'That's poetry!'

I shrugged modestly. 'We Cockneys put our style on the songs we sing.'

'Get the fuck out of here! Let's go to dinner. I'll be dressed and ready in ten minutes.'

When I told her what I had been reading all day she came alert. 'Baldwin has been on my mind since I woke up. This is my third book and he's published fourteen. When I first started my first book he told me, "Writing a book is like shitting bricks, and the bricks get bigger all the time".' She relapsed into reverie for the rest of the drive.

Maya was in great form at dinner; food and company uncorked her good humour after the frustrating day. Then when dinner was over she suddenly became serious and fixed Derek with a theatrical and imploring stare. 'I want you to do me a big favour, Dek.'

21

'If I can, My, what do you want?'

She smiled suddenly. 'Show me some of your work.'

'Ah no, My, you don't need to see my snapshots.'

Mary nodded across the table at me. 'Come on, sweetie, clear the dishes with me.'

When we had stacked the dishes by the sink Mary went upstairs and brought down a box of photographs. She set them down on the table in front of Maya. As she went through them Maya selected some and laid them out on the table. I knew them well. They were his pictures from 1968, the 'days of rage' in Paris. He had packed a bag and headed for France within a couple of hours of the first reports of the protests. He had not waited for an assignment and, impressively, had not bothered to pick up expense money. He had stayed in Paris until he was satisfied he had the record he wanted. Maya continued to lay out the pictures and rearrange them until the eight-foot-long table was completely covered. 'This is a book, Dek.'

'Tell him, Maya,' said Mary.

He was genuinely embarrassed. 'Just snapshots for my own trips down memory lane. Nothing to put on a coffee table.'

Mary and I went to wash the dishes. When we returned the conversation had moved on to the inner city riots that had followed the murder of Martin Luther King. Maya was talking about Baldwin's courage in taking a visible and vulnerable stand to advocate reason and compassion, trying to stem the rage. 'Was that reported over here?'

'Yes,' said Mary, 'but it wasn't a big story.'

'The picture editors were scrambling for photos though,' said Derek. 'We thought he might be killed. That would have been the story.'

'You could have been right. The Whites or the Blacks could have killed him.'

When we came down early next morning Derek was already at the dining-table skimming through the newspapers. Maya asked to use the phone to call Baldwin. 'I woke up thinking about him again.'

Derek nodded, still intent on the papers. 'Use the phone in our bedroom if you want privacy. Maar's already left for work.'

'This one's fine. Can I dial direct to France?'

'Get the operator. It's simpler.' He gathered up the papers and beckoned me away. 'Let's get a cup of tea, mate.'

22

We went out onto the tiny back patio and arranged chairs so we could take advantage of the thin morning sunshine. 'Nice dinner,' I said. 'Thanks.'

'Nice evening.' He nodded towards Maya in the dining-room. 'Super lady.' I nodded. 'Are you going to America when she goes back?'

'She hasn't asked me.'

'You need permission? You getting soft, mate?'

'I don't know how the Black and White mix works over there.'

'If you don't go you'll never find out, will you?'

Maya soon joined us. She was smiling and jaunty. 'I got him. He was home by the phone.'

'Everything alright?' asked Derek.

'Fan-fucking-tastic! It's his birthday next week. I told him about Paul. He said: "I think I ought to meet this man, Maya".' She chuckled. 'Wouldn't it be a groove to visit him for his birthday? How far is Nice? About a thousand miles? A two-hour flight?'

'More or less,' said Derek, 'but this is a holiday month. Why don't you get on the blower and see if any flights are open? Take anything you can, mate.'

I spent the next fifteen minutes on the phone, mostly on hold, but finally I booked two flights on Air France four days ahead. I told Maya and she nodded contentedly, then as an afterthought asked how much the tickets cost. I told her. She shook her head. 'We don't need to fly first class.'

'That's not first class.'

'They've made a mistake. It's only like flying from . . . San Francisco to Phoenix. That's got to be wrong.'

Derek shook his head. 'That's what it costs, My.'

'For that money and a few dollars more we could buy a little second-hand car and drive, see something of France together and have our own transport to hand when we got there.'

'There you go, mate.'

'I suppose we could do that.' She sounded less than enthusiastic.

Derek stood up and rubbed his hands with satisfaction. 'Make a trip of it, Maya. Let's see, take the night ferry, pleasant couple of days driving, three or four good meals along the way. Perfect. Wish I was going with you. Come on, let's go inside and get busy. Time to get out the maps and the Michelin guide.'

His enthusiasm soon infected Maya and before long all horizontal surfaces were filling up with maps, cook-books and travel guides. When

23

they started to read each other recipes for obscure Provençal dishes I took that as my cue to go and look for a car.

I headed for Paddington to seek guidance from Lew Dixon, a street-wise Irish polymath who rarely left his apartment before noon. At nine o'clock he was dressed the same way he always had been in the fifteen years I had known him; dark suit, white shirt, sober tie and well-polished black shoes. When I told him I needed an economical and inexpensive car to get to the South of France and back his eyes lit up. 'You and Maya taking a trip?' I nodded. 'Oh, lovely, mate, lovely. When are you planning on leaving?'

'In two or three days.'

'This isn't the best time. Late September would be perfect.'

'It's James Baldwin's birthday next week and we're going down to wish him many happy returns.'

'Oh, lovely.' He smiled. 'And you're right. Late September would be a little late for birthday greetings. So you're off to meet James Baldwin. What a privilege! I wish I was going with you. I'd very much like to hear his thoughts on the Nixon administration.'

'I'll make a point of listening carefully to everything he says on the subject and you can debrief me over a few Scotches when I get back.'

'That's something to look forward to. If you think about it, Baldwin drew the road map for the American debacle in Vietnam when the war was still a very covert operation. You see his thesis . . .'

'Not to change the subject, Lew, but today or tomorrow I have to buy a car.'

'What does Maya drive back home?'

'I never thought to ask.'

Lew shook his head. 'Of course you never were a carburettor man. I think that's the secret of such little success with women as you *have* had. The geezers stand around talking about cars and you slide off and chat up the birds. Sooner or later some lonely woman takes pity on you. Talking of women, does Germaine know you're on with Maya?'

'We haven't talked. None of her bloody business anyway.'

'True. But I'm seeing her next week. She's thinking about buying a house, and Morty's thinking about godfathering the deal. What do I say if your name comes up in conversation?'

'Let your conscience be your guide. You'll cough your guts anyway. I need a car. So counsel me.'

'Maya probably drives a Cadillac.'

'Who the fuck cares. She's not going to ship it over.'

'Some of the largest and most profitable Black-owned businesses in the United States are Cadillac dealerships. It's interesting how that came about . . .'

'Do you have a Guinness in the kitchen? And an egg?' I beat a raw egg into a glass of Guinness and enjoyed a refreshing draught. 'Tell me about Cadillac dealerships . . . I know there's no way I can stop you.'

'In 1912 Cadillac brought out the first car with an electric starting motor. They went for the semi-luxury market. Think about it. With an automatic starter motor you don't need a chauffeur to crank the engine. The luxury market doesn't care. The driver gets you from here to there. But the semi-luxury market drive themselves.'

'Gotcha.'

'But the cars didn't sell well. In those days Cadillac dealers were contractually prohibited from selling to negroes. The theory being that if Blacks were seen driving Cadillacs the larger White market would boycott them. But that didn't work. Cadillac was failing. So Mr Cadillac, whoever he was, switched sides. He went flat out for the Black middle-class buyers. His strategy worked and Cadillac was saved. And today the proportion of Cadillac owners among upper income Blacks is still significantly higher than among their White economic counterparts.'

'How do you know all this, Lew?'

'I subscribe to a couple of American car magazines.'

'Of course. Why did I ask?' Lew bought and read more magazines than anyone I had ever known. 'Nice story, but fuck it. I need a car that starts first time, has good brakes and gets about twenty-five to the gallon.'

'What about an Austin Mini Countryman? The shooting brake version . . . or station wagon as the Americans term it.' He led me over to the bay window that looked out on to the street. There it was parked by the kerb. 'Come on. Let's go for a drive.'

'I didn't know you had gone into the used car business.'

'One of the chaps needed money for his defence fund. But it's for sale. I advanced him three and a half. He doesn't need a car. Her Majesty's Prison Service will be accommodating his travel needs in the immediate future. I've had it greased, changed the oil. The tank's full. Brakes are about one-fifth worn. If you want it. Four hundred quid. Let's go.'

After about twenty minutes I drove on to the bank and gave Lew four hundred pounds. He handed me back fifteen pounds. 'I forgot to mention the spare tyre is shot. Buy a new one and have a drink for the road. Let's go and see Maya, I'd like to wish her godspeed. We'll stop and get a bottle of Scotch on the way.'

Derek and Maya were up to their eyes in cooking what, judging by the number of pots in play, promised to be a complex meal and a delicious one going by the aromas. Maya looked very happy. Lew greeted her with an Irish boisterousness that was his habitual public mask. 'Having a grand old time are you, Maya? Rattling the pots and pans, eh?'

She beamed. 'This is the first time I've cooked, really cooked since I left the States. Why don't you blokes get out of my way and take a walk to the pub while I have fun here. You'll stay to lunch, Lew?'

He accepted and I mentioned we had a car. Maya came out to inspect. As she towered over the tiny station wagon her face was a study in dismay. I tried to accent the positive. 'It gets very good mileage.'

'I'll bet,' said Maya.

'It's more roomy once you get in than you'd guess . . . well . . . from looking at it.'

'It must be.'

'What do you drive back home, Maya?' asked Lew.

'I have a Buick Skylark.'

'Lovely. Two-door with a fastback silhouette. What colour?'

'Red, like a fire engine.'

'Perfect. Just the colour to give it that oomph. You'd classify that as a touring car, wouldn't you, Maya?'

'It's a little bit sporty.'

'And wouldn't *that* be just the car to drive down Route Nationale Deux?'

Maya nodded wistfully. Lew patted the Austin's tiny hood and in a voice full of phoney blarney said, 'But *this* . . . this will be an adventure.'

Maya started giggling and shooed us off to the pub.

Lunch was leisurely and delicious and inspired stories of memorable meals in foreign parts. Maya presided benignly over the table and Derek bustled to his bookshelves for background material to flesh out the anecdotes. When Lew was trying to describe the exact location of a restaurant in the industrial suburbs of Nice in which he had eaten an unforgettable fish dinner, Derek amazed us by producing a large-scale map of Nice and its environs. Then Lew amazed us equally by locating it on the map, right down to which side of the street it was on. 'Try and get there if you have the time.'

'Any particular table we should ask for, Lew?' I had been his straight man for fifteen years.

Lew deadpanned. 'The window table on the right as you go in has a wobbly leg. You're liable to spill your wine if you fill the glass too full. Apart from that just keep away from the kitchen door and you can't go wrong.' Maya got the giggles again.

As soon as lunch was over she was eager to plan a dinner feast. Derek set a chair for her beside the cook-books, poured her a Scotch and gave her a notepad to make a list of the provisions she would need. Then he went out to the backyard to enjoy the afternoon sun and Lew's Scotch.

'Well, mate, what's the decision? Are you off to California when Maya goes back?'

'What's the hurry? You want to rent my room out?'

'You should go,' advised Lew. 'There aren't that many adventures in a lifetime and you can't let chances slip by. Not at our age.'

I left them chatting on the patio and sat in the sunshine on the small backyard lawn. 'Not at our age,' Lew had said, and his casual phrase had caught my attention. I looked over at Derek and Lew and there *was* a little grey hair on both their heads and their hips were thickening, just like mine. Middle age was sneaking up on me on cat's feet and I had not noticed. Well, an inter-racial love affair in California ought to concentrate the mind and bring a sense of urgency to my cocooned life. I went over and got a drink.

'What's the verdict?' Lew asked. 'California there you go?'

'Yep. California here I come.'

'You'll have to curb your habit of losing fights in bars, mate. It could be terminal over there. A lot of hand guns around in the wild and woolly West. But if you *do* fall off your barstool Dek will have plenty of snapshots and Mary's already researched your background.'

'True. What do you reckon I'm worth, Dek? Quarter of a column inside page?'

'I think we could puff it up to eighth column, front page and two pics. As long as you're dead of course . . . soon.'

'Of course. Let's go and see if Maya's ready with her list.'

27

Lew was in an expansive mood and insisted not only on buying provisions for dinner but buying them from Harrod's absurdly expensive food department. With reflexive frugality I mumbled that we could get everything from the store round the corner but Lew stole her heart by blarneying that, 'a great cook deserves to create with the finest ingredients'.

CHAPTER TWO

SOUTHERN FRANCE: AUGUST 1972

Very little preparation was needed for our trip, just pack a couple of suitcases, buy a new spare tyre and point the car south towards the Dover ferry. I forgot to buy the spare tyre.

The night passage to Calais was tortuous; a long wait to get on the ferry, a long wait for a truly awful dinner aboard and a longer wait to drive off at Calais. In spite of all the obstacles and distractions I contrived to drink plenty of wine. As Maya drove us out of the French Customs station I fell into a vinous slumber. When I awoke, feeling chipper and refreshed, the car was stationary. Ahead, as I looked up, was a road sign that read: Chartres/3 km. It pointed to the left. Maya was waiting to make the turn.

'Ah, Chartres, the cathedral and lunch. I'll take over the driving now, if you like.'

She started to giggle. 'Mister, you have a nerve . . . you've been slumped in a drunken stupor for the last four hours and you wake up sounding like a character in a British World War Two movie. She mimicked the clipped accent of the British officer class: 'Chartres, eh! Damn good show, Johnson. I'll take over the bridge now. You go below and get some rest.'

I was giggling now.

'I have to give you credit though, your recuperative powers are terrific . . . matched only by your ludicrous male arrogance.'

'Touché, as we say in Chartres.'

We parked and looked at the world-renowned Rose Window, from the outside. A glorious meld of medieval craftsmanship, artistic vision and religious devotion. A felicitous confluence that makes the whole greater than the sum of the parts.

'Shall we go in?'

'We can.' She sounded less than enthusiastic.

'*This*,' I framed the view with my fingers like a comic movie director, 'is the BIG PICTURE. Now, as I see it, we have two choices: we can stay focused on the BIG PICTURE and find an unpretentious restaurant where the excellence of the food is a revelation . . . or we can explore every aspect of this sublime cathedral, immerse ourselves in every detail. An hour, two hours, and we will barely have scratched the surface. However, by that time the restaurant kitchens will be closed and lunch will be a cheese sandwich at an unpretentious bar tabac.'

Maya nodded. 'I think it's important to keep focused on the BIG PICTURE.'

There was an unpretentious restaurant on a medievally narrow street in the shadow of the cathedral. Lunch was delicious and what made it a special delight was the glowing happiness of a middle-aged French couple at the next table. While we were choosing our meal the waiter brought them a whole baked fish. It was broad and fleshy and at least eighteen inches long from lips to tail. Maya looked at it and raised her eyebrows in wonderment. 'Maybe they have friends to join them,' I whispered.

The husband went to work with his knife and fork and filleted off a generous helping for his wife who watched his every movement with soft, loving eyes. Then he took an equal portion for himself. The process was repeated twice in the next half hour until every shred of flesh was consumed. From time to time the waiter stopped by their table to chat with them. All three were of an age and looked as if they had been friends from schooldays. Next came the *tarte aux fruits*, twelve inches in diameter, and they ate the whole thing with unhurried delight.

'That,' whispered Maya, 'is a truly happy marriage.' For the first time the idea of marriage surfaced from my subconscious. I wondered what Maya was thinking.

As we drove south the afternoon heat rose in a haze from the tarmac. Maya held the speed at a steady sixty miles an hour and soon black smoke came seeping out of the dashboard vents. We pulled off into a lay-by. I explained that English cars were not designed to

30

function at continuous high speed in intense heat. She was incredulous. '*This* is intense heat? Sixty miles an hour is high speed?'

'Let me show you something.' I raised the hood and pointed to the tiny engine. '*This* is all that's pulling us to St Paul de Vence.'

She was overcome with compassion. 'Poor little thing. My sewing machine has a bigger engine.' We held a steady forty miles an hour for the rest of the afternoon until we turned off the highway to Roanne where we planned to stop for the night.

Roanne was a large and once flourishing city that had been a centre for textile manufacture but had wilted since the invention of nylon. Across from the railway station was the Railway Hotel, a monumental nineteenth-century commercial hotel that appealed to both of us as a romantic place to spend the night. It was silent as the tomb. A desk clerk came out of a back office and seemed pleased to see us. We checked in and asked him when dinner was served and he told us that the dining-room had been closed for years. When we asked him to recommend a place for dinner his eyes twinkled mischievously. 'There is an excellent restaurant just to the right, on the corner . . . but,' he tapped his finger to his eyelid, 'I suggest you look at the prices before you go in.'

Maya was highly amused. 'Just because we're wearing jeans and T-shirts he thinks we're a couple of penniless hippies.' She swaggered down the street with a comic jive walk. 'Shoot! There's nothing short about me but my hair, and I cuts it! Man, we've got money we ain't even spent yet! Tell *us* it's expensive — shiiit!'

We looked in through the restaurant window. It was completely empty of customers but every table was beautifully laid out with spotless linen, heavy silverware and sparkling crystal. Three or four waiters, elegant in evening jackets, stood at their stations. We read the fixed-price menu posted in the window. Dinner was about forty dollars a head. Our mouths dropped open. Lunch had been about ten dollars for both of us. We went back to the desk clerk and humbly asked him to suggest somewhere cheaper. He directed us to a bistro in the town square.

Dinner was nourishing and tasty. Out of curiosity we peeked in at the corner restaurant before returning to the hotel. Every seat at every table was full. 'Amazing,' I said.

'Where do they all come from in a backwater town like this?' We asked the clerk the same question.

'From everywhere. From Paris, from Dijon.'

31

'Paris. That's two hundred miles away!'

'True. People come from all over the world.'

'What's the name of the restaurant?' asked Maya.

'*Les Trois Gros Frères,*'

Maya clapped her hand to her head. The clerk was laughing.

'I can't believe we're staying fifty yards from the greatest restaurant in the world and we've just eaten in a greasy spoon bistro.'

'We're a stylish couple. We did it our way.'

The next afternoon we got a puncture. Lew had been exactly truthful, the spare tyre was shot and canvas was showing out of the wounds. We turned off the highway at the next exit and drove through back roads looking for a village with a service station that could repair the punctured tyre. The landscape was bleak; narrow roads wound among scrub-covered hills to lead to other roads that led to other roads. We were in *Maquis* country. Maya studied the baleful scenery with gloomy distaste. 'This is worse than Appalachia. The hell with it. Let's get back on the freeway and take our chances.'

'We'll be alright. That last signpost had the name of a town. We should be there in a few minutes.'

The town turned out to be a handful of houses, a bar and a solitary gas pump in front of a ramshackle workshop. I parked beside the pump and got the wheel out of the car. No one appeared. I leaned the wheel against the car and went through the open door into the workshop. It was disordered, dirty and deserted. When I approached the neighbouring house a fierce-looking dog snarled and barked from the porch but no one came out and no curtains moved. Maya was sitting rigidly upright, her eyes wide and alert. I reached through the window and honked the horn. Nothing stirred.

'This place is like the wreck of the *Marie Celeste*. But this *is* France. I'm going up the road to the bar. I'll find someone there.'

Before I reached the bar a raw-boned country boy in greasy overalls came out and headed towards me. I asked him if he could repair the tyre. He shrugged and said, 'Maybe.' He looked at the tyre, at Maya, at our luggage, at Maya's mink coat folded beside the suitcases, at me, at Maya again and then without a word went into the workshop. Through the open door I watched him pick up the telephone. I waited by the car. Maya leant across and pushed open the driver's door. 'Let's go!' Her voice and mien were urgent and serious.

'Let's get the tyre fixed first.'

'My hinkety doesn't hench me right.'

'What does that mean?'

'Please. Let's get out of here. Now!' I swung the wheel in on top of the suitcases and off we drove. We were silent for about ten minutes until the highway came into view. I whooped with illogical triumph: 'Back on the road again!'

Maya grinned. She gave me a sly wink as I watched her out of the corner of my eye. 'Remember what Hannibal said when he was crossing the Alps?'

'. . . er, what was that now?'

'Fuck 'em!'

'Ah . . . actually I was thinking of what he said after the battle of Lake Trasamene.'

'What was that?'

'They'll never catch us now!'

She clapped her hands and plopped a big kiss on my cheek. 'I think,' she said, 'I'm going to try very hard to keep you around for a while.'

'You won't have to try very hard. In fact you won't really have to try at all.'

We drove the next few miles in happy silence. Then I sensed her looking carefully at me. 'You didn't think I was crazy to want to get out of there?'

'It crossed my mind for a moment.'

'But you saw the way he looked us over. I've seen eyes like that before, just casual cold hatred.'

'All we wanted was a tyre fixed.'

'That has nothing to do with it.'

'You're right. A woman's hinkety . . . that's the word? . . . is better than a man's certainty. Those are the badlands. In World War Two the French resistance fighters used to hide out there. Even the Nazis couldn't establish law and order in those hills. So why take a chance on being robbed?'

'Or worse,' she shivered. 'That's the *Maquis* country then? I *knew* it.'

'That's where the Drummond murders happened. Back about 1950 a young English family, husband, wife and young child were on a camping tour. They camped the night in those hills and were never heard from again. Their dead bodies were found weeks later, shotgunned and

33

beaten to death. It was big news. The British government put pressure on the French government. For months there were investigators all over the hills but . . . nothing. *Omerta* is the rule there, just like Sicily or Corsica. About ten years later an old man whose family lived nearest to where they were killed made a public confession on his deathbed. He said he had killed the wife when she resisted his sexual advances, then killed the others and robbed them.'

Maya shivered again. 'I knew it. My hinkety doesn't hench me wrong. M'm m'm.' She reached back among the luggage for a cook-book. 'Let me read you some general observations on the foods and wines of Provence.'

'That will soothe our nerves and whet our appetites. How's the eating at Jimmy's by the way?'

'I don't know. I've never been with him in his own domestic setting. However, I'm sure the drinking will be fine.'

We arrived in St Paul in the late afternoon. A soft Mediterranean breeze was refreshing the streets. Town folk were out enjoying a stroll before dinner and we joined them, happy to stretch our legs and savour the satisfaction of a long journey successfully accomplished. Whoever said it was better to travel hopefully than to arrive was not driving an Austin Mini. Maya looked more relaxed than at any time since leaving London. 'You know we could buy a little house in France and I could write and cook and you could build and write comic strips. You could teach me how to build and I could teach you how to cook.' We held hands and contemplated an idyllic future together. St Paul was working its magic on us.

'It's so . . . un-dangerous here . . . Malcolm's dead, Martin's dead . . . Hampton and Jackson murdered and slandered in death and *so* many more. Nixon in the White House, the new emperor of a bad new world . . .' Her good mood was vanishing.

'Why don't you phone Baldwin and get directions to his house?'

She brightened up, took a deep breath and stretched up to her full height, a routine for shaking off depressing thoughts that I had come to recognise.

'That's the ticket. That's the jolly old ticket.'

She turned into the next bar to find a pay phone and I sat down at a sidewalk table and ordered a bottle of champagne. She soon came out smiling. 'Bernard Hassell is coming to join us. You'll like him.'

'Lovely. What about Baldwin?'

She giggled. 'You'll like him too. Jimmy's been off somewhere since lunch. He'll be back sometime. He forgot to tell anyone we were coming. That's par for the course. Everything will be just fine.'

While we waited for Bernard Hassell, Maya briefed me on the social infrastructure of the Baldwin household. Bernard handled the day-to-day practicalities. He made sure Baldwin had an ordered and secure place to write, and fended off the vulpine and vulturine freeloaders who made grabs for Jimmy's celebrity coat tails.

'Bernard was a professional dancer who eventually settled in France. I'm sure he and Jimmy were lovers at one time and from time to time but essentially they're friends. They complain about each other like an old married couple. But it works for them. Dancers learn discipline *and* they learn how to make their pennies stretch. He anchors Jimmy's life.'

I recognised Bernard easily enough, a gracefully muscular Black man in his forties. He spotted Maya in a moment and came briskly to our table. Somehow he contrived to wear blue jeans, a cotton shirt and rope-soled espadrilles with more elegance than most of us achieve in five hundred dollar suits, Asser and Turnbull shirts and Gucci loafers. He kissed Maya on both cheeks. 'What a lovely surprise!'

Maya chuckled. 'We didn't plan a surprise.' She introduced us, we shook hands and he patted me on the shoulder. 'A second lovely surprise! Welcome to our annual *fête de chaos*.'

While we enjoyed the champagne he entertained us, describing the disorganised comings and goings in the household with witty exasperation. I suggested that Maya and I find a room in town rather than add to the confusion but Bernard would not hear of it. 'Out of the question. Absolutely. Jimmy would never forgive me . . . or you. I'll just shuffle a few guests around. What are your preferred sleeping arrangements?' He twinkled his eyes at Maya. '*À deux*?' She smiled and nodded. 'Then I shall prepare the bridal suite.' He patted me on the shoulder. 'Don't worry, dear boy, it's just Jimmy's birthday. Happens ever year. Are we ready? I'll lead the way. Just follow *La Vieille Dame*.' He pointed to an elderly and immaculate car parked nearby.

'Is that the household limousine?' asked Maya. 'What is it?'

'A venerable Mercedes. A recent acquisition of Jimmy's.'

'Very nice. Jimmy doesn't drive it of course?'

35

'How I wish that were true. But, Monsieur Baldwin is taking driving lessons.'

'Oh my God! How is he doing?'

'Terrifying us all.'

'At least it's a good, solid, safe car.'

'It needs to be a Sherman tank, dear.'

A short and pretty drive brought us to a comfortable stone-built farmhouse with some casual additions and a couple of outbuildings converted into living quarters all set on a fair-sized hillside lot with some ancient terraces. In the typical Mediterranean style the workaday buildings were laced into graceful unity by walkways and walled patios and dressed in pungent and abundant vegetation.

Maya surveyed the scene appreciatively. 'I'm very happy for Jimmy. God knows he deserves it. I know it's been a struggle.'

'Maya, I don't think he'd ever have bought it if he had known. Compared with this real estate transaction, a Vietnam peace treaty would be a handshake deal. And of course he's going to have to write a book a year until he's eighty to pay for it. But, what to say? Here we are. Take a look around while I make your sleeping arrangements. Help yourselves. Jimmy's house is your house.'

Maya headed unerringly for the kitchen. It was large and sunny and had probably looked the same way for fifty years. It had the perfect country ambience that decorators can approximately reproduce for the price of a princeling's ransom. She was soon pulling out drawers and taking inventory of the equipment. She nodded her approval: 'Someone around here cooks.'

I poured us a couple of drinks from a plastic bottle of dark red table wine and we sampled it. 'H'm, boisterous little vintage.'

'Almost rough,' said Maya, wincing as she swallowed.

'Bloody hooligan to tell the truth. Bernard was stretching the pennies a little too far when he bought this little darling.'

I refilled our glasses nonetheless. 'The second glass may be tamer. We'll never know if we don't try.'

The bridal suite turned out to be the spartanly furnished upper storey of a converted barn. The double bed had been stripped and the folded bedclothes and fresh linen were set on a wooden chair beside it. We unpacked, made up the bed, washed off the travel dust and took along a bottle of duty free Scotch as we went to look for the rest of the company.

We found Bernard and three other men lounging quietly in a large comfortable living-room. The scene reminded me of a railway station waiting-room where travellers, coincidentally together for a while, dribble out conversation until they are carried off to their separate destinations.

Maya and I were half a dozen steps into the room before we were noticed, but when her presence was recognised it galvanised the company. Bernard and the two other Black men sprang to their feet. A young White man lounging on a sofa, dressed in singlet and shorts, lounged back a little more and flexed his muscles.

The youngest of the Black men, about twenty years old I guessed, glided across to Maya, hands held out, paused a yard away from her and turned to Bernard silently imploring introduction. Bernard introduced him as 'Felix, a dancer, who will be *very* good as long as he works *very* hard.'

Bernard introduced the other Black men as 'Cecil Brown, the writer. I know I don't need to tell you about him.' Maya nodded and exchanged the briefest of handshakes with Cecil and the slightest of smiles before she removed her attention. The louche young Italianate, who had still not risen, was introduced as 'Bud . . . an . . . actor.' Bernard made the word sound like the most transparent euphemism for 'whore'. Bud nodded once and moved his left hand slightly. Well, well, I thought. One big happy family. It was a good thing we weren't living in an Agatha Christie whodunnit or there would be a dead body in the study before this party was over.

I offered to go and get glasses and ice for the company but Bernard overruled me on the grounds that he would do it better. Maya settled in an armchair and Felix squatted adoringly beside her. Cecil looked me over as if he was trying to categorise me. He was a medium-built thirty-year-old, already thickening around the middle. Too many hours at the typewriter perhaps, or too many good times. Bud ignored us all and I assumed that he thought he was projecting rampant sexuality and coiled menace.

'Do you live round here, in France?' asked Cecil.

I noted that he spoke of our proud host nation as if it was a neighbourhood in a town called Europe. A New Yorker, I guessed, by the sound of him. 'No. I live on the north side, across the Channel, in England.'

'England? How is it there?'

'It's okay. But the weather's better round here. We just drove over an hour ago.'

'Alright!' Bernard was back with ice and glasses. He poured minute drinks for Cecil and myself. 'We must save some for Jimmy. Have you noticed how much Scotch costs in France?'

'Once, years ago. I never ordered it again. I stick to Ricard 45 in Provence, Calvados in Normandy and wine everywhere in between.'

I nodded a toast to Cecil. He looked at me as if he was seeing me for the first time. 'What's your second name?'

I told him and spelt it at his request.

'Was there an article about you in the New York *Village Voice* earlier this year. And a picture?'

'Yes.'

'You were a nude centrefold?'

'Yes. The nude centrefold in *Cosmopolitan*. European edition.'

'Like Burt Reynolds.'

'A month ahead of Burt.'

He slapped me on the shoulder. 'Alright! You're famous! So what did you get out of the deal?'

'A few laughs.'

'And hot and cold running women in every room, huh?'

'I'd love to say "yes" but it didn't work out like that.'

'That wasn't much of a picture of you in the *Voice*.'

I shrugged. 'Unfortunately it did me justice.'

He nodded towards Maya. 'Does she know about it?' I nodded. 'What does she think?'

'A few laughs.' We looked each other over and both smiled.

The surly actor stirred out of the sofa and slouched over to the nearby table where Bernard had set the bottle of Scotch. He plucked it up with the arrogance of a movie gunfighter in a Wild West saloon. As he turned back towards his perch I cleared my throat. 'Ahem. That's not your fucking bottle . . . put it back. And wait till you're *fucking* invited.'

He hesitated and then complied with my request and went back to the sofa.

'Peckerwood cocksucker!' said Cecil in a stage whisper. 'He wouldn't have done that if we were fucking White.' I raised my eyebrows. 'Shit, you don't count. You're with Maya. You're an honorary nigger.'

It was the first time in my life I had heard a Black man say the word 'nigger', except on a movie soundtrack or a Richard Pryor comedy album. It gave me something to think about. In the first few days of our friendship Maya had made it unequivocally clear that the word 'nigger' was anathema to her and pointed up her revulsion for the word with an apposite anecdote.

She had, she told me, been sharing an intensely pleasurable moment with a Black manfriend and he had said, 'You're my big nigger and if you get bigger, you'll be my bigger nigger.' She had promptly put him out of her bed and out of her house at pistol point. I had duly noted her linguistic Rubicon.

'What,' asked Cecil, 'would you have done if the dipshit had ignored you?'

I shrugged. 'Nothing . . . or torn his arm out of the socket and beaten him to death with it.'

'That's a good line. Can I use it.'

I laughed. 'It's public domain where I come from.'

Cecil told me that he had written a successful novel called *The Life and Times of Mr Jiveass Nigger*.

'Quite a title.' Now I understood Maya's frigid reaction when they were introduced. He had high hopes of selling movie rights and soon we were deep in a 'favourite movie' conversation and still were when Baldwin and friends swept in.

Baldwin did a double take when he saw Maya, then swept over to embrace her. He became theatrically flustered like an old man undone by an unexpected visit from a beloved niece. She played off him, fawning like an adoring teenager. They were obviously having a fine time and I suspected that they had played the scene many times before. Maya introduced me and his face lit up with renewed delight. He went over to a sofa and insisted I take a place beside him, then sat back and let the conversation buzz around him while he smiled and listened. He carried his years lightly; on the eve of his forty-eighth birthday he was trim-figured with broad, bony shoulders and narrow hips. His face was little changed from the familiar youthful photograph on the book jackets. His tailored dark blazer and worsted slacks were enviably unwrinkled after hours of wear. A bright silk cravat, knotted at the throat, set off his sober outfit with a raffish touch.

Maya drew the company around her like a magnet attracting iron filings as she described our drive south from London. It became a series of comic misadventures and the car shrank in the telling to a shoebox on wheels powered by a flashlight battery. Baldwin rocked with laughter at every turn in the tale.

When her story was over and conversation spread and fractured around the room I understood very little of what I heard. There was

39

a high level of veiled flirtation and a general recognition of names unknown to me. After a few minutes I got up and went across the room so I could watch Baldwin from a discreet distance. Maya had told me something of his personal history and I knew that ten years earlier he had been one of the 'best and brightest' in the Kennedy circle.

What if? I wondered as I watched him. What if Dallas had just been another political stopover? What if Robert Kennedy had been running for re-election now? Where would Baldwin be and what would he be doing? Probably not in a French farmhouse chatting with people in whom his interest seemed no more than polite. I could picture him as a poet/politician at the court of Henry VIII, another ruler who liked to surround himself with the best and the brightest while they pleased him. Baldwin had the look about him, lean-featured, bright, guarded eyes and an air of quirky vanity. The look one sees gazing out of sixteenth-century paintings in London's National Portrait Gallery. That was it. His portrait would fit right in between Wyatt and the Earl of Surrey.

Cecil Brown came over and joined me. He nodded towards Baldwin. 'You know this business of the writer as a celebrity is really all a crock. In the end it's just the work that counts. Just the words on the pages. I'm thinking of doing an article on it.'

I shrugged.

'What do you think?' he asked.

'I think it takes all sorts to make a literary world.'

'What do you mean?'

'I mean there are good writers who are good at being celebrities like Charles Dickens and some who are good at being private people like Jane Austen. And writers who might have done better out of the limelight like Oscar Wilde and others who might have profited from timely recognition . . . some "Mute, inglorious Miltons". Were you thinking of Baldwin as the peg to hang your article on?'

He nodded. 'You read a lot?'

'I used to read more. Years ago I majored in English Lit. That how I learned to talk heap shit like a radio.'

'Let's get together tomorrow and let me pick your brains.'

'I'll look forward to that. By the way, would *you* like to be a celebrity?'

'I don't know.' He grinned. 'I'd like to try.'

Maya and I made an early night of it. I awoke around seven, went over to the uncurtained window and inspected the morning. The stone-walled room was pleasantly cool to me which meant cold to Maya. I took her fur coat and spread it over her for a cover. She mumbled gratefully and settled back into sleep.

I planned, if no one was about, to walk into town and find a bar for coffee and a Ricard 45 but Bernard was already at work in the vegetable garden. He took me to the kitchen for coffee and rolls, introduced me to the motherly French housekeeper, gave me directions to a repair shop that would fix the punctured tyre and briskly excused himself saying, 'This place doesn't run itself, contrary to popular opinion.'

'If you let me know what you want done I'd be more than happy to put in a morning's work. I'd enjoy it . . . I was bred for stoop labour.'

He smiled. 'So I noticed. Sturdy peasant stock. Thick legs and deep chested . . . but I'll be fine. You just look after Maya.'

I found myself a sunny spot on a low stone wall and settled to enjoy my breakfast in the fragrant morning peace. A moment later Baldwin came out of the main house. His quick walk was almost a trot. He was dressed in narrow, wrinkled black jeans, black turtle-neck sweater and sandals; artist's uniform, Paris, Rive Gauche, *circa* 1950. The good old days.

He waved and gave me a bright distracted smile: 'Bonjour and happy birthday, Jimmy.'

For a moment he seemed puzzled, then smiled again and thanked me. He disappeared into his workroom. What a wonderful time those good old days must have been for him. What company: Sartre, de Beauvoir, Signoret, Montand, Genet, Camus . . . was Camus there? or was he still playing soccer in the bleaching Algerian sun? . . . and Baldwin. The young Baldwin with a first novel already in the making, ready to step into the spotlight.

I was staring out over terraced hillside and reshaping it into the Paris that I had first seen twenty years earlier when the present Baldwin brought me back to the present. He had come and sat unnoticed beside me on the wall.

'My dear Paul, I forgot to tell you last night. A German TV crew is filming a birthday interview with me today. Lunch at the Colombe d'Or with a few guests. You and Maya must join me. It's the best lunch in town.' I thanked him and he went back to work.

41

'No,' said Maya, when I took her coffee and told her of our lunch invitation. 'I wouldn't do that to Jimmy.'

'Do what?' I had been looking forward to the best lunch in town.

'Take the limelight away from him. It's his birthday, he must be the star.'

'Fine. We can just sit there and smile and enjoy the food.'

'You don't understand about performance, do you?'

'No, not subjectively. I've never been on stage in my life, except if you count the boxing ring . . . but there wasn't usually much of a crowd then, and God knows I wasn't much of a performer.'

'Performance is central in Black culture. When you come to Black America you'll see that. Little girls in Harlem jumping rope, a Black minister in the pulpit, Ali in the ring. We *work* at performance. It's not showing off, we *create* by performance, we polish, we extend. Dizzie Gillespie or Leontine Price are not making music, they are creating a musical *performance*. And, modesty aside, I am a very good performer. That TV camera will come to me, and I will seduce it. I'm a better performer than Baldwin. No, it's his day. We'll stay home.'

I got the tyre fixed in a leisurely fashion, sat over coffee and a Ricard while I picked my way through a couple of stories in the *Journal de Sud* and it was still only ten o'clock when I got back to the house. Maya and I strolled into town and did some shopping and sightseeing. She bought bread and cold meats and wine and cheeses while I watched the housewives selecting tomatoes and peppers, one by one with fierce concentration, like diamond merchants picking over a parcel of uncut stones. It was a familiar enough scene but I never tired of it. What were they looking for? How could they tell what a tomato would taste like without tasting it?

It was all a mystery to me. It had all been a mystery to me thirty years before when my mother would ask me to go into the victory garden and pick three or four *nice* tomatoes or a couple of *nice* lettuces. 'Pick *nice* ones mind,' she would always say as I went out the back door. What did she *want* from me? What exactly did she *mean* by nice? Questions like that give a seven-year-old kid a lot to think about. I always played safe by picking the largest and most appropriately coloured; red for tomatoes, green and white for lettuce, red and green for apples, black for blackberries, etc. And when I brought them back to her she always said, 'Oh, those *are* nice.' So why do you have to remind me every time, mum? You know I always do nice work. Lighten up, mum!

We returned with our purchases and the housekeeper and Maya began to inspect them. The housekeeper used her full repertoire of shrugs, smiles, sniffs and pouts to critique the groceries. I wondered if the French had always been like that? Did French prehistoric cave-dwellers, back from a day-long expedition gathering nuts and berries and leaves, lucky enough to have killed a squirrel and a couple of field mice, have to turn over their haul to some dyspeptic earth mother who picked it over sniffing and shrugging, 'Was this the best mouse you could catch? Where did you go for these berries? Tut, tut, tut.'

I was soon given a basket and sent out to gather tomatoes and peppers from Bernard's garden. 'I'll pick nice ones.' I assured them as I left the kitchen.

Between the kitchen and the garden I met with Cecil Brown. He looked half-stunned from sleep. 'What time is it?'

'Towards noon. Just woken up?'

'Yes. I guess jet lag finally got me. I've never had it before.'

'Come and help me pick some vegetables.'

'What do you mean, *pick* vegetables? I'm a New Yorker, man! We pick *up* vegetables. From the A & P.'

'It's easy. I'll show you.' I explained my size and colour guidelines and we started prowling the vines and bushes. Before too long he held up a tomato for my inspection.

'How's this?'

'That's a *nice* one, Cecil.' We continued to prowl and pick.

'You know that phrase you used — "mute inglorious Milton" — is that Alexander Pope?'

'Thomas Gray. Same century. *Elegy in a Country Churchyard.* Gray is sitting in a cemetery at dusk thinking about the meaning of life. He looks around at the tombstones and wonders how many people buried there could have been great writers or political reformers or monstrous tyrants if only they had not been born to drudging poverty and obscurity. Stop me if you've heard it before.'

'Go on.'

'On the other hand, he says, the famous and powerful all end up in a cemetery anyway. "The paths of glory lead but to the grave."'

'So Gray was a bluesman.'

'In a nutshell. Good line. May I use it?' We laughed and decided we had done enough food gathering for the day.

'Let's go and get a shot of Scotch. It's the sovereign cure for jet lag.'

43

We took our drinks out to the sunshine. I raised my glass and toasted Jimmy's birthday.

'Where is Jimmy? Where's Bernard?' I told him about the German TV crew. Jet lag vanished. 'I need to be there. Can you drive me, you know where they are?'

'I'll find them. Come on, let's go.'

'Let me get changed.'

'You look fine.'

'Let me get changed, man.'

Half an hour later he reappeared. 'How do I look?'

'Very spiffy.'

'But do I look *right*? Do you think this jacket is alright?' He was wearing a dark brown soft leather jacket that looked very expensive.

'It's a beautiful jacket.'

'But for where I'm going?'

'Perfect. It says you're street-wise, but classy. The understated trousers and plain expensive shoes hint at sensitivity and hidden depths.'

He grinned. 'How about my hair?' His medium-length haircut looked sculpted. 'How's the back? There's only one mirror in the bathroom.' He twisted his head round for my scrutiny.

'You have a couple of tiny dents there.'

He pulled a large, wide-toothed comb from his hip pocket and held it out to me. 'You know how to fix Black hair?'

'I've watched Maya. You want me to try. Sit down on the wall over there.' I picked and patted out the dents, then stood back to survey the result. 'Modesty aside, I do nice work.'

When we got to the restaurant I gave his hair a final touch while we sat in the car. 'Now,' I said, 'you're ready to become a celebrity in Dusseldorf, you know, Dusseldorf on the Upper East Side. Take the Rhine Bridge and have exact change ready. It saves time at the toll.'

He started laughing. 'Fuck you, you snotty English bastard. But listen, I want to get something going for a sale of the German language rights of *Jiveass*. You gotta hustle, man, you gotta hustle.' In he went and I hustled back for lunch.

When the restaurant party returned, Maya and Baldwin went off to his workroom for time alone. I had eaten myself into a semi-comatose state and was glad to go upstairs to the bridal suite for a siesta.

Two hours later Maya joined me. Her heart to heart with Baldwin had been restorative and encouraging. They had talked of *Giovanni's Room*, his second novel that had been rejected by the publishers of his successful first novel. It was a *roman à clef* about a tortured and destructive homosexual passion, set in Europe with a White American narrator/protagonist, but change of skin colour did little to conceal the autobiographical foundation of the story. I had never read it and knew nothing of it but the title from the 'List of other works by . . .'. But as Maya struggled with *her* second volume of autobiography it was easy to see why she would seek his counsel.

'We had a great talk. I knew I could count on Jimmy to get to the heart of things.'

'What did he say?'

'He said, "Write the fucking book, Maya".'

'Sound advice.'

' "And when you've finished it get on and write the next one." '

Very sound advice.

'Well, that,' I said, 'seems to cover all the points.'

The rest of the day was a free-form party. Local friends and admirers came by to wish Baldwin happiness. Maya sang, recited poetry, told jokes and kept the celebration moving along at an unflagging pace. At three o'clock we went up to bed.

As she undressed she packed her clothes. 'I'm ready to go back.'

'Well, the tyre's fixed and the car's running as well as it ever will.'

'I'm ready to go back to America. Will I see you there?'

I nodded.

'For sure?'

'For sure.'

She smiled and kissed me. She undressed till she wore nothing but her shoes and continued to pack. I watched her with rising pleasure.

> *How graceful are your feet in sandals*
> *Oh queenly maiden*
> *Your rounded thighs are like jewels,*
> *the work of a master hand.*
> *Your navel is a rounded bowl*
> *that never lacks mixed wine.*
> *Your belly is a heap of wheat,*
> *encircled with lilies.*
> *Your two breasts are like two fawns,*
> *Twins of a gazelle.*

Like most of my hormonally deranged twelve-year-old Catholic schoolmates I had been a keen student of the *Song of Solomon* and the biblical description of the 'navel' as a receptacle for 'mixed wines' was a scholarly crux that we debated at length. The more knowing among my companions were of the opinion that 'navel' was either a mistranslation of, or a euphemism for, vagina since 'mixed wine' was to be found there. Over the years I have found myself favouring their interpretation more and more.

Maya became aware of my gaze and postured prettily, then thrust forward her biblical navel and smiled a whorish invitation that erased my concern with textual analysis for the rest of the night.

I awoke around seven as usual and slipped out to the kitchen for coffee. The housekeeper had not arrived or was not coming. I made coffee and took up my perch on the wall in the sunshine. Baldwin soon came hurrying out of the house, headed for the workroom. He was wearing the same black outfit. He saw me and stopped.

'Up so early?'

'Best part of the day.'

'For me too.'

'Coffee's made. May I bring you a cup?'

'Where is it? Where do you have to go?'

'The kitchen. A short walk.'

'Then let's walk there together, my dear Paul.'

We set our coffee mugs on the wall by the vegetable garden and rehearsed the highlights of his birthday party.

'Maya's visit was the loveliest treat of all. Thank you for bringing her.' He smiled and stroked my cheek with the back of his knuckles. 'The only thing I missed was the children.' I had not seen a child since I had arrived and for a moment his conversational triple jump nonplussed me. 'When I'm in New York with my family there are always *children* around. I *like* children around. You have children?'

'Two teenage sons in London. They live with their mother.'

'You see them?'

'No.'

'But you think about them?'

'Of course.'

'And one day you'll see them. Or you won't. But you have them. I wish I had a child.'

'It's not that difficult. You're only forty-eight years and one day old.'

'True. It's not that difficult. But also true, it's not that easy.' He had the European mannerism of using a cigarette as a conversational prop. His hands were large for his small build and long-fingered. He held

46

his cigarette between extended fingers and waved it like a conductor's baton as he led a silent orchestra for a moment. We admired the view in silence.

I broke the silence. 'Do you work in the garden much?'

'The garden?' I nodded towards the neat rows of vegetables. 'Do you think it would be a good idea?'

'Things grow so well here. And the climate is wonderful, most of the time.'

'It *is* wonderful most of the time but most of the time I'm not *here.*' He lit a fresh cigarette with a flourish. 'When I go into that workroom I'm not *here.* I'm there or there or there. I'm wherever my characters are. I'm an actor playing three or four parts, and directing. And designing the sets . . . and sewing the damn costumes.' For a moment he dealt with his cigarette. 'It keeps on getting harder, my dear Paul. When I started writing I knew a great deal and I was blessed with ignorance. I could write it this way or that way or the other way. But now I know very little and I'm cursed with knowledge. After thirty years I have thirty ways to write a sentence . . . and that means thirty ways to be wrong. Have you ever written?'

'I've hacked out several hundred thousand forgettable words.'

'Published?'

I nodded. 'And paid for, and the bloody money spent.'

'Ah, the bloody money. Airline tickets, taxes, telephone bills, loan payments . . .'

'And just one small typewriter to pay for it all.'

'Just one small typist. I don't think I'd be very good at gardening. I'd pull up the plants and water the weeds or whatever is wrong, and Bernard would be upset with me and send me to bed with no supper . . . I think I'll stay this side of the wall. Do I have to work the day after my birthday party?'

'I won't tell. Some more coffee?' The suggestion did not excite him. 'There's a fat corner left in the last bottle of Scotch. I stashed it in the kitchen for just such an occasion.'

He smiled and stroked my cheek again. 'So young and yet so wise, and the sun is under the yard-arm and risen over the hill. Let's away to the kitchen!'

The bottle was about a quarter full. I poured us drinks.

'Do you know the Irish definition of a gentleman? A gentleman throws away the cork when he opens the bottle. This is not a full bottle, but I am not fully Irish or for that matter completely a gentleman. But we'll make do.' I flipped the bottle cap into a trash box.

'Maya and I talked about you yesterday.'

'Nothing but good of the living I hope.'

'Nothing but good. But she didn't tell me how you two came to meet. You met in London?'

'In an interesting way.'

'Of course. All love affairs have interesting beginnings. Do I get a story while we drink? All the details?'

'She rescued me. I was a damsel in distress and Maya was the Black Knight in shining armour who galloped up and swept me away on her charger.'

'I like this story. What was your distress?'

'I was backed up against the wall by a gang of radical feminists about to give me a verbal mugging.'

An American editor had recently paid me a respectable advance to write a book and for the first time in my life I had a literary agent. Up till then I had sold my hack work direct to editors I had known for years. Soon after I got an agent I got my first invitation to a literary soirée. I was unfamiliar with polite literary society. I knew no one at the party but my agent. For a while I chatted with strangers whose attention was elsewhere and eavesdropped on conversations that sounded well polished by wear. Most of my *own* attention was on a tall Black woman in West African dress and her handsome middle-aged companion in tailored English tweeds. They had commanded the room with their presence since I had arrived and interested me far more than anyone else in the room. Four women whose intense and unadorned demeanour indicated that they were radical feminists had gathered near the Black woman so I moved to the edge of the group and sipped my wine with a vague party smile hoping to introduce myself to the fascinating couple.

I was not really listening to the women's conversation and when one of them turned on me like a prosecuting counsel snapping the trap on a perjured witness, I was caught completely off guard and all I heard was '. . . do you disagree?'

'I'm sorry, I didn't catch the question.'

The group's spokeswoman's eyes hardened to a killer's stare like a boxer intimidating his opponent at the weigh-in. She spoke slowly and

IN GOOD COMPANY

carefully like an adult authority figure trying to communicate with a retarded child. 'I asked you if you disagreed with what I was saying. That . . . was . . . the '. . . question.' Her gang bared their teeth in lupine smiles. On a tougher street corner they would have been popping their switchblades.

I sensed I was in for a polemic thrashing but I had no intention of going down without a fight. 'Let me rephrase here. Unfortunately I didn't hear the statement that immediately preceded your question. Would you be so kind as to repeat it?'

'I said: "The male sex's innate drive to senseless violence from Ghengis Khan to Hiroshima is the root cause of the misery and suffering in the world." Do you disagree?'

'Not enough to argue the point. And please don't ask me now when I stopped beating my wife.'

I heard a basso chuckle from the Black woman. There was a moment of silence as she stepped forward to address the group. 'I suggest it is unwise to deny to any section of humanity the penchant for violence, the capacity for evil or the savagery to hate. I think of the Bitch of Auschwitz torturing Jewish children to death, I remember middle-aged White housewives in Little Rock lining the way to the high school to spit and throw stones and scream filthy insults at nine Black children as the National Guard escorted them to the schoolhouse door to do nothing more than claim their legal right to an education. But these are matters of pith and moment better discussed at another time and in another setting. I came here for a party, some good wine, good company, some joy and some LAUGHTER!'

Her voice was extraordinary, the timbre of West Africa with the mellifluous accent of Western America, each word enunciated with unstudied clarity. She stopped the conversation stone dead, then, right on cue, turned from the silence with an actor's gesture of dismissal, smiled broadly at me, held out a strong right hand at the end of a strong right arm and said, 'Hullo, I'm Maya Angelou.'

I took her hand and gave her my name. She repeated it with American courtesy. It sounded altogether better when she said it. I just wanted to listen to her talk. Her voice was an exhilarating change from the mumbled consonants of middle-class English and Cockney vowels hog-tied by glottal stops. With another perfect minimalist gesture she brought forward her tweed-suited companion. 'And this is my dear friend, Sonia Orwell.' I reached for their glasses.

49

'Since we came for wine let me get you some more.' I returned and delivered the refilled glasses and raised mine in salute. 'Thank you, Maya Angelou, for saving me from a good verbal whipping.'

She raised her glass and said with soft-toned weariness, 'The world doesn't need more bullies.'

'I felt like a punched-out sparring partner looking across the ring at a sadistic young title contender bent on chopping me into dog meat. Then, just as the bell rings, young Joseph Louis Barrow ducks through the ropes, shuffles into the centre of the ring, hands low, no fear, no need for defence. A left hook to the jaw . . . "The Bitch of Auschwitz!" A short right to the heart . . . "Little Rock housewives!" An uppercut to the point of the chin . . . "Neither time nor place" . . . and it's all over.'

Maya was smiling and looking at me with interest. 'Do you know much about Black Americans?'

'Very little. I've read a couple of books and I read the English papers.'

'But you called Joe Louis by his full name.'

'Joseph Louis Barrow? That's correct, isn't it?'

'Absolutely, but very few Whites know that, and not too many Blacks.'

'Oh that. I was crazy about boxing when I was a boy and read all the fight magazines I could get hold of. A lot of the articles were about Black fighters, of course. I guess I remember it from those days. I couldn't understand half the stuff I read, though.'

Maya was grinning. 'Give me an example.'

I thought back to when I was a ten-year-old carefully reading every word of the latest copy of *Boxing News,* cutting out pictures for my scrapbook. 'Black-eyed peas!' Maya's eyes widened and she chortled with delight. 'You see, I read that before every fight Joe Louis would eat a lucky meal, steak and black-eyed peas. I tried to imagine what black-eyed peas could possibly look like and why they were lucky? I still don't know. Then there was the business of picking cotton. Ike Williams had a special Bolo punch and I read he developed his punch practising on sacks of cotton and his strength picking cotton as a boy. That puzzled me. What did cotton look like when it wasn't on a cotton reel and how did picking it develop your muscles? How did picking cotton compare with carrying a hod for example?'

Maya nodded knowingly. 'It compares, to say the least.'

That sounded like first-hand experience. 'Have you picked cotton?'

'Yes.'

'How's your right hook?'

'Adequate. Have you carried a hod?'

'Oh yes.'

'How's *your* right hook?'

'Patchy. My timing comes and goes . . . er . . . your voice?'

She murmured, 'Yes?'

Was that coquetry in her eyes? My heart bumped. Was this beautiful and extraordinary woman flirting with me? 'Er . . . are you an actor . . . or a singer?'

'Yes.'

Sonia Orwell, who had observed our exchanges with good-natured tolerance, decided to intrude hard information into the conversation. 'And besides being an ex-cotton picker with an adequate right hook, Maya is one of the most vivid and graceful writers it will ever be your good fortune to read.'

'Really? Are you published over here?'

'Not yet.' She made it sound like a simple matter of waiting for the inevitable, as if I had asked her before dawn if the sun had risen.

'Where can I get your books?'

'If you give me your address I'll call my manager in New York tomorrow and have his office express them to you.'

Sonia produced an elegantly minute notebook and a silver propelling pencil for me to write my address.

'And if *you* give me your phone number i can call you with rave reviews once I have read them.' She told me the number and Sonia offered the notebook again. I shook my head. 'No thanks, I'll remember it.'

Maya sniffed in mock pique. 'Do you always go around remembering ladies' phone numbers?'

'No. But I'll remember *yours*. It's easy. The last four digits are 2337. Twenty-three is the age I'd like to be. Thirty-seven is the age I am.' She looked me up and down with theatrically carnal eyes.

'Thirty-seven is a wonderful age,' she said softly.

Sonia's upper-class English stiff upper lip was getting stiffer as she watched our blatant and public flirtation. She started to, 'Er . . . er . . . er' and look at her watch. Maya ignored her.

'Maya, we really must be going.'

Maya nodded but kept her eyes on mine. 'You don't have to wait to read the books before you call.' I shook hands with them and they left.

I went to say goodbye to Giles Gordon, my agent, and thank him for the party. He invited me into his office for a glass of Scotch and the good news that he was well on with a deal to sell the British rights of my book-to-be. I thanked him for the good business but my mind was elsewhere. 'Tell me what you know about Maya Angelou. Is she your client?'

'No, she's Tony's client. She should be published here. She's written an autobiographical memoir of a young Black girl growing up in rural Arkansas in the Depression. I think the trouble we're having selling it is that it's different. The publishers are looking for the next *Soul on Ice* and it isn't an angry book. It's lyrical and pastoral and funny. There's a beautiful description of the cotton pickers going out to the fields in a soft southern dawn and working through the day, then trudging home at nightfall. It's a prose poem. There's a chapter on the Blacks gathering around the radio in a store listening to the Joe Louis-Max Schmelling title fight, praying for a victory for their race. That could be a one-act play. It's different . . . but unforgettable. I'll rustle you up a copy and you judge for yourself.'

'That's alright, she's having a copy sent to me.'

He raised his eyebrows. 'Is she now? Well, well. I noticed you two seemed to be hitting it off.'

'We have a lot in common. She picked cotton and I carried a hod and we both admire Joe Louis.'

He laughed. 'How did you get on with Sonia?' I shrugged.

'I think she's an insufferable snob. Can't stand the woman. You know who she is, don't you?'

'No idea.'

'She's George Orwell's widow.'

'I didn't think George Orwell was the marrying kind. She must have rare powers of persuasion hidden underneath that tweed suit. Or adaptability.'

'They married in his declining years. She nursed him more or less.'

'Good for her. Ironic though. The road *from* Wigan Pier led in the end to Sonia. Life's a crapshoot.'

'I'll give you a piece of advice. If Maya Angelou offers you any hints on writing, take them to heart. Good luck with everything. And don't forget to write. Final piece of advice. Just write something every day. Anything.'

I took a taxi across town to my favourite Paddington drinking club. Settled at the bar and mindful of my agent's parting advice, I wrote a cheque for five pounds. Bella the barmaid gave me a Guinness boilermaker, my change and a message from Lew Dixon that he was driving to Devon for an estate auction the following day and would like me to share the driving and keep him company. Normally I would have jumped at the invitation to enjoy sea breezes, country scenery and Lew's Irish wit for a few days. But my mind was on Maya. Bella noted my hesitation. 'The weather's nice in Devon this time of year,' she encouraged.

'Very nice, but tell Lew I need to stay in London.'

'Something cooking?'

'Maybe.'

'A woman, huh?'

'Good guess.'

'No guess, it shows.' She flirted her eyes. 'You're looking good this evening.'

'You look tasty yourself, kiddo,' I flirted right back.

Baldwin was smiling when I finished the story. 'That's it?'

'That's the story.'

He applauded softly. 'So many ways it could have happened differently. Maya could have left the party half an hour earlier, you could have gone to Devon the day before.'

'The web of fate, Jimmy.'

'Yes.'

'One loose end. My friend Lew, the one I might have gone to Devon with. He's a devoted student of your works and has the highest opinion of your political insight. I promised him I would note carefully your comments on the Nixon administration and retail them to him on my return. I'm empty-handed. Or empty-minded. Can I get a quote?'

He stopped smiling. 'Nixon. Where to begin?' He worked his cigarette elegantly for some moments. 'His name is Lew?'

I nodded.

'Tell Lew the new Nixon is nothing new,

To jog his memory,

Tell him THIS

Whitacker Chambers,

Alger Hiss.'

We clinked glasses. It had been a wonderful summer, but it was over.

53

CHAPTER THREE

Maya's letter to London and the plane taking me to San Francisco must have passed each other somewhere out over the Atlantic, so when I called her from a pay phone at the airport the news in her letter was news to me. She had contracted to play a lead role in a Broadway play and would not be in San Francisco in the near future. It did not surprise me that my travel plans would have to be rejigged — that was just another strand in Spinoza's good old web of fate. I had anticipated a peripatetic visit and relished the prospect. The surprise was that she had switched from being a blocked and distracted writer to being a leading actor on Broadway. When I tried to get more information over the phone she said sweetly that she would explain everything when I got to New York and that meanwhile I should enjoy a couple of days in San Francisco in the company of her son.

'Just wait by the kerb outside the TWA International arrivals. I'll call him as soon as you put the phone down. He'll be there in about half an hour. He'll be driving my red car. Guy will take care of you.'

Guy had grown impressively since I had met him as a new-born babe in the final pages of *I Know Why The Caged Bird Sings*. He was about six foot four with Herculean thighs, a gladiator's neck and a broad-featured, powerful head atop of it. He was clearly his mother's son and I spotted him immediately as he got out of the sporty red Buick. He scooped me and my bags from the sidewalk and we were away and gone.

55

'Would you like to go to my mother's house in Berkeley? Everything's ready there. I changed the sheets and stocked the fridge and the liquor cabinet . . . there's a spare room in my apartment . . .'

'The spare room sounds inviting. If it's no trouble.'

'You're invited, and very welcome. So that's settled. Are you exhausted? Ready to crash? Or would you like to see some San Francisco nightlife?'

'I'm probably exhausted but I just don't know it yet. Let's do the town.'

'The City.'

'The city.'

'New York is a town. San Francisco is THE CITY and it's *never* Frisco.'

'Gotcha!'

He proudly guided me through San Francisco as if it were his private estate. We saw the Purple Onion where Maya had been a headlining calypso singer, the Hungry I, Enrico's and other landmarks of a past era that had fossilised into tourist attractions. After a couple of hours and half a dozen stops at clubs and jazz bars we were drinking coffee at the Café Vesuvius when he asked me, 'What are your intentions towards my mother?'

'We were lovers in London. I'm in love with her and I hope to marry her. However, I haven't mentioned marriage to *her* so I'd appreciate your discretion.'

He raised his cup to me. '*Omerta.*'

I raised mine. '*Grazzi.*'

'Let's keep going, there's plenty more to see.'

In Guy's energetic and amusing company my two-day stay stretched to four days and then five while I scarcely noticed the time passing. He had taken a week's leave from his job at the Kaiser Medical Center and with princely courtesy seemed ready to spend it entertaining me. I watched him hold his own in a quick, tough game of chess at the No Name Bar in Saulito, a place I knew from a Hunter Thompson article in *Rolling Stone* magazine. He had slaughtered me at Scrabble, guided me through a revolutionary war zone around the Berkeley Campus, the Black Panthers' territory in Oakland. We swapped stories about hard-time travels in Spain and adventures in London. With his Italian-American girlfriend we went on shopping expeditions to supermarkets where the abundance overwhelmed me and then we cooked huge meals that were shared by friends who were completely unhomogenous.

He knew no more about his mother's New York plans than I did. At twenty-eight years of age he was wildly proud of his mother's achievements and gently tolerant of what he regarded as her amusing eccentricities. I suspected that he thought of me as the latest of those eccentricities.

He endeared himself to me by wearing workshirts, boots and jeans wherever he went. When I brought up the subject of Maya's distaste for work clothes apropos of the history of Blacks in America he just laughed. 'My mother is my mother and I'm me. Anyway, half the time she wears the same clothes she used to wear in Ghana. Tribal robes wouldn't suit you, Paul. You don't have the gait.'

We got to the airport in good time to have a few drinks before my flight departure, then ambled over to the gate, loose and laughing. Waiting travellers and quick-moving passengers, newly arrived, fixed their eyes on us for a moment then went about their business with downcast eyes, quickly intimidated by Guy's linebacker presence. I had forgotten about that during my days with him. He was a big guy. And he was Black. I thought about the first night I had walked down Sloane Street with his mother.

My flight was called and we shook hands at the entrance to the covered way to the plane. 'Time to send you on to New York . . .' He scooped me up by the waist and made as if to throw me on to the plane. People around us froze in terror, then loosened into twitching panic. Guy set me down and winked. *'Vayas tu con Dios.'*

'Y tu, amigo.' I had a lonely flight to New York.

Maya was staying at the Algonquin Hotel. There was a message for me at the desk. Maya had gone to pick up her mother from the airport. 'Please go up to the suite and make yourself comfortable.'

On my previous visit I had gone to the Algonquin for a drink in the bar in search of round-table ghosts. Being grandly ushered up to a suite was a very nice way to come back to New York.

Within an hour Maya and her mother arrived. Unlike Guy, Vivian Baxter was easily recognisable as the glamorous and independent woman I had met in *Caged Bird*. She carried her years as elegantly as the mink jacket draped around her shoulders. She was charming but reserved, and certainly reserving in her judgement on me. I suspected she did not approve of my shoulder-length hair or my white skin. Maya had told me that her brown-skinned mother had always had the darkest-skinned husbands and lovers . . . 'Blacker the berry, sweeter the juice.'

57

Maya talked about London friends, Guy, the airlines I had flown on, the weather in San Francisco, everything but the play she was going to act in. When I tried to get information about it she shushed me and said we would talk about it later.

'Why don't you call for drinks? My mother likes Dewar's White Label on the rocks . . . and ask for the room service menu. Let's be comfortable and eat in the room tonight.'

We ate medallions of beef, excellently cooked and beautifully served. Maya and her mother analysed the ingredients of the sauce and all the details of the meal with the professional intensity of practising chefs. Food seemed the common ground on which mother and daughter had agreed to meet. Their conversation reminded me of my occasional meetings with my father when we would contrive to have an agreeable time discussing construction techniques and new materials and by tacit agreement avoid any reference to our diverse personal lives. As I watched them together I would never have guessed they were mother and daughter. Vivian Baxter's hair was long and straight, Maya's short and curly, her mother was six or seven inches shorter, aggressively elegant, expensively bejewelled and unapologetically self-centred. I doubted that she had ever said, 'Tell me about yourself' to anyone in her whole life. She reflexively rearranged her clothing and adjusted her posture in a routine of subtle sexual display. Vivian Baxter neither looked her age nor gave the slightest nod of acknowledgement to the passing years. I thought she was great.

Next morning Maya was ready to talk about her immediate future and the unlikely circumstances that had created it.

'There was vague talk about my acting in a play before I left for London but I didn't bother with the details because Gerry Purcell promised me I wouldn't get the part. He said he was asking for terms that no producer would ever accept. "Just forget about it. Go off and write the book." So that's what I did. There are all sorts of deals and offers floating around all the time and I don't get into all that. That's what I have a manager for. And right up to the last minute I never thought it would happen.'

'What went wrong?'

'Several things. I met Charles Bloch, the producer, and I liked him. The part interested me, and finally Charles drove the last nail in the coffin of my reluctance by saying he would drop the production if I didn't take the role.' She laughed, 'Modesty aside, he's right. I don't know anyone else who could play it better. I play Mrs Elizabeth

Keckley, a Black woman of course, who stood by Mary Todd Lincoln in her troubled times after Lincoln's assassination. She had *bought* herself *and* her son out of slavery with the money she had earned and saved dressmaking. She went on to become the First Lady's confidante and couturier. Geraldine Page plays Mary Lincoln. Just the two of us on stage for two and a half hours. Geraldine's husband, Rip Torn, is directing.'

'Rip Torn!'

'You know him?'

'I'm a fan. He and Eli Wallach are my two favourite non-leading American actors. They always seem to get more out of their parts than the writers ever put in. Yes, I'm definitely a Rip Torn fan.'

'How about Geraldine Page?'

'I think I know the name . . . I associate her with Tennessee Williams . . . but I don't think I've ever seen her in anything.'

'Well, when you do, you won't forget her. Ms Page on *stage* is Hell on wheels. Anyway, rehearsals start next week. We open in the New Year and that's all I'm going to say right now. Meanwhile, we've got an apartment at the Chelsea Hotel. That should make you feel at home, it has a kitchen and a realistic rent. My mother will help us settle in. Your hair seems to have grown healthily since I saw you in London.'

'Yes, my winter coat, I guess.'

'It might be nice to get it trimmed.'

'I'll do better than that, I'll get it shorn. In answer to your unspoken question, my long hair is not a political statement or even a style. It's just lack of a haircut.'

She kissed me and grinned. 'Thank you. I was nervous about bringing the subject up.'

'I'll attend to the matter forthwith. Tell your mother top of the morning for me . . . and reassure her that I've gone to find a barber who knows how to cut hair short.'

She laughed. 'Smartass! We're all lunching with Gerry Purcell. Let's meet downstairs at noon.'

'Whereabouts downstairs?'

'In the lobby. We'll be the two very attractive Black women drinking Dewar's White Label.'

I dressed in light grey flannel pants with four puffy pleats at the waist and a soft-shouldered woollen jacket. It was a bold-patterned red, blue and cream number cut high in the back.

'New clothes?' said Maya.

59

'Yes. Yves St Laurent finest ready-to-wear. It's the *dernier cri* in London.'

'Really? We call that an Eisenhower jacket here. It, er . . . looks comfortable. Most truck drivers wear them.'

'Well, casual elegance seems to be the keynote this season. And I wanted something warm for winter.'

She laughed. 'That's your idea of warm winter clothing?'

'I was planning on wintering in California.'

I had a premonition that my new clothes would soon follow my long hair into oblivion. I was disappointed. My outfit had been a great success the first time I had worn it to go shopping in London.

I had gone to a Bond Street shoe shop and been brightly welcomed by the salesman and then fawned on when I asked him to select a couple of pairs of shoes to complement my outfit. Half an hour later when he had finally satisfied his fastidious taste and I started to write a cheque I had automatically reached in my wallet: 'Let me give you identification.'

'Sir! We do not require identification from a gentleman wearing Yves St Laurent trousers *and* an Yves St Laurent jacket.' He plucked the cheque from my fingers and glanced at the name printed above the signature. He beamed. '*Thought* so!' He gave my forearm a playful tap. '*Loved* the pix in *Cosmopolitan*, Paul.'

The barber was hung over like a dog and camp as a row of tents. As he chopped away he paused from time to time to gaze at the mirror and inspect his skin for blemishes while he muttered about his wild excesses of the night before. I was uncertain about customer etiquette in that situation so I just waited silently until he was ready to carry on with his task. In the end I was pleased with his work. His hands shook as if he was in the advanced stages of Parkinson's disease and that had resulted in a pleasingly shaggy accent to my coiffure that was in keeping with my general theme of casual elegance.

There was still an hour till noon so I bought newspapers and went into a diner fitted out in chrome and plastic for coffee and a read. The stools at the counter were filled by sturdy working chaps on early lunch-break. Most of them wore soft-shouldered woollen windcheaters in bold, bright plaids. Damn you, St Laurent!

I joined Maya and her mother at a table by a low oak partition that separated the lounge area from the passageway that led to the registration desk and the dining-room. From the radiance of Vivian's greeting smile I judged that she approved of my haircut.

She was in a talkative mood and I sat back and enjoyed listening.

The upper half of a grey-haired Black man's face appeared slowly above the partition. I glanced at Maya. She had seen nothing. A moment later it appeared again in a different place. Our eyes met and the head rose a couple of inches, a finger rose to the lips begging silence. Maya had seen nothing. The face sank out of sight again. There was a rustle of movement behind the partition. She looked over; the face and the dashiki-clad trunk supporting it popped up above the partition. Maya's mouth fell open then stretched in delight. 'Dizzie!'

He reached over and hugged her across the partition, then came around to join us. Not only could Dizzie Gillespie create a musical *performance,* he could get a slapstick skit out of a chance encounter.

'When I kept seeing half a face over the partition and no one else noticed I thought delirium tremens had finally got me,' I said when he left.

'They don't call Dizzie "Dizzie" for nothing,' said Maya. 'And he's mellowed a lot.'

Lunch across town was a light-hearted pleasure. Gerry Purcell, who up till then I had known only as a gruff voice on the other end of the transatlantic phone, turned out to be a charming and witty host. In person he was a slab-shouldered, middle-aged man who looked like a Roman emperor who employed the services of an excellent tailor. His shirtmaker was pretty good, too. The food was honest Italian and the service as exceptional as I had expected because Maya had already told me that he and his sisters owned the restaurant. After lunch Maya and Vivian went off to the piano bar with one of the sisters for a drink, leaving Gerry and I to our coffee. I thanked him for the meal and complimented him on the food. 'We try. We don't kid ourselves we serve the very best food in New York but we try to give value for money. I'm very glad you enjoyed it. You're welcome here whenever you're in New York. You're on your own . . . with a friend, can't think where to eat, my sisters will always take care of you. Just sign the bill. Anything else you need, call the office. If I'm not there Ruth will always take care of you. Speak with Ruth. Anything you need now?'

'Well, I was thinking of asking you for the name of your tailor.'

He laughed. 'I was thinking of asking *you* the name of yours. I like the pleats in the pants, and that's a beautifully cut jacket. Perfect detail; the sewing on the button holes is perfect. We don't do work like that in America any more. Cardin?'

'St Laurent.'

'The European casual look. Very elegant.'

Okay, St Laurent, the governor just signed your reprieve.

'I don't think Maya likes it.'

He grimaced and shrugged. 'What does she know? You look good.' He chuckled. 'You wouldn't look right in a dashiki, anyway.'

For a few moments we trod conversational water, then he asked me about my reaction to Maya's news about acting on Broadway.

'Mainly surprise.'

'We were all surprised. We were asking for terms that almost embarrassed *me*! I kid you not. I was feeling my ears getting hot as they kept agreeing to everything. But the producer is right. They got a bargain. Maya *can* be great in the part. Not just good but *great*. You understand me? Maya can *create* the part. The audience will come into the theatre knowing nothing about Elizabeth Keckley, but when they walk out they will remember her for the rest of their lives. They will never forget her.'

As he became intense and repetitive he began to lisp slightly. His upper lip had the fold of an old scar that I guessed was the relic of corrective surgery in childhood.

'Geraldine Page is one of the established *greats* of the New York stage, but Maya can blow her right *off* the stage. I'm not saying she *will* but she can! Maya can blow her right into the aisles. I kid you not. I don't believe Geraldine can sustain the energy level any more. Quite frankly I don't think she's got it any more. In fact, Maya may have to draw back. You understand what I'm saying? She may have to come back and come down to keep the performance in balance.'

Gerry sounded like a fight manager talking about his protégé's prospects against a fading champion. Maybe it was like that. It would certainly be interesting to see.

'What about Rip Torn as director?'

He grimaced and shrugged. 'Your guess is as good as mine. Quite frankly I don't think the play *needs* much directing.' Maybe refereeing, I thought. 'The truth is Rip Torn came in the package. You want Geraldine, you take Rip. It's a trade-off. Who knows? He may be outstanding. It's his first time directing on Broadway as far as I know, he may be great.'

He stretched back in his chair and let his intensity evaporate, beckoned a waiter. 'Have a drink, Paul. You like Valpolicella?'

'Lovely.'

'Two glasses . . . Maya tells me you're writing a book. Will you be able to write here?'

'Sure. Maya's going to be busy and I'll have nothing else to do.'

'Will you need an office to work in?'

'No. All I need is a chair and a table and a warm dry place.'

'Good. I'd love to see anything you've got ready to show. I really would. Sincerely.'

'They printed a chapter in the European edition of *Penthouse*. I'll walk over to your office and drop a copy off.'

'Call before you come and I can show you around. It's nothing luxurious, but it's comfortable. You know the address on Fifth Avenue?'

I nodded. He smiled. 'Welcome to New York.'

According to an inscription carved in a granite plaque set in the exterior wall, the Chelsea Hotel was the first co-op building in New York. That was in 1882. By the look of it, the lobby got its last coat of paint in the same year. As Maya had predicted I felt very much at home.

However, the apartment she had rented was spacious and freshly painted. It was on the third floor and so we had no need to use the elevator, which was fortunate because Maya was nervous of elevators and the one in the hotel was usually out of order anyway.

Vivian Baxter inspected our new lodgings with the same unenthusiastic gaze she had focused on me at our first meeting. Without a word she went to the bedroom, changed into comfortable houseclothes and set to unpacking and getting the place in order.

'What do you want *me* to do?' I asked as she started to scrub down the kitchen. She looked up at me with a dazzling smile.

'You can make Momma a drink, baby.'

Vivian was a decisive woman who could not have played Hamlet to save her life. She had decided she liked me and thereafter that was that. Like all her decisions it was final. A woman's right to change her mind was not a privilege she ever invoked.

Maya was one day away from starting rehearsals and tied to the bedroom phone, so when the doorbell rang while I was making drinks I opened it to a fine-looking Black woman.

'Good morning. I'm Dolly, Dolly McPherson.' She held out her hand. 'And you must be Paul.'

Dolly was Maya's boon companion and I already knew quite a lot about her from Maya's stories. In spite of, or perhaps because of, the fact that she had never married, she was a fascinated admirer of men. An academic all her adult life who had worked and travelled extensively in Africa and Europe, she had never learned to drive a car or cook anything much more complicated than an egg and she had certainly never taken a walk on the wild side.

When Maya had been contemplating autobiographical schizophrenia to avoid admitting her youthful indiscretions, Dolly had been the model on whom she had planned to base the 'good girl' half of her literary personality. I was fascinated to meet Dolly. She was a voluptuous beauty with a dark, flawless complexion that glowed with deep red tints, impeccably groomed and gorgeously scented.

She declined my offer of a drink, saying that it was too early for the hard stuff. It was ten o'clock. Vivian glanced at her with cold mocking eyes. 'Shiiit! The right time to have a drink is when you feel like it.'

Perhaps *both* the models for Maya's bifurcated autobiography were right there in front of me.

While Dolly puttered busily, sending me on errands for flowers, paper doilies, room fresheners, picture hooks and table mats — always one item at a time — Vivian cleaned, set the kitchen to rights, cooked a three-course lunch with provisions she had brought in with her, drank Dewar's White Label and, in what free moments Dolly's errands allowed, told me stories of her days running gambling joints up and down the West Coast, from Anchorage, Alaska, to the Mexican border.

Lunch was superb. When I thanked Vivian she just murmured, 'I'm happy you liked it, baby,' and flirted her eyes.

'Yes, Mum. It was delicious. Tell me, how did you cook the chicken?' asked Dolly in a tone of earnest inquiry. Vivian stared at her. Maya started to laugh. 'What would it all mean to you if she told you, Dolly?'

Dolly's deep red highlights got a little redder. 'Oh Maya, stop teasing.'

Soon after lunch Vivian was ready to catch a plane to the next destination on her transcontinental swing back to California. I put Dolly in a cab back to her apartment. We were settled in. That evening Maya was quiet and moody as she leafed back and forth through the script of the play. She had some hard work ahead of her and she was taking a considerable gamble. She had never acted on Broadway before and it was more than ten years since she had played off Broadway in Genet's *The Blacks,* but she was not worried about being stage rusty because, as she explained, her lecture tours were really a one-woman stage show. Acting was not the challenge. The play was the thing!

It was called *Look Away.* A phrase from 'Dixie', a Confederate Civil War song ('I wish I was in the land of cotton', etc.) that author Jerome Kilty had presumably chosen to point up the fact that the wife of the president who had freed the slaves was a southern belle raised by a Black slave mammy in Kentucky.

Kilty had written two other successful two-character plays. His first, *Dear Liar,* which I had seen in its London production, was a skilful scissors and paste job. He had scissored excerpts from love letters between George Bernard Shaw and Mrs Campbell and pasted them up to 'create' a theatrical recitation. When I saw it I thought Kilty was sliding by with a slick piece of *littérature trouvée.* One actor playing Shaw recited bits of Shaw's letters to the other actor playing Mrs Campbell who recited bits of her letters to him. The actors were skilful, a delight to watch, and it made for a 'civilised' evening's entertainment. The theatrical equivalent of curling up in an armchair with *Reader's Digest* for a good read . . . and about as satisfying. Kilty had repeated a winning formula by pasting up *Dear Love.* This time he had clipped and pasted the love letters between Elizabeth Barrett and Robert Browning, also out of copyright.

Look Away was a breakaway for Kilty. The letters between Mary Todd Lincoln and Elizabeth Keckley were workaday communications for the most part and even the best clipper and paster could not hope to fluff them up into a full-length drama. So this time he actually had to get the typewriter out of the case and do some writing. The dramatic moment in the two women's relationship that he chose was June 1876, the last night Mary Lincoln spent in the lunatic asylum where her son Robert had arranged for her to be incarcerated so that he could get control of her considerable estate. The two women reminisce. That essentially was the play.

History was not on Kilty's side. In 1868 Mrs Keckley, miffed at not being paid for her services to Mrs Lincoln when Mrs Lincoln finally received her share of Abraham's estate, had published a book called *Behind The Scenes: Thirty Years a Slave, Four Years in the White House.* Mary Lincoln was miffed in turn and never had anything to do with the 'coloured historian' again. Mrs Keckley went back to Washington and continued where she left off being a successful dress-maker to the city's new élite. Undaunted by history, Kilty deftly solved the problem of bringing the two women together eight years after their last recorded contact by borrowing a piece of theatrical legerdemain from Thomas Cullinan who, in 1969, had written a play called . . . *Mrs Lincoln.* Cullinan set it in the lunatic asylum and has characters from her past appear as in a dream to talk about the old days. So, Kilty has Mrs Keckley turn up for Mrs Lincoln's last night in the asylum 'as in a dream'. Problem solved.

I had to tip my hat to Jerome Kilty. As a fellow hack scribbler forever counting the words and looking for an easy way out to complete an assignment I had to acknowledge the man was Hall of Fame material. Cool Hand Kilty.

He had another winning card up his sleeve. The play he wrote could have been titled *Scarlett O'Hara in her sunset years. All alone with my old Black faithful slave mammy.*

It was a bankable idea. White Americans are patently infatuated with the gallant myth of the slave-peddling old South. Black Americans, understandably, are not. But a producer can fill a Broadway theatre without them.

When Maya explained all this to me, my first unspoken thought was, 'What's a nice Black girl like you doing in a crummy play like this?' She soon enlightened me. 'Honey, if anyone thinks I'm going to be the new Butterfly McQueen they are in for a surprise. I am going to walk out on that stage and pay Mrs Elizabeth Keckley her long deferred due. You ain't seen revisionist yet!'

'A hard go of it though, you're one against the mob.'

'Honey, my religion teaches me that one person with God constitutes a majority . . . and as Hannibal said when he was crossing the Alps . . .'

'Fuck 'em.'

'You said it, kiddo!'

As I watched her dress on the first day of rehearsals, she moved with untypical deliberation (one of her engaging talents was the knack of being dressed and out the door looking fine in about two minutes flat). Her self-absorbed, slow movements evoked an image of a movie gunfighter slowly loading his Colt peacekeeper and carefully strapping on his gun belt before stepping out on dusty main street at noon . . .

or a matador patiently fastening himself into his *trace de luces* and meticulously folding his cloak so that it hangs just right before he struts out on to the sand of the bullring . . . or maybe Hannibal on an Alpine pass looking down on the fertile plains of Lombardy.

We were silent as I walked with her to the corner. She gave me a quick peck on the cheek as I helped her into the cab. I gave the Black driver the theatre address, he looked me up and down and barely nodded. As I turned back to get on the sidewalk I heard him say, 'What are you doing with the *enemy*, sister?' I nodded to myself. 'I *hear* where you're coming from, brother!' And in my own limited way I really did.

Back at the Chelsea, I rolled a sheet of paper into my typewriter and thought about writing. I was faced with the 'Kilty Dilemma'. Sooner or later I would have to write something. I just wished I had his moves, but we can't all be superstars. Then I realised it was the right time for a drink because I felt like having one. I settled in an easy chair with a decent bottle of light breakfast wine, found a pop music station on the radio and pondered the interesting process of actors subverting an author's intent.

About fifteen years back I had spent a long summer converting a dank and cavernous basement in a Victorian town house into a modish apartment for a young Cockney actor named Alfie Lynch. Alfie had time on his hands most days and took to hanging around on the job site. He was a cheerful and unassuming young chap who quickly made himself popular with the work crew. They had no idea he was the owner of the apartment and the goose that laid their golden pay packets every week, or that he was a star in a West End musical hit show. They probably would not have believed him if he had told them. Actors, after all, were people like Laurence Olivier or John Gielgud, not young tearaways in sweaters and jeans. The consensus among the crew was that Alfie was an unemployed relative of mine good for running errands. They sent him out for cigarettes, beers, sandwiches, had him bring tools and materials and tipped him generously.

We made friends and, away from the job site, I socialised occasionally with him and his fellow actors in Joan Littlewood's Theatre Workshop Company. *Fings Ain't Wot They Used To Be,* the musical that was making them all fat and prosperous, had started out in Joan Littlewood's off-West End theatre as a Brechtian drama. It was a play about London gangsters with a heavy social message (i.e. criminals are really the victims of the society they despoil) and written in dreary earnest. When the company started rehearsing in their workshop way, they perked up the dialogue as they went along. Then they went for a few laughs but the damn play still did not work because the characters sounded like a bunch of weary ex-cons who had done far too much hard time in Pentonville Prison. The dramatic tension just would not tauten. They played it for more laughs — the over-the-hill gang that never could shoot straight. It was getting better. Then they borrowed melodies from a few Cockney pub songs, added some funny lyrics that rhymed, worked up some raunchy dance routines and . . . a hit was born. The rest was a long run and record royalties flowing in by the barrowload.

One of Alfie's and his pals' party turns was to play a scene as it was originally written and then reprise it in its final form. They were pretty good subverters. I had no doubt that Maya would be pretty good herself. She had said that she was the best actor she knew to play Elizabeth Keckley and the more I heard about Mrs Keckley the more I agreed.

Contemporaries had described her as a 'tall mulatto of regal bearing'. By her skill and business acumen she had bought herself out of slavery in Virginia. Maya's paternal grandmother had parlayed her cooking skills, from baking pies to sell to workers in the local cotton gin in Arkansas, to ownership of the Negro Quarter's only general store. She had secured the future of her disabled son, Willie Johnson, by shrewd hard work. Mrs Annie Henderson and Mrs Elizabeth Keckley were both tall and of regal bearing and not that far apart in time. I had the feeling Mrs Keckley was not the only tall Black woman whose memory would be honoured when Maya stepped out on the stage on opening night.

Lou Reed's hit record *A Walk on the Wild Side* was playing on the radio so I stopped pondering and gave my full attention to enjoying it. There were some great songs around in those days: *Killing Me Softly With His Song, Lean On Me, Drift Away, He Ain't Heavy He's My Brother, Papa was a Rolling Stone*. They don't write them like that any more. Of course if I were interrogated by a hard-eyed panel of Inquisitors I would have to admit that being very in love and feeling very alive warped my perception and made me overvalue the songs. But having admitted that I would have turned aside, like Galileo in similar circumstances and muttered, 'And still they move me'.

The damn typewriter just sat there on the table and the blank paper rebuked me. Oh well, there comes a time when you have to bite the bullet and face the facts. I finished my drink, got out of my comfortable chair, put on my jacket and went out for a walk. I was sick of looking at that damn typewriter and that was a *fact*.

CHAPTER FOUR

CALIFORNIA, BY WAY OF BROADWAY: 1973

I was pecking away at my typewriter, feeling diligent and productive when Maya swept into the apartment like a sudden storm. I had not expected her for another two or three hours. 'Hi, short day at rehearsals?'

'For me. I walked out.' Vertical folds of sullen anger bracketed her mouth.

'Walked out as in "take this job and shove it!"?'

She nodded sourly. 'Well,' I said, 'I've been watching the TV weather reports and Northern California looks very nice this time of year.' She nodded and absentmindedly pecked me on the cheek.

'It's not come to that yet, but the shit is going to hit the phone any minute now. Let's get out of here. I wish Baldwin was in town.'

I cleared my typewriter and papers off the dining-table and we were out the door in two minutes. We strode through the chilly damp afternoon, heading, by unspoken consent, for Greenwich Village. 'Why did you walk out?' I asked.

'Fucking *Dixie*! I don't want to talk about it now. I want to sit in a bar with a bottle of red wine. I want to talk to a Black friend, preferably a southerner. If I'm going crazy I'd like to know.'

'Sam may be home by now.'

'Good idea. Sam will be able to tell me.' She hooted sudden laughter. 'We *know* Sam's an expert in craziness!'

Sam Floyd was one of my favourite new friends in New York. A

69

debonair forty-year-old bachelor whose twin passions were golf and grand opera, he was actually an undercover tenured college professor who camouflaged his identity by posing as a tireless disco dancer, boisterous tippler and quick-tempered street swaggerer. In those days a lot of academics had gone undercover, just to avoid boring discussions about the latest flood of student demands and assaults on faculties, campus be-ins and trash-outs. I 'made' him one tipsy evening in a toughish Lower East Side bar. My lips were loosened with whisky and without thinking I misquoted a couple of lines from *Prufrock*. It caught Sam off-guard and he corrected me reflexively and continued the quotation for another dozen lines before he realised what he was doing.

'You're wrong, Sam.'

'Sheeiit, the hell I am. I'm teaching a class in Eliot and Pound this semester.'

'You're what?' He realised his mistake and looked furtively at the George Raft and Sylvester Stallone look-alikes mumbling at one another around the bar. He dropped his voice to a murmur. 'I'm a professor of English Literature at Queen's University.'

I hooded my eyes and put my finger to my lips. 'Your secret is safe with me. The rat turd bastards can tear my fucking windpipe out and stuff it up my arse but I'll never squeal.'

Once his cover was blown he was a ready source of information I was grateful for. Many of the references everyone else understood went by me, but when Sam was around all I had to do was raise an interrogative eyebrow and he would succinctly footnote it for me. I hoped Sam was home and available.

Maya and I settled in a near-empty bar a couple of blocks from his Horatio Street apartment. We made a start on a carafe of gritty red wine that tasted as if it had been fortified with paint stripper and then she went off to phone him. A few minutes later Sam strutted in looking amused and arrogant. The barman greeted him by name and handed him a wine glass. He sipped the wine and then turned his attention to Maya. She brought us up to date on the play's progress in rehearsal. It sounded a mess but perhaps rehearsals always were — construction sites look a mess too, but things get built in the end.

'You haven't read the play, Sam, but there's a pivot when Mrs Lincoln/Geraldine Page comes down stage and in a senile memory of her happy southern girlhood in Kentucky starts singing *Dixie* . . . I wish I was in the land of cotton and shit forth . . .'

'That's why it's called *Look Away*, after all,' said Sam.

'Of course. I/Elizabeth Keckley stay upstage and do some things with the forty-six packing boxes of bits and pieces that represent what's left of Mary Lincoln's life. It makes a sort of sense.'

'Go on.' Sam sipped his wine and winced.

'This afternoon Rip comes up with a new move. He wants me to come down stage, put my arm around her shoulders, sitting *behind* her of course, and sing along with her, smiling like a fucking coon. I wouldn't do it, Sam.'

'Dumb of Rip Torn to imagine you would.'

'He said, "You *have* to try it, Maya".'

Sam stretched back and grinned. 'And you said, "Boy! Ain't nothing I *have* to do but *die*!" and walked out of the theatre.'

Maya nodded, her eyes looked teary. 'My question is, Sam, was I right or am I crazy?'

'Those are two questions. Do you want them answered in the order posed?'

'Smartass,' said Maya and kissed him on the cheek.

'I'll answer but first of all I'd like to ask Paul a question.' His large and slightly protuberant eyes stared hard into mine. 'Did you or did you not order this lousy wine?'

'Well, Sam . . . Maya said . . .'

'Just answer yes or no.'

'Yes.'

'Tut, tut. The Mafia ships this garbage from Italy as ballast in oil tankers. It'll kill you.' He turned to the barman. 'Isn't that right, Tony?'

'What's that, Sam?' He repeated his allegation. 'So you found out? Who talked? Give me a name, Sam.'

'I'll give you a name. Chivas Regal, three over, water back. And I want to see you break the seal on a new bottle.'

'That'll be the day. I've never seen a new bottle of Chivas in this place yet. But then I've only worked here fifteen years.'

Maya was cheering up. 'Yes, you were right,' said Sam. 'Asking a southern Black to smile and sing *Dixie* is like asking a Holocaust survivor to sing the Horst Wessel song in a Munich beer hall. If you *did* do it, every reviewer would pick up on the "fascinating ironies" and every Black intellectual in New York would be on your case. You'd spend the rest of your time explaining why you gave credence to a cracker's fantasy of happy slaves singing on massa's plantation. You were right.'

'Thank you, Sam.'

'Alice Childress . . . *Trouble in Mind* . . .' I raised an enquiring eyebrow. 'A play about a play with antagonism between a White director and a Black cast. Rehearsals get stormy.' I nodded. 'Let me give Paul some more background. *Dixie* was the anthem played in 1861 at Jefferson Davis' inauguration as President of the Confederacy. If the South had won the war they'd be singing it at Rebel stadia before the ball games and Maya and I would be picking cotton.'

'Gotcha, Sam.'

'I've thought about the consequences since I walked out but at the time I just reacted.'

'Of course. Like Rosa Parks,' said Sam, and I raised an eyebrow.

'Where were you on 1 December 1955, Paul?'

'It was winter, I was at college . . . so if it was a Wednesday or Saturday I would have been playing soccer. Any other day of the week I was probably playing ping-pong in the students' union lounge and thinking about the essay I should have been writing.'

'At least you were thinking about it. I wish I could say as much for most of my students. Rosa Parks wasn't so lucky. She had been working all day as an alteration seamstress in Montgomery, Alabama. When she got on the bus she sat down in the front. The bus driver told her to move to the back of the bus. She refused. The police came and took her to jail. Black women in Montgomery got together and asked the local ministers to organise a bus boycott. There was a meeting and a young and little-known minister named Martin Luther King gave a speech. Four days later, on the day of Rosa Parks' trial, the boycott started. On 13 November 1956 the courts declared the Jim Crow law segregating the races on the buses unconstitutional. The American Constitution was 180 years old and it had taken White judges that long to figure out something that Rosa Parks had known since she was ten years old.'

'Gotcha, Sam. Let's have another drink.'

'Good idea but let me use the bathroom first.' His eyes flickered at me out of Maya's sight. His message was clear.

'I need that too,' I said, and we excused ourselves.

Sam rinsed and doused his face at the wash basin and then studied his dandified self in the mirror. 'Has Maya eaten today?'

'Probably something at the theatre. A snack probably.'

'This is all a tempest in a teacup really. Maya's upset but she'll get her way. The important thing is not to let it blow up into the Third

World War. It's not a good idea for us to sit here drinking for the rest of the day.'

'What do you suggest?'

'Let's go back to the Chelsea and cook something and cool out before the storm clouds gather again. Why don't you arrange that?'

'It would be better coming from you, Sam.' He nodded.

Once we were back at the hotel Sam started work in the kitchen. That provoked Maya to change into work jeans and take over. The therapy of food preparation worked very well and the conversation drifted into happy talk. Sam entertained us on the rented piano. Sam knew her very well. They had been lovers for a while and friends much longer. I hardly knew her at all. Day by day as she rehearsed she climbed deeper into the persona of an elderly nineteenth-century Freedwoman, stern, dignified and puritanical. She moved 'old'. Sometimes when we made love I felt I was being unfaithful in another century to the woman I had met an ocean away in this one. It was the stuff that fantasies are made of.

Gerry Purcell soon called and Maya arranged to meet him at seven. For half an hour she retreated into herself, humming and swaying as she worked in the little kitchen. Sam and I talked about the London he knew from reading but had never visited.

We arranged to meet up at the Paparazzi at eight, put her in a cab and started to walk and drink our way along the twenty-odd blocks to the restaurant.

At the first bar I thanked him for his perception and tact in the other bar earlier. He shrugged it off. 'Maya's a pussy cat. Have you met Nina Simone yet?' He rolled his eyes and started laughing.

'Do I want to?'

'You'd probably have her eating out of your hand. Of course she might bite it off at the elbow. Nina *is* crazy. You know her stuff?' I did.

'She and Ray Charles were superstars for my generation in Europe.'

'Ray Charles has something she doesn't have, or vice versa. Maybe it's genius but I honestly don't know which of them has it. Come on, let's go and tease Gerry about his golf game.'

Maya was in a good mood and dinner was lighthearted. Mrs Keckley was back in the Playhouse dressing-room and Maya was her old self again. When she and Sam went off to the piano bar Gerry and I had our ritual glass of Valpolicella at table. He wanted to talk about what he had read of my book. He was predictably flattering. 'What's your promotion budget?' I had no idea if there was one. He asked who my editor was. I told him. 'Has his wife seen you yet?' I shook my head. Gerry grinned at me with his bared teeth clenched on the filter of his cigarette. 'Well, that's something that will be interesting . . . how are you getting along with Sam Floyd?' He was watching me carefully.

'Fine, Gerry, just like you and I get along.' Gerry and Maya had been friends for years and lovers for a while. I had the feeling he was jealous of Sam.

'Are you still married to Germaine?'

'Yes, but I'm going back to England soon. My visa runs out next month. I planned on getting a divorce while I'm there.'

'You anticipate any problem with the divorce?'

'None at all. She told me the only reason she hasn't already divorced me is to protect some other innocent woman from the misfortune of marrying me.'

'She's full of shit! If you're going back, think about the timing though.'

'I was going to wait till the play opened.'

'Think some more about that. Have another glass of wine.' The ever-hovering waiter was at the table in the flicker of an eyelid. 'You heard what happened today with Rip, I'm sure.' I nodded. Gerry became fierce as he always did when any of 'us' was challenged by any of 'them'. 'Maya was right of course. Maya was absolutely right. I kid you not. Maya had right on her side. I wish I'd been there. I'd have broken his other fucking leg . . . that's just a joke.' In an earlier career Gerry had been a New Jersey labour union negotiator and some of the mannerisms lingered. He sipped his wine and dismissed his ferocity. 'But that's all settled. Anyway . . . this is just the start . . . they're only what . . . about half way into rehearsal . . . about three weeks? Things will get worse. You understand what I'm saying? Every day the tension will move up another notch. It's not Maya, or even Rip. It's performance. Have you ever been around performers going into a show?' I had not. 'Boy, I can tell you, it's an experience. I'm not just talking about Broadway or La Scala or London West End. It's *any* show. Believe me. Two or three times a year I put T & F shows into Vegas and Reno . . .'

'What's a T & F show?'

'It's Tits and Feathers. Just little filler acts, you know, three girls with high heels and feathers and cleavage and a fag dancer with his crotch stuffed. It's not the New York Ballet . . . but it makes no difference. It's a performance. It gets crazier and crazier till the opening.

And this is a play! Sudden death, live or die by the reviews. I kid you not, it will get worse.' He started to tick off items on his fingers. 'It's Broadway. Charles Bloch is a first-time producer, a cherry from Los Angeles. You understand what I'm saying? Rip Torn is a first-time director. No out-of-town try-outs. They're going in cold. The stars are Black and White. The White star is married to the director. *And* did you know this is the *third* play about Mrs Lincoln on Broadway this season? Can you believe that? . . . I'm running out of fingers.'

'What's your suggestion, Gerry?'

'Spend Christmas and New Year with Maya, that's very important for both of you. The play opens second week in January. Don't be around for the opening night. Watch a preview after New Year and then . . . get out of Dodge. Let's see how Maya and Sam are doing next door. The waiter will bring your drink.'

Maya had taken over the piano bar mike to everyone's patent delight. Gerry watched for a few moments and then excused himself, smiling paternally.

She was working the room like the pro she used to be. I wished I could have seen her years ago when she was a coloured chanteuse at Mr Kelly's or the Blue Angel. One day I would ask Gerry about those days.

That night Mrs Keckley was out of town and I made love to a slightly hard-bitten club singer who was a bit of a tart and much smarter than you would ever have guessed.

She was silent for a while over breakfast and then she clapped her hands together. 'I know how I'm going to do it!'

'Do what?'

'Sing fucking *Dixie*. Don't ask. Wait till opening night. Pick me up at the theatre. Let's have drinks out before Dolly comes to dinner.'

'Lovely. See you at five.' She wished me good typing and was gone with a spring in her step and a sway in her hips. I wondered who I would be meeting at five o'clock. Mrs Keckley had not called home in a while.

I tidied the typewriter away early and did some modest Christmas shopping. There was only a week left and shoppers' tempers were getting frayed. After two hours in the Manhattan retail arena the Playhouse Theater was a welcome dim-lit oasis. At least the tensions were under the surface there. Rehearsal was winding down. Geraldine and Rip were front stage left having a half-hearted quarrel. Maya was standing upstage right, immobile and erect as a sentry outside

Buckingham Palace. Gerry stood in centre front stalls like a cobra reared to strike. Charles Bloch sat at the far end of the front stalls with a relaxed smile on his face that may have been utter bewilderment. Electricians and stagehands were doing busy work. I was within a yard of Gerry before he noticed me. He held his hand out for a touch handshake and raised his eyes to heaven. Without a word he walked away and headed back up the aisle. Charles waved me over and smiled a welcome.

I had visited rehearsals twice before and met Charles and his wife Zeta on my first visit. They were both in their late forties, soft spoken, tanned, healthy looking, amused at the world and each other. Gerry had introduced me as Maya's very good friend from London and they had seemed genuinely pleased to meet me. 'Are you in the theatre?' asked Zeta.

'No. All I know about the theatre is how to buy a ticket and watch the show.'

'That sums up our knowledge, too,' said Charles laughing.

But this evening Charles was alone. We sat and watched while Rip and Geraldine wound down their spat. She went upstage to sit beside the pile of packing cases and he limped off noisily tapping his walking stick on the boards. I noticed that the stick had no rubber tip to mute the dramatic impact of his tortured progress. As he dragged himself past us, his right leg encased in a filthy old plaster cast, his face clenched in misery and anger, he passed close enough for us to smell his sweat but ignored our presence and went on to talk to a technician about lights.

Different lights played on Geraldine for a few minutes and that was the end of the rehearsal. Maya waved at me and went off stage. Rip came and slapped me on the back and shook my hand. 'Maya said you were coming. Ready for a drink? Give me two minutes. I'll tell the girls where we are.' He hobbled off jauntily.

'Will you join us, Charles?'

'Nooo . . . thank you. I think I'm ready to just slip away and escape into real life. Do you know why I'm producing this play?'

'A psychotic urge to lose money?'

'You must have been talking to my wife,' he laughed. 'The *conscious* reason was to show my friends, especially my New York friends, how easy it is to produce a successful Broadway play. No experience needed. Just good California know-how.'

'But what idea gave you that idea?'

'I did it in the movies. Picked a winner first time out. I read the manuscript of Arthur Hailey's *Airport.* I thought it would make a great movie. Arthur gave me an option. Chuck Heston's a fellow tennis player and he agreed to play the lead. I had a script written, hired a producer, some friends joined in and we put up some money. We went to the bank and borrowed the rest. *Airport,* the movie, was made. After a while I started receiving large cheques. It was as simple as that. No strain, no pain. My tennis game got *better.* I can always tell when I'm under stress because my backhand goes to pieces. Of course, my friends all made a great deal of money too, so they kept pestering me to do it again, but I said let's do something different. Let's do a Broadway show, it'll be fun.'

Charles was impressively wry and amused for someone with several hundred thousand dollars in play.

'How's your backhand these days?'

'Terrible. I'm snatching at the ball and I haven't done that in years. Enjoy your drink with Rip.'

We went to Au Tunnel round the corner from the theatre. In memory of his Texas roots Rip ordered bourbon and branch half and half, so to show my solidarity with the proletariat I ordered a boiler-maker, in memory of my construction worker days. Unfortunately Au Tunnel was an upmarket bar-restaurant, owned and operated by a family of French immigrants, and not only was the ethnic and social significance of our choices lost on the bartender but he had not the faintest idea what we were talking about. We reordered and defined our drinks in specific terms.

I felt overdressed in Rip's company. His ill-fitting and stained polyester pants were ripped up the leg to accommodate his dirty and disintegrating plaster cast, his tweed jacket was without shape or buttons. I also felt overwashed.

'How does Maya feel it's going?'

'She was in fine fettle when she left for work this morning.'

'She told you about the singing business?'

I shrugged. 'I've only been in this country two months. Some of the niceties of old grudges escape me . . . now if we were in Belfast drinking a pint of porter in the Fortress pub in the Falls Road district having a similar discussion I would be on firmer ground.'

'Are you Irish?'

'Like your bourbon and water, half and half. Torn's an Irish name I think?'

'I believe it is.'

'And Rip's a nickname?'

'No, it's my given name. There's been a Rip in our family for the last three generations.'

'It's a grand old name. You know when Maya told me you were directing I was very excited.'

He looked me over warily. 'Why?'

'I reckoned I'd get a chance to meet you. I'm a fan. I told Maya that you always seem to get more out of the parts you play than the writers put into them.'

I had his attention. 'What do you mean exactly?'

I had rehearsed my theory of acting in moments of solitude at the Chelsea when the practice of writing got tedious. Now I was ready to try it out on someone in the business.

I tucked my chin in, clenched my cigarette between my teeth in the corner of my mouth and stared straight ahead with a squinty-eyed, Clint Eastwood thousand-yard stare. 'There'sh two shortsh of actorsh in thish world. The flat wallsh and the bumpy wallsh. The flat wallsh do a job. The bumpy wallsh *act*.'

Rip squirmed around on his bar stool, cocked his head on one side and looked up into my face, ferret eyes flickering, lips twitching in an ingratiating smile. 'Blondie, we're friends. You can tell me, Blondie. We've always been friends. Tell me the name. The name, Blondie. Just tell me the name of the film where the Oscar's hidden?'

We started giggling.

'Now just tell me the difference between a fucking flat wall and a bumpy wall.'

'Okay. You throw a tennis ball straight up against a flat wall and it comes straight back at you. You do it again it comes straight back again. But if you throw it against a bumpy wall it will bounce off at an angle and you have to duck or reach or step to catch it. It's more interesting that way. A television series like *Hawaii Five O* is pure flat wall acting. The dialogue bounces straight back among the actors. *The Good, The Bad and The Ugly* is flat wall, bumpy wall and a combination of the two. Lee Van Cleef is flat wall, Eli Wallach is bumpy wall and Eastwood is sometimes flat and sometimes bumpy. You're bumpy wall.'

'Well that's not exactly how they taught it at the Actors' Studio but I'll take the compliment, buddy. I'm not getting many these days. Thanks.' He gestured for another round of drinks.

The barman set them down with pride. 'Boilairemakaire, and Bourrrbo' an' brrranch, 'alf an' 'alf.'

Rip grinned. 'Bumpy wall barman.'

'Definitely.'

Maya and Geraldine soon arrived. Maya was shoulder to mid-calf in mink and strutting sassily. Gerry looked as if she was wrapped in a small horse-blanket, one from a Shetland pony perhaps. Her grey-blonde hair was stringy and dirty, her jeans did not quite zip at the fly under her pot belly and her blank eyes and unco-ordinated walk reminded me of a concussed soccer player wandering around the playing pitch after a brutal clash of heads. I wanted to hold three fingers up to her face to see if she could count. Except that once in a while her eyes focused with deadly sharpness.

The patron came bustling out of the dining-room and headed straight for Maya, who was obviously the sort of customer he had in mind when he invested his life's savings in a high-class restaurant. '*Mademoiselle Angelou, quelle plaisir!* You will be dining with us tonight?'

'Unfortunately not, because we have a guest for dinner *chez nous* tonight. But . . . this is what I am planning to cook . . . I need some advice.'

'*Bien sûr, Mademoiselle . . .*' He snapped his finger to summon a waiter and led Maya off to a table.

'You boys have a nice time?' said Gerry in a menacing voice.

'Lovely,' I said.

'Paul told me I could act and proved to me he can't. But I'm grateful. It's nice to hear a compliment for a change.'

'You complaining?'

'Of course I'm complaining.'

I inserted myself between them. 'Here are the fight rules. On a knockdown you go back to a neutral corner; break clean from the clinches; no hitting on the break but defend yourself at all times. Shake hands now and come out fighting. What do you want to drink, Gerry?'

'Bud in the can.'

A waiter was serving Maya champagne.

Over dinner Maya told Dolly McPherson every detail of the *Dixie* crisis. Dolly puffed with outrage at every turn of the tale. She started planning to organise her students to picket the theatre. Red skin tones glowed out of dark brown cheeks and neck and her body heat was perceptible from where I was sitting across the table. In all the years since I had first heard the old gag 'God, you're lovely when you're

79

angry' it had never before occurred to me that it was a sexual innuendo that really meant that the man would like to bring the woman he was flattering to the same pitch of excitement in bed. My mind meandered for a while as Dolly's anger ripped on unabated. Maya started playing Devil's advocate for Rip. I erased irrelevant images from my mental movie and got into the conversation.

'It's really a play within a play, Dolly. You know, like Alice Childress' *Trouble in Mind*?'

'It *is*!' Maya wiped a quick smile off her face and leaned forward. 'Explain that more, Paul?'

'It's the basic premise of the play. Whites and Blacks read different implications into script and there's a . . . a . . . a . . . how shall I say it? . . . an antagonism between the White director and the Black actors who are rehearsing a play.'

'Exactly,' said Dolly. 'Alice Childress was right on time.'

'When *was* that play written, Paul?' asked Maya sweetly.

'Written or produced . . .?'

'It was produced in 1969,' said Dolly promptly.

'I shook my head. 'Are you sure, Dolly? I didn't think it was quite as recent as that. For some reason 1967 is the date that sticks in my mind. I'll have to check my notes.'

Dolly folded her lower lip up over her upper lip and gazed at the ceiling with intense concentration. 'I'm certain it was '69, Paulo.'

'You're probably right, Dolly,' I conceded.

'You know, Maya, it's really a sad commentary on our educational system when Paulo, an Englishman, picks up on an analogy that I honestly don't believe one in ten of my students would have drawn.' She closed her eyes and shook her head rapidly. 'I won't even begin to talk about the faculty. I'm not sure any of them could *spell* Childress.'

'Paul can do that,' smirked Maya.

'C H I L D R E S S E.'

'No E at the end. Gotcha,' said Maya.

'As I was saying before I was so rudely interrupted. C H I L D R E S S. Even though you feel certain about the date I'm going to check my notes, Dolly.' S M A R T A S S mouthed Maya out of Dolly's sight.

'What set of notes are you going to consult, sweetie pie?' honeyed Maya. 'Your notes from your work at the Paddington Bar-Users' Institute for Afro-American Studies, or the Wandsworth Common Negro Ensemble Theatre?'

Dolly froze in concentration and scanned back through her memory files for the two unfamiliar centres of learning. Then she reddened to a sunset glow. 'Shame on you, Paulo! You're teasing me. I trusted you, dammit!'

'White man ask you where you goin'; you tell him where bin, chile,' said Maya between giggles. 'Sam Floyd is Paul's one and only connection for Black literary history in this town. We had drinks yesterday and *Paulo* has a facility for *parroting*.'

Dolly's eyes sharpened their focus. 'How is Sam? Has Nina caught him or is he still running?'

'In hiding, I think,' said Maya.

Dolly squirmed around in her chair as she giggled. 'Oh Maya!'

'You know that Gladys Knight song . . . *LA Was Too Much For The Man*?'

'Oh Maya!' Dolly quivered with delight for a moment, then sat up and sang out with operatic force, 'Nina was too much for the Sam.'

Maya leaned forward and sang in a throaty chanteuse voice, 'He's gone back to a better face and time.'

Dolly's eyes widened. 'Is he back with Linda?'

Maya shrugged and looked innocent. 'He mentioned that she enjoyed the opera last week . . . but my name ain't Lit, I ain't in that shit. No ma'am, I don't get in folk's mess.'

I cleared the table and washed the dishes while the ladies updated their ongoing research in human relationships. As I did my chores I pondered, not for the first time, how different Christianity would be if Bible classes studied The Gospel According to Mary Magdalene . . . 'And it came to pass in those days that John, who had been hitting on Matthew, went to Jesus and said that Martha . . .'

It was nice to see Maya having an unbridled good time. Good times were thin on the ground as we approached the New Year. Christmas was squeezed in between rehearsals. Julie Harris had opened in *The Last of Mrs Lincoln* on Christmas Eve to respectful reviews that were unlikely to sell many tickets. As Gerry had predicted the tension kept moving up a notch. Maya was in character as Mrs Keckley almost all the time and when I told her I was going back to get a divorce she just sniffed and said, 'Good. I don't chippy with other women's husbands.' Obviously she was not the same person who wrote a poem about adultery that ends:

81

IN GOOD COMPANY

They went home and told their wives
That never once in all their lives
Had they met a girl like me.
But, they went home.

She was putting on weight and moving with statuesque dignity. Geraldine was still reading her lines some of the time and interrupting the flow of rehearsal with petty requests to get her husband's attention. The dialogue was not bouncing well between them. Maya believed that Geraldine was faking incompetence to lull her into complacency and that on the opening night she would come out firing on all cylinders and try to steal the limelight with a bravura performance. Maya was planning to do the same thing.

I booked a low-cost flight on Laker Airlines and found myself daydreaming about London a great deal of the time. We spent New Year's Eve at the hotel with Dolly McPherson. Maya spent about ten hours in the little kitchen making head cheese from scratch, endlessly stripping meat from pigs' ears, and spicing and simmering it. There were black-eyed peas boiling on the stove. We were going to have a traditional meal to bring good luck for the coming year. At last I understood why Joe Louis ate black-eyed peas before a fight. Head cheese turned out to be the same as the brawn of my childhood. It was my least favourite sandwich filling, eaten only during the worst food shortages of World War Two and then only when we had run out of delicious Spam.

Previews started right after New Year. A preview is more than a dress rehearsal and less than a first night. The audience pays a few dollars and takes a chance on the quality of the show. Audience reaction is carefully monitored by everyone with an interest in the production because preview audiences are generally knowledgeable and experienced, like the crowd that buys tickets to watch a boxer's public workouts before a title fight.

Sam and I went together to the first preview. Geraldine was an audience favourite but she was still plodding through her lines. Maya joined her front stage for the singing of *Dixie* but stayed deadpan and silent while Geraldine sang feebly. The audience was unexcited by the scene, they were New Yorkers to the bone and as far as they were concerned she could have been singing *The Wearing of the Green*, or *Greensleeves*. The single bit of business that excited them most was Maya cutting cloth for a dress for Mrs Lincoln. The whole move took about a minute and all the while Maya was looking at the audience and

82

not at the cloth until she held it up cut precisely into the panels of a dress. It was a feat of legerdemain that made them gasp. They might not care about Civil War history but they knew the rag trade. Maya had practised for hours in the apartment using old *New York Times* sheets, scotch-taped together. She was definitely bumpy wall.

When it was over Maya got a little more applause than Geraldine but the audience was enthusiastic for both of them. Sam and I stayed in our seats as the theatre emptied. He was deep in thought. 'It's an unsatisfying play . . . or am I missing something?' he said at last. 'Mrs Keckley visits Mrs Lincoln on her last night in the asylum. They talk about old times . . . some they shared and some they didn't. Mrs Keckley starts to make a new dress and fix Mrs Lincoln up so that she looks good when she leaves. That's it. It's like an excerpt. But where's the rest of the play, climax, denouement, catharsis? Was Aristotle that wrong? What was Mrs Keckley doing making a dress in a lunatic asylum?'

'Mrs Keckley is a figment of Mary Lincoln's imagination.'

'So it *is* all a dream. I thought it had to be, but . . . oh well, it just isn't much of a play. What do you think?'

'I'm with you, kid.'

In the foyer Charles Bloch and Zeta were accepting congratulations. They were smiling as usual. Rip was limping painfully and touting for sympathy. He was working his stick and cast like a master. The crumbling cast was obviously no more than a stage prop because it had long since ceased to give any support to his injured leg. We left word with Gerry that we would make our way to the Paparazzi and went off to do some male bonding in a bar.

It was my first flight on Laker Airlines and I enjoyed the challenge of trekking all over the airport to find the cubbyhole office to check in, carrying my bags across miles of tarmac and crossing swords with snooty young women who spoke in the strangled accent of London and the Home Counties and held unshakeable belief in their pre-eminence on the evolutionary ladder. I felt I was back home in the UK already. I was used to hard travelling and the whole thing was a bit of an adventure. There was plenty of time to strike up acquaintance with fellow cheapskates and, in truth, it was a relief to escape the relentless American efficiency that had engulfed me for the past two months.

Until I got on the plane.

That was a shock. The wear and tear evident throughout the craft made it seem impossible that it could survive one more flight across the Atlantic. Given the choice I would rather have hitched a ride on the *Spirit of St Louis* with Charles Lindbergh. Once we were airborne I unbuckled my threadbare seat belt and joined the line for the rest-room. We were a talkative and nervous bunch and all of us flying Freddie Laker for the first time. When it came my time to use the toilet I noticed that not only was the carpet covering the threshold worn through to the metal sub-floor but the metal itself was shiny as a barber's razor and sagged ominously when I stepped on it. I felt very glad that Maya had cooked us a meal of black-eyed peas just two days before. This one flight would exhaust my whole year's supply of good luck.

'How was your flight?'asked Mary when we finished hugging on the front steps of her house and settled at the familiar dining-room table with a bottle of wine and two tumblers.

'Just fine. But don't buy stock in Laker Airlines. The day they run out of first-time flyers that bastard can padlock the door and make a run for the border.'

'That bad?' I nodded. 'He's a hero, you know. Cheeky Freddie, the spirit of British pluck and daring.'

'Yeah, another miracle from those wonderful people who brought you the *Titanic*.'

'Anyway, you're here. Let's crack a bottle and drink a toast.'

'Before you open the bottle . . . I have a taste for a warm Guinness and a Wall's pork pie. Let's stroll to the Hope and Anchor.'

'Whatever your heart desires, sweetie. Let me write Derek a note.'

We settled in the pub lounge and I brought her up to date on my news. The coincidence of three plays on Mrs Lincoln appearing at the same time caught her journalist's attention.

'Why? There must be a reason. That's like three plays in the West End on Queen Victoria and John Brown or whatever his name was. What's special about Mrs Lincoln? And why now? *You* want to sell this story?'

I shrugged. '*Mia historia es tua historia*. Feel free.'

'Alright. Tell me about Mrs Lincoln, leaving out no detail, no matter how seemingly insignificant.'

I aired my newly acquired knowledge of American history and then Mary summed up. 'She was an extravagant, frivolous woman whose husband was probably seriously unfaithful. He was strongly hated and adored and shot to death while he was in office. She was mistreated by Congress, and drifted through the remaining years of her life. One son died young, one was a greedy bastard who had her locked up in a lunatic asylum for a year. Some parallels there with Jackie Kennedy. Maybe that's the hook for the story. Maybe that's what made three writers go back to the history books and see what happened to her after Lincoln's death.'

'By jove, I think you've got it.'

'Well, I'll hawk it around among the hacks. I'm sure one of them can beat it up into a column and buy us a curry dinner and a bottle of wine. How's the play itself?'

'Like Laker Airlines. I don't think it will fly for long. Maya's fine in it. Her reputation won't go down with the ship.'

'Are you two going to get married?'

'I'm going to get divorced.'

'Well, that's a start. Can I be maid of honour? Derek can be your best man. That's a good excuse for us to have a holiday in the States.'

'I think you have to ask Maya about being a maid of honour but first I have to ask her to marry me.'

'Get on with it then. Germaine is going to be pissed off.'

'She won't worry.'

'She won't worry but she'll be teed off.'

Derek soon joined us and he was concerned about Maya's reaction if the play flopped. 'Maya takes everything personally. You know she's got one layer of skin less than the rest of us.'

'It'll be disappointing. A lot of work and worry down the drain.'

'Perfect time to ask her to marry you. She'll be vulnerable.'

'Oh Maar!' said Derek.

'Phooey! That's how you caught me.'

'Why?' asked Germaine, when I told her I wanted a divorce.

'It's tidy, that's all.'

'Are you still on with Maya?'

'Yes.'

'I hope she knows what she's doing. I think we should have a woman to woman talk. Is she here with you?'

'She's in New York.'

We set the legal processes going.

IN GOOD COMPANY

I phoned Maya on 8 January. The review in *The New York Times* had been lukewarm and cursory but the acting had been praised.

'What happens now? Do you keep on going as long as you draw an audience? Do plays pick up on Broadway by word of mouth?'

'I don't now. Charles Bloch has called a meeting for later today. Call me tomorrow. I'm in a very strange place right now. I'm . . . I'm . . . lost for words for once. Love you. 'Bye.'

Charles Bloch cancelled that show that day. He thanked everyone for their outstanding work, paid up guaranteed salaries on the spot, and told everyone that he respected them too much to submit them to the painful process of dragging out a failed play to cut his losses. Then the caterers brought in the champagne.

'Charles and Zeta are a very classy couple.' Maya sounded as if she was crying.

'That was my impression. Funny too.'

'I don't feel real. It's as if Mrs Keckley vanished without trace and I don't know who I am . . . and I'm drunk . . . and I wish you were here. Come back soon.'

Derek called me from Fleet Street to read me Clive Barnes' review. Maya's acting was unequivocally but briefly praised. 'There is the strength and cool sweetness of Maya Angelou which is very lovely.' Mrs Keckley was described as a 'cool and contained Black woman who loves (Mrs Lincoln) sufficiently to take care of her'. Geraldine was similarly praised, so was Rip's direction, the lighting and the sets. The play just did itself in, along with the surfeit of Mrs Lincoln on Broadway that year. Derek brought the newspaper home so I could study it before I talked with Maya again. The title told the story: 'More about Mrs Lincoln'. Geraldine's characterisation was described as 'slightly bitter, very faded and with a sadness that is very fine indeed'. As to the direction and the play itself it said, 'Rip Torn has directed with naturalistic skill. It is the nature of the work that two actresses come out and deliver what are virtually set pieces to the audience.'

'Sounds like a lot of hard work for nothing,' remarked Derek. 'Have you read the opinion piece on Nixon's second term? Here it is.' He pushed the article to me across the dining-room table. It was titled 'A Nation Unready for Le Grand Richard' by John Brademas, who was a Democratic Congressman.

'What about it?' I asked.

'Read it, you idle bastard.'

It was an outline of the ways in which Nixon would try to establish an imperial Presidency in his second term and why he would be opposed by Congress. It all seemed familiar stuff to me.

'So what's new?'

Derek pointed to a paragraph in the last column. It dealt with Nixon's plans to censor TV news by a backdoor manoeuvre that would be blocked by a Congress opposed 'to the still unexplained Watergate campaign tactics'.

'Is that break-in still news in the States? I thought that was all over and forgotten.'

'Little bits and pieces keep coming up in the papers but Nixon will be sworn in this month and then it'll probably be all over. No one talked about Kennedy stealing votes in Chicago very much after the inauguration as I recall . . . it was Camelot all the way.'

'But see where it's positioned in the story, right along with censorship of the press. That sounds like what's-his-name is flying a trial balloon. You know he's got suspicions and he's hoping someone can come up with some proof. Clip the stories for us when you go back. It might be a nice piece for Mary to try in *Private Eye*.'

Maya was composed next time we spoke. She was ready to go back to California. We discussed timing and travel arrangements then she said, 'Guess who turned up in New York?'

'Baldwin?'

'I wish. No, that wife of yours. What's with her anyway?'

'I think she wanted to have a woman to woman talk.'

'Sheeit!'

'Well, the divorce won't take long.'

'Sooner the better.'

I made arrangements to emigrate. I went through my wardrobe and threw away whatever of it friends would not accept as work clothes, gave Derek my modest collection of obscure reggae records, donated a few pieces of furniture to the Wandsworth Common household, closed my bank account and changed the modest proceeds into dollar bills and traveller's cheques. Sewed a couple of thousand dollars in bills into the lining of an old black leather overcoat to obviate pointless discussion with the British Customs service about archaic currency regulations, paid the solicitor for the divorce, renewed my US visa and finally went over to Maida Vale to visit Sister Anna. She was a Ghanian friend and extended kinswoman of Maya's who had been keeping some of

Maya's clothes. Maya had asked me to bring them to the States. I had an old-fashioned canvas wardrobe/suitcase that was divided down the middle. I packed Maya's clothes in one side and mine in the other.

US Immigration was giving me a hard time in New York. UK Customs had written in my passport that I was taking 250 pounds sterling out of the country and they wanted to know how I was going to survive for three months in the USA on that. It was a fair question. The line behind me was impatient. They were decent middle-class English folk for the most part, and they were ashamed of me in my old black leather overcoat for causing a scene.

'I have friends in the States. And I have more money, trust me.'

'Don't ask me to trust you, show me.'

'Okay.' I pulled up the bottom hem of my coat and ripped open the lining and fished out a handful of bills and dropped them on the desk. I reached back in for more.

The immigration officer started laughing. 'Alright, alright. I trust you. Get going.'

I truthfully told a fierce-looking Customs woman that I had nothing to declare. She bridled and brusquely ordered me to open my bags. The first one she reached in was my canvas suitcase and she pulled out one of Maya's full-length dresses. She held it up and measured it against my height. It was just about right.

'I'm bringing some clothes in for a friend.' Her face squinched up. Then she pulled out a pair of Maya's high-heeled shoes. We both took about the same size in shoes. She threw them down on the table as if they were contaminated with bubonic plague. 'Get out of here you filthy pervert.'

The connecting flight to San Francisco was uneventful.

We moved into Maya's pleasant rented bungalow in the Berkeley Hills and both set to writing in earnest. We never discussed *Look Away*. The memory was almost wiped from the slate, but not quite.

Some months later I was out working in the yard when Maya came out to tell me that she had just had a call telling her that she was nominated for a Tony award for best supporting actress on Broadway.

'Talk about the proverbial band aid for a slit throat . . .'

'But you must have made a pretty big impression for a one-night stand.'

88

She grinned and twitched her lips saucily. 'I guess someone thinks I've got some good stuff. Wanna try me, big boy?'

But our little joke vanished fast. She stared away glum and miserable. 'No wonder actors are crazy. I won't make that mistake again.'

CHAPTER FIVE

A TRUE BELIEVER. SAN FRANCISCO: APRIL 1974

Before the 1849 Gold Rush, when San Francisco was still a rough and tumble seaport, the Berkeley Hills across the bay were blanketed by redwoods and oak trees. When San Francisco mushroomed and Gold Rush money fuelled a construction boom, the trees were felled and milled and barged across the bay. Within a few years the hills of San Francisco were blanketed with timber-built houses and the Berkeley Hills were bare. They were soon replanted with fast-growing eucalyptus trees that had been introduced into Northern California from Australia. The trees were very sappy and stored their own water through the long dry summers; their root system was shallow so they thrived in rocky soil. By the time I saw them the Berkeley Hills were pretty as a picture again. Maya's cottage in the shady hills was pretty as a picture too. The dining-room had stunning views across hills and water to the Golden Gate Bridge.

I set up my typewriter at the dining table and Maya, who wrote long-hand, made herself comfortable in the bedroom. It was surprisingly cold in Berkeley that winter, and very conducive to staying indoors and working. For recreation Maya cooked and I grocery-shopped; friends and neighbours visited. Sometimes we went to a movie on Solano Avenue or made a daring foray across the Bay Bridge to San Francisco but most of our time was given to industrious hibernation. It was the winter of our content. It turned out to be a winter of disaster for the eucalyptus trees. The cold snap broke all records. It turned tree sap into ice and all over the bay hills eucalyptus giants blackened and froze to death. As usual Nature was having the last word. We should have left the buggers in Australia where she put them in the first place.

Somewhere in that happy time we decided to get married. After that I proposed and then we went down town and bought a ring.

I say 'we' bought a ring but the plural pronoun is probably inaccurate. We had pooled our money in a joint bank account and my modest contribution was probably already spent. Maya always seemed quite untroubled by money, as she explained when we left New York. Of all the things we would find to quarrel about, money would not be one of them. Gerry Purcell's office handled all major bills and transferred spending money into our account as needed. Maya employed a secretary who came to the house two or three days a week and a part-time housekeeper. It all seemed very grand to me, but she was convinced that her lifestyle was almost eccentrically modest. A cousin made her dresses, she drove a three-year-old car, we dined on chicken most days and drank California jug wine. Compared with our neighbours we were living at subsistence level. That was all fine with me, except for eating chicken all the time. My palate was homesick. I started having fish-and-chip supper dreams and after a few drinks I would get teary-eyed thinking about Wall's pork pies and Mary's roast beef dinners. Maya was a fine cook, let me make that perfectly clear, and her repertoire was impressive, she just liked chicken and rice more than I did. Every grocery list started off 'Fryer chickens'.

I was writing to Derek one day: '. . . another stereotype confirmed; as I suspected Black folks live almost exclusively on fried chicken and rice'. Maya read the letter over my shoulder and was outraged. 'How can you say such a thing? I've never even cooked you fried chicken.'

'What did we have for breakfast yesterday?'

'Chicken and rice fricassee au fine herbs.'

'And lunch?'

'Smothered chicken, country style with boiled rice.'

'Dinner?'

'Poulet au citron à la moroccaine, au ris.'

'What are you planning for lunch?'

'Chicken Kiev . . .?' she said in a very small voice and started to giggle. 'But all that does not alter the fact that you are propagating a dastardly lying racial slur against poor helpless Black folks. We do not live on fried chicken.'

'But I buy fryer chickens every time I go to the store. So we're eating fryer chicken every day. And rice with every meal.'

'Poor baby. You think that fryer chicken and fried chicken are the same thing?'

'Fryer . . . fried . . . freyered, you mean I haven't had fried chicken yet?'

'I'm going to cook you fried chicken for lunch. No. I'm going to *teach you* how to cook it. You've never had fried chicken in your life?'

'No. We had two chicken dishes growing up, roast chicken and left-over roast chicken.'

I learnt how to cook fried chicken. It was delicious. No wonder Black people eat it all the time.

After that I started cooking alongside Maya sometimes and buying potatoes, which she called Irish potatoes because Black people have a stereotyped notion that the Irish eat potatoes all the time. We cooked meat-loaves and London broils and potatoes ten different ways as occasional variations on chicken and rice. I stopped having fish-and-chip dreams. With the menu problem solved there was no further impediment to our marriage and we started planning the wedding.

Gerry Purcell was going to give her away and Derek was going to be my best man. Guy and some friends who called themselves the Berkeley Irregulars were to provide the music. Jessica Mitford was in charge of making lists. Her husband, Bob Treuhaft, who was Maya's lawyer, set about unearthing proof of her divorce from her first marriage.

We were going to be married in the back yard so as soon as the cold weather broke I started a crash programme clearing and planting. I built new redwood fences. Bob was over one day and was impressed by my work enough to ask me if I would like to build them another bathroom in their Oakland home to work off a six-hundred-dollar debt for legal services that had been lying fallow for some time. His timing was perfect. I was well ahead with my book, yard work was in hand and it would be a nice change to get out of the house and work on something more challenging than redwood fences. I jumped at his suggestion.

I turned up full of beans at eight o'clock the following Monday. Jessica was already typing away at the dining-room table (one day, perhaps, I would meet a *real* writer who worked in a book-lined study).

'Thrill of thrills,' warbled Jessica. 'A bathroom is coming, a bathroom is coming! Bob's making coffee in the kitchen. Come along, I'll show you where the drinks are so you can help yourself as required.'

The kitchen was in disarray, with dirty dishes and glasses everywhere. She waved vaguely at the mess. 'Do ignore the state of things. I'm suffering from a bad case of housewife's block this morning.'

'For the last thirty years,' muttered Bob.

'Oh dear,' she sighed. 'A woman's work is never done.'

'Not in *this* house,' muttered Bob.

She showed me the drinks cupboard and poured herself a nip of vodka. 'What about you, Paul dear, a splash of something to help the coffee down? Why not, I say! Why not?' I helped myself to three fingers of scotch and went to work.

By the end of the day I had hacked off plaster and cut holes in walls and ripped up floorboards and generally made a fine mess. 'Most impressive,' said Jessica as she surveyed the destruction. 'I *do* hope you're coming back tomorrow to finish it.'

'I was planning on leaving it this way.'

'Something to that, it *is* rather dramatic. But I *did* so long for a bathroom. Oh dear, me girlish hopes dashed again. What about a splash of whisk to wash the dust down?'

We settled to a cocktail hour in the kitchen, now immaculate after the housekeeper's visit. Jessica was mildly tipsy on 'splashes of vod' and wanted to talk about her current book, *Kind and Usual Punishment*, a critical survey of the US penal system.

'Have you spent much time in prison, Paul?'

'None so far. Just a few overnights in jail.'

'What a pity. One is always on the lookout for a nugget of first-hand experience. I've just about finished at last with this tome and done much more research than I planned to and still there are fascinating questions. I have the highest regard for my ex-convict friends, salt of the earth and all that, but they can be annoyingly unreliable.'

'The nature of their calling I suppose.'

'Yes . . . you wouldn't consider being a research assistant, I suppose? I mean going to prison for a while. After you've finished the bathroom of course. I'm sure Bob could get you convicted of something. He's a defence lawyer. He does it all the time.'

'It's a handsome offer, Decca, but it would foul up the wedding plans.'

'You can get married in prison. It happens all the time.'

Bob returned about six and examined the destruction and asked a few knowledgeable-sounding questions that revealed his profound ignorance but would probably have swayed a jury. We went downstairs and I finished my drink and he started cooking dinner with tense concentration. 'Bobby loves to cook,' explained Jessica.

'Self-preservation,' muttered Bob.

By the end of the week the bathroom was shaping up nicely. The plumbers had roughed in the pipe work, the doorways were cut and formed, the wiring was in and the walls framed out. I had nailed up a few boards of clear redwood tongue-and-groove to give Bob and Jessica a preview of the finished effect. 'Oh the wonder of it all!' said Jessica. 'Why can't you be something useful like a carpenter, Bobby?' He muttered something under his breath that I did not catch.

While we had cocktails he broached the subject of remodelling the kitchen. 'We could swap labour again. There must be someone you want to sue . . . oh, that reminds me . . .' He paused for effect, shaded his eyes with his right hand and tilted his head back. We waited while he ordered his thoughts. 'Ask Maya to call me very soon. I need to talk about her divorce.'

'What about her divorce, Bobby?'

He paused for effect again. 'Perhaps I should talk to you anyway. In a sense you're my client and it concerns you . . . I suppose . . .'

'You're *my* client, Bob. The relationship between Handyman and Homeowner is confidential and privileged. And of course a sacred trust.'

'Get to the point! What about the divorce? Get on with it, Bobby. For heaven's sake!'

'About the divorce? There never was one. Maya's still married to Angelopoulus.'

'Are you sure, Bobby?'

'Decca! Of course I'm sure!'

'Lord love a duck!' I said. 'Ain't that a turn up for the book!'

'This makes the imminent wedding more fascinating than ever, if that were possible,' said Jessica.

'It makes it bigamous,' said Bob.

'A felony offence, my dear Paul. *Now* are you ready to reconsider my offer of a research fellowship at San Quentin? You see I told you Bob could get you convicted of something.'

'Your offer's looking better all the time.'

'The important thing while you're in the slammer is to take copious notes. Of course your mail will be censored and your cell liable to spot searches . . . but lavish bribery can take care of these details. We will spare no expense. Your relationship with the prison gangs will be of *particular* interest. The Black Guerrilla Family will be ambivalent towards you because you're married to Maya. So will the Aryan Brotherhood for the very same reason. With sufficient tact and charm you will be able to move freely on both sides of the battlefield, so to speak.'

'Or you might be found dead in the showers,' said Bob. 'Your legal expenses will run high. You can remodel the kitchen while you're on bail pending trial . . .' He shaded his eyes and tilted his head back. 'There are some interesting implications in civil law. You could sue Maya, her husband could sue you . . . there's the matter of their community property accumulated over the past twenty-five years . . .'

'Who would get custody of Guy?' I asked.

'Good *question*!' said Jessica. 'Perhaps we could adopt him, Bob? He plays an awfully good game of Scrabble.'

'The simplest thing would be to call off the wedding.'

'Don't be ridiculous, Bobby. I've already ordered my frock.'

Maya decided to meet with her husband forthwith. I thought that was a good idea. 'I don't chippy with other men's wives,' I told her and quick as a flash, and witty too, she stuck her tongue out and thumbed her nose at me.

Tosh Angelopoulus still lived in San Francisco and gracefully agreed to a prompt divorce, but of course it could not be finalised before the wedding date we had set and so instead of a wedding we decided to have a celebration. The Revd Cecil Williams would say something appropriate, we would have a fine old party and sometime later we would get a licence and discreetly tie the legal knot.

By way of introducing me to Cecil Williams we went next Sunday to Glyde Memorial Baptist Church in San Francisco. She had arranged reserved seats in the front pew. When we got there I understood why that was necessary. The church was jam-packed, the aisles were full and worshippers were perched rump to rump on every window-sill. The congregation was an unsolemn kaleidoscope, a Joseph's coat of many colours. We were conducted to our seats by two muscular ushers two minutes before the start of the service. Maya was recognised and the congregation started applauding. She stood up and faced them and applauded herself to them. The stage filled with musicians and choristers. Music started and Cecil swept in flanked by six black-suited Black gunmen. They fanned out and took positions around the stage, genuflecting and scanning the congregation with radar stares, right arms held across their chests, hands on shoulder holsters. 'I'm talking about LOVE!' boomed Cecil in a pleasing baritone. His oblong face was fringed by a flamboyant beard and topped by an unruly fan of black hair. In his flowing robes he could have hidden out in the Sistine Chapel ceiling among the Old Testament prophets and no one would ever have spotted him. The sermon was interspersed with vocal encouragement from the congregation. I paid little attention to it, but then my concentration would have lapsed if I had been present at the original Sermon on the Mount. My years as a Catholic altar boy had immunised me to sermons long ago. There was fine singing, concert-quality instrumental numbers, then Maya was brought up on stage, spoke for a few minutes and was applauded to the rafters. Everyone had a fine time.

After the service we went to the church hall and browsed among the booths set up there by a dozen charitable organisations under his ministry. I was impatient to meet Cecil.

In the years that followed I got to know him fairly well and came to the conclusion that he was probably a saint. He had graduated from a Southern Texas College and come to take over a staid and poorly attended Church in the Tenderloin. Photographs of him at that time show a clean-shaven, buttoned-down, serious young man. However, as soon as he realised that his appearance was a barrier in his dealings with his poor and disenfranchised parishioners, he had shed his three-piece suits and taken on the style of San Francisco street people. He started organising activities in the church hall, feeding the hungry, finding jobs for ex-prisoners, helping drug addicts become ex-drug addicts and sheltering the homeless. The Sunday services were really weekly block parties. The rest of the week was solid, hard work of corporal mercy. The poor may be always with us, but that will not be Cecil's fault.

His ministry was not unique but it was effective. He was successful at persuading the rich and powerful to part with money and goods because they could see where the money was well spent. He and his wife lived in a small apartment in a so-so neighbourhood. He drove an inexpensive car and probably spent less on clothes in a year than some of his patrons spent on pet food in a month. He

97

was diligent and efficient, too. It takes more than good intentions to provide five thousand Christmas dinners for the needy. When the Symbionese Liberation Army demanded millions of dollars ransom for Patty Hearst, Cecil had negotiated and organised food distribution on which the money was spent. He was absolutely undiscriminating about race, sexual proclivities, social status and past sins.

Not that everyone loved him. The trustee board of Glyde Memorial, scribes and pharisees to the bone, repeatedly tried to kick him out. Homophobes, racists and all-purpose crazies sent a constant stream of hate mail and death threats to the church. His bodyguards were there for a very good reason.

One day he called and invited me to lunch. Maya was away so I automatically suggested we waited until she was back.

'This is something I want to talk over with *you*.'

I went to the church and, after being pat-searched by a bodyguard, I was escorted into his office. He asked me where I wanted to eat and I suggested Julius Castle, up on the hills overlooking San Francisco Bay. Great food, great view and expensive for a saint so I insisted lunch be my treat.

Once we had settled to our meal he told me that he and his wife were breaking up. I was not altogether surprised. Lately she had been drinking a lot and taken to drawing me aside at parties and tearfully explaining how she had sacrificed her budding career as a concert pianist to devote herself to their marriage. The conversation was becoming a ritual. She would seek my sympathy as a fellow nonentity. I would nod and listen and she'd go on a crying jag and Cecil would take her home.

I was not looking forward to the rest of the lunch talk. It is not that marital break-up conversations embarrass me but I am just no good at them. All I can contribute is occasional bromides like *'Es la vida'* and 'Faults on both sides'. However, it turned out that he wanted to talk about Gerry Purcell rather than his failing marriage. The question came out of nowhere. 'What do you think about Gerry Purcell?'

'We get along fine. We like each other.'

'But what do you think about him professionally?'

'He was president or chairman of the American Managers' Association for some years. He 's not a fly-by-night. Well respected. Mostly he manages performers. Maya's kind of the odd one out.'

'Who else does he manage?'

'Eddie Arnold, the country singer; Jay Leno — he's a young stand-up comic. He plays here once in a while. Al Hertz the trumpet player — I'm not sure if he still manages him. And then a lot of run-of-the-mill Las Vegas acts . . .'

'Do you think he'd take me as a client? And if he did do you think it's a good idea?'

'What is the idea, Cecil? What would you do that you're not doing now? You work every day of the week.'

'I want to make some money. I've been working for nothing for ten years and now it's time for me to do something for Cecil.'

'You planning on marrying again?' He nodded. 'So you'll need money. I wish you and Jan all the best.'

'Why do you say Jan?'

'Isn't she the one?'

'Yes.'

I shrugged. 'Anyway, to get back to the subject, what's your idea?'

'I want a TV ministry.'

'You mean like Oral Roberts?'

'Yes. What do you think?'

'It's mysterious to me, but apparently if you go on TV and ask people to give you money, a lot of them do. Personally I'd rather buy a wino a hot meal, but I'm a lapsed Catholic agnostic, and what do I know? You want me to talk to Gerry?'

'Would you?'

'If that's what you want. He'll be out in Reno next month. I'll set it up then.'

I was disappointed in Cecil. I selfishly preferred him as a saint, but of course he had every right to make a legal buck like anyone else. I talked with Gerry who remembered him from the wedding and surprised me by being fascinated with the idea.

'Where his church? Berkeley?'

'San Francisco. Big one. Very big congregation.'

'Refresh my memory, who's the mayor of San Francisco?'

'Joe Alioto.'

'Alioto? Well, that's a start. We've got the mayor . . . just joking. You know the time might be right for a Black TV preacher. You understand what I'm saying? The timing might be right. You know I was at the meeting when Billy Graham was picked to be America's evangelist. It was down to a short list. They were auditioning like actors. Graham got the nod. That man was packaged and marketed like a soap powder.'

'Cecil's not like Billy Graham.'

'That can all change. We'll talk with him.'

Gerry and I attended a Sunday service at Glyde Memorial, then went to the Hilton for coffee while we waited for Cecil.

'You know when I'm at a show I always spend more time watching the audience than the performers. You know what I'm saying? I'm watching the audience reaction. Cecil got that crowd, he turns them out . . .' he grimaced. 'But it's hard to pick out anything memorable. It's hard to remember what he said. You understand what I'm saying?'

'Don't look at me. I wasn't listening too much.'

'Cecil needs some catchy sayings. You know Maya's line: "A people thrives and survives in relation proportion to the heroes and sheroes they keep alive." That always gets quoted when she lectures. "Sheroes" catches your attention. You hear what I'm saying? Then there's that other line: "Living Black is not just surviving, but thriving and thriving with some passion, some compassion, some humour and some *style*." That's always quoted. Cecil needs some catchy sayings. Maya could write him some. They'd be called "Cecilisms" . . . people would read them in the paper and start saying "Have you heard the latest Cecilism?" ' He was very pleased with his coinage. 'People would turn on the TV and get the latest Cecilism. Just a catchy line. People don't want much. They have no attention span anyway.'

I shook my head and opened my eyes wide awake. 'What was that you were saying, Gerry?'

He laughed politely. 'But seriously . . . he's very San Francisco. That means fruit and nuts to the rest of America . . . but he's a handsome man . . . Well, we'll see.'

Cecil soon joined us and we made small talk and Gerry and he set a future meeting.

I never talked with either of them again about TV evangelism but I like to think that Cecil was taken up to a high place for lunch, Top o' the Mark on Nob Hill perhaps, and tempted with the vision of all the TV networks of the world and that he resisted the temptation. Whatever happened he is still at Glyde Memorial and still feeding the hungry and comforting the afflicted. It has been that way for the best part of thirty years now.

If it turns out that I have got hold of altogether the wrong end of the stick and St Peter gives me a hard time at the pearly gates, I am counting on Cecil putting a word in for me. After all, I did buy him a very fine lunch.

CHAPTER SIX

A BACK-YARD WEDDING.
BERKELEY, CALIFORNIA: MAY 1974

Our favourite rock and roll song while we were falling in love was Dobey Gray's *Drift Away* . . . 'Give me your beat, boys, and free my soul. I want to get lost in your rock and roll and drift away.' We chose it for our wedding anthem and Guy and his musical friends pliantly rehearsed, although they obviously regarded it as chewing-gum music. The trade-off for them was that they would play as back-up band at the reception after the wedding and the chance to appear with Taj Mahal and Abbey Lincoln at Berkeley's Rainbow Sign Club was enough to buy their tolerance of our middle-aged banality.

Preparations moved along smoothly. Weddings were a rarity among our friends and everyone was eager to get into the act. Derek and Mary arrived from London as promised. Gerry Purcell arrived in good time to double check the catering arrangements, and anything else that anyone would let him interfere with. Ruth Beckford, the doyenne of East Bay dancers, drew from her experience with Katherine Dunham's dance troupe to choreograph the 'Celebration'.

Derek, Gerry, Bob Treuhaft and Ruth's husband Cero took me out for a bar crawl on the wedding eve and I got pie-eyed. Maya stayed at home with her lady friends and also got pie-eyed. When I got back to the house we had a quick effortless row and she stormed off into the night to her mother's house in Stockton. Breakfast was a low-key affair but I had no doubt that a strong-minded woman like Vivian would not allow the cancellation of an event she had been looking forward to for weeks. They arrived late morning, Maya with a cruel hangover and a sour mood. I was in the same condition.

The wedding was set for three o'clock. When Cecil arrived at two o'clock we were all crowded in the small house staring at the rain pelting down and soaking the back yard. Cecil was undismayed. 'The rain will stop.' He raised his arms like Moses by the Red Sea and ten minutes later the sun came out. Cecil took the miracle in his stride. 'Right on time, just like the weather forecast said, "Showers heavy at times clearing by early afternoon".' After that everything was wonderful. Another story-book wedding. We honeymooned for the night at the Claremont Hotel in the Oakland Hills and then enjoyed our guests for the next two weeks.

No sooner was Maya's second volume of autobiography at the printers than she started gathering and writing material for a second volume of poetry, but she was restless. Putting together a volume of poems is a sporadic business without the satisfying grind of writing a book. A young theatre director, Robert Greenwald, asked her to write her own version of Sophocles' *Ajax* for his theatre group in Los Angeles and she accepted the job without hesitation. We bought a copy of the play in translation and took turns at reading it for a couple of days. The theme of the play was clear, 'Those whom the Gods would destroy they first make mad'. The plot was simple. Ajax the Greek and Hector the Trojan meet in single combat and just as Ajax is about to deliver the *coup de grâce* Hector is saved by divine intervention. Ajax is enraged at the gods for fixing the fight and storms off in a fury. In his madness he hallucinates that a flock of sheep are his enemies and slaughters them. When he comes to his senses and sees what he has done he is so ashamed that he falls on his sword and kills himself. The topicality of the play at our time and in our place was as clear as the theme. The revolutionaries of the Sixties were going off their rockers in droves in the Seventies. Just down the road in Oakland the Black Panthers were in disarray. Those who had survived the onslaught of harassment, ambush and imprisonment orchestrated by the police were riven by the systematic covert subversion instigated by J Edgar Hoover. No Black friends I talked with doubted for a moment that Black opponents of the White establishment were being systematically poisoned with mind-warping drugs from the Pentagon's secret arsenal of psychological weapons. Those whom the White gods would destroy they first make mad. It was not debated, but simply noted as a twentieth-century version of the covert genocide that White settlers in California had perpetrated by giving smallpox-infected blankets to native Americans under the guise of charity.

Maya and I talked about that sort of thing quite a lot but it was not helping her write the play. I dredged up schoolboy memories of the theory of Greek drama, the unities of time, place and action, and the function of the chorus. I reached down a little deeper sometimes when the jug wine was tasting good, and recalled the BBC Schools' Broadcasts I had enjoyed as a nine-year-old, listening in the air-raid shelters while the rocket bombs were banging about outside. We all enjoyed the radio plays based on stories from the *Iliad* and *Odyssey*. They seemed relevant in those World War Two days in South London.

Maya discoursed learnedly on African influences on Greek culture and the cultural carry-over of West African story-telling tradition epitomised by Aesop's Fables. We had some good talks but her deadline was looming and the play was not written. She was writing every day, and yellow pages were getting filled up but her Muse was taking a long lunch break.

'What this damn play needs is help,' she said. 'It needs Ray Charles and the Raylettes singing chorus and Dizzy Gillespie playing trumpet. The Joffrey Ballet would be useful too.'

We stopped talking about the play because that was not doing any good. *Not* talking about it was not doing any good either, to judge by Maya's deepening gloom. A phone call from Nina Simone provided a moment of light relief. Maya was incommunicado behind the walls of writer's block so I answered the phone. 'Nina here, you must be the Englishman. You treating our sister right?'

'Best I can.'

'You better goddam treat her right or you'll answer to us. Put my sister on the phone.'

'Let me take a number and she'll call you back.'

'Put her on the fucking phone.'

Maya got on the phone. 'I'm trying to write a play called *Ajax*,' she said. And then she listened. And then she started to giggle. When she got off the phone she told me the joke, mimicking Nina's throaty anger. ' "Right on! Write fucking *Ajax*. Get those honkeys where they live! Right in their soap powders and toilet cleaners." ' I thought it was a good quip. Maya disagreed. 'Nina was serious. She thinks I'm writing a play about detergents and bleaches. But she has a profound need to be pissed off. She came here to stay with me for a month and left after a few days. One morning she just said: "I'm catching the next plane back to New York. I can't stand all this fucking niceness here." And she was gone. The lady sings the blues. Nina is interesting . . . the trouble with Ajax is that he is *not* interesting. He's just a blunt instrument, a killing machine. He's Sonny Liston and I want Mohammed Ali.'

'The class at St Anselm's Catholic Preparatory School shared your opinion as I recall. We thought Ajax was a dummy too. The one we liked was Odysseus. He was a good wrestler. We liked that. And he was always called "Cunning Odysseus" or "Odysseus the trainer of wild horses". We liked that too. Now I think of it, I suppose everyone liked Odysseus. That's why Homer spun him off as his hero in his own series and Virgil did a Latin knock-off. James Joyce relocated him in Dublin . . .'

Maya was not listening. Her eyes had settled into the thousand-yard stare. 'A tamer of wild horses . . . that's just what my great-grandmother Kentucky Shannon was. We don't know much about her except she walked out of slavery when she was a seventeen-year-old girl and turned up one day in Arkansas. She knew how to train wild horses and she started a family. "A trainer of wild horses".'

'Was she from Kentucky?'

'Don't talk!'

The creative process is mysterious but I thought I saw a light bulb shining above her head just then. She went back to the bedroom and the yellow pads.

I searched around and found an atlas. It was a long way from Kentucky to Arkansas. I liked a nice walk as well as the next person. I used to do walking tours, a hundred and fifty miles a week or so in Normandy or Scotland . . . but Kentucky to Arkansas! A teenage Black girl without a road or a map or an inn or . . . did she have shoes? In the chaos of war's end? The chaos of slavery's end? Just thinking about it put me in my place. Quite an Odyssey.

The play was soon written and Maya was pleased enough with it to take Sophocles' name off the credits. It was simply *Ajax* by Maya Angelou.

We went down to Los Angeles for the pre-production and stayed for the whole thing. I think Maya wanted to get back in the saddle again after being badly thrown on Broadway. Kentucky Shannon would understand.

Robert Greenwald and Maya were an odd couple who hit it off from the start. He was in his early twenties, about five foot six and slightly built, a scholarly young man who listened more than he talked. The first time I visited the rehearsal room and watched the two of them together I knew that this was going to be a good time for Maya. The cast was young, racially mixed and full of team spirit. Rehearsals were like training sessions of a sports team, and not just because everyone did calisthenics from time to time. The shared ambition of the cast was to perform a winning play rather than scramble for the limelight. I added my 'cake theory' to my 'bumpy wall' theory. There are two sorts of actors in the world, those who try to grab a bigger slice of the cake regardless of what it tastes like, and those who try to bake a better cake by improving the ingredients and getting the mix right, even if they only have a dozen lines.

The part of Odysseus was played by a young Black actor who certainly looked as if he would do well as a middle-weight wrestler. I had seen his type around the boxing gyms in my youth. In street clothes you would hardly give him a second glance but if you watched him taping up his hands for ten seconds you would know he was going to be very good inside the ring. His realisation of Odysseus was rounded and complete. You were looking at a man who could tame horses, outwit the Cyclops and hold Penelope's love. Everything about the play was just as fine.

Maya's spirits were refreshed. Her confidence was coming back. The opening was a success and the audiences for the two-week run were knowledgeable and appreciative.

While Maya was occupied in theatrical midwifery I enjoyed the leisure to be a tourist in Los Angeles. When I had first planned on coming to California, friends in England had told me how wonderful San Francisco and how dreary Los Angeles would be. Experience proved otherwise. Our occasional visits to San Francisco were a bore to me and Los Angeles was a delight. If Maya wanted to move there any time that would be fine with me. The prospect of moving to LA was not at all far fetched. Maya had a dream on hold, an ambition to build a Trojan horse that would get her inside the walls of Hollywood. It would not be easy. White males had virtually total control over the making and distribution of movies and television programmes. It was no secret, of course, but how to get inside the walls certainly was. Sydney Poitier could be the most popular film actor in the world but White men made the films he played in, built the sets, rigged the lights, produced and directed, designed the billboards on Sunset Strip and sold the popcorn.

105

She often told the story of the first film she had written, *Georgia Georgia*. It was a subtle story of a Black expatriate singer in love with a White photographer, set in Sweden and made in Sweden. The director was Swedish. It had been a nightmare of failed communication and the final product was an uneven mish-mash. After that she promised herself that one day she would make a film the way she wanted to make it. It might not be a good film but it would be hers. You have to control the horse if you want to ride it.

The failure of *Look Away* temporarily disillusioned her with performance but *Ajax* had put the twinkle back in her eye. Maya's decision to write her life story was a decision to mine a rich but limited vein of ore. At some point she would face the prospect of writing a book about herself writing a book about herself, unless she spread her wings and explored new skies.

Our mood was upbeat when we got back to Berkeley. It was time to make changes and we decided to buy a house. In my innocence I thought this would be a simple and straightforward business. We had a brief discussion with Gerry Purcell about money, how much cash down and how much a month for mortgage payments we could afford. There were realtors' 'For Sale' signs all over the place. We engaged a realtor who was a friend of Bob and Jessica and like them an ex-communist, radical, civil rights activist. That made Arlene Slaughter something of an oddball in the real estate profession.

Well into the 1960s selling real estate was an absolutely segregated occupation. White realtors were called realtors and Black realtors were called realtists. They had their separate associations and worked in separate parts of town and observed a cold peace. Arlene, who had come out from New York to work as a riveter in the Oakland shipyards during World War Two, was feisty and Jewish. When the war work was over she switched to cocktail waitressing and studied real estate in her spare time. She married a Black jazz pianist, started a family and then, with time on her hands, joined a firm of Black realtists and started selling houses. She thrived at the work and opened her own office as a White Realtor. Then she hired a Black salesman and all hell broke loose. Her office windows were shot out, her 'For Sale' signs were torn and trashed, and her phones jammed with hate calls. Being a feisty New Yorker all that was the perfect cure for the housewife blues. She started 'block busting'. It worked this way. She would target a street in an all-White neighbourhood with a house for sale. She had a waiting list of Blacks with money and desire to buy such a house and a list of sympathetic Whites with the money to buy it too. Bob and Jessica were on that list. The Whites would negotiate the purchase and take out a loan and on the day the deal closed they would transfer title and loan to the Blacks who moved in forthwith. The first things the Black families carried out of the furniture van into their new home were pump-action shotguns and hunting rifles, displayed ostentatiously for the benefit of the White neighbours peeping out behind their curtains. It helped to discourage them from burning crosses on the front lawn, but that still happened from time to time. The next stage of the block-busting process was for her Black salesman systematically to call every householder on the block in his thickest and gruffest accent and explain that they had just sold the house on their block and ask if they would like to put theirs up for sale. Someone, anxious to get out before prices went to hell in a hand-cart, would put their house up for sale. The all-White offices had no Black customers and no Whites would buy into a busted block so greed overcame bigotry and they listed their house with Arlene. After that came the domino effect and Arlene moved on to the next block. It was fought like the battle of Stalingrad, block by bloody block, with no quarter asked or given by either side. The tide turned when the White realtors realised that they were losing millions of dollars in sales and started hiring Black sales people themselves, another triumph for greed and the American Way.

When we engaged Arlene to find us a house, the battle was a memory for the most part, albeit a recent one. Her street-fighting, bareknuckled energy was channelled into the fight to empower single women to buy houses and get loans. However, the idea of Maya and I buying a house was too good to pass up. Like an old warhorse hearing the bugle call to battle, she charged back into the fray. We plodded through $200,000 houses in the Oakland Hills that we could not afford overlooking golf courses where we would not be welcome to play a game that we did not play anyway. Arlene enjoyed every minute of the owners' discomfort as they tried to act naturally in Maya's presence and only succeeded in tripping over their prejudices at every turn — but we wanted to buy a house not prove a point. We wished her joy of the struggle and put the project on the back burner.

Maya went off on lecture tour and left me to my own devices. I was soon caught up in the Senate Watergate hearings and baseball. I justified my idle hours in front of the television set by telling myself that I was studying the American system of government and the American national game. Sometimes when I had been studying jug wines too

107

searchingly it became difficult to distinguish one from the other. Both went on for ever. All the players had tremendous reputations until they messed up. There were double plays, unforced errors and walks. Erlichman and Haldeman went to jail on a double play. Slugger Nixon made an unforced error and the relief pitcher, Gerry Ford, came in and walked him to a pardon. John Dean was voted Most Valued Player for the Senate Dodgers. When the game was over Nixon had lost but it was not clear to me who won. The commentators all agreed that the system of checks and balances had won out but it seemed a matter of blind chance to me. A sharp-eyed security guard in the right place at the right time; a stool-pigeon who called himself Deep Throat betraying his colleagues for reasons unknown; a conservative President who liked to let his hair down in private and record himself plotting felony in the colourful language of a Mafioso wise guy; and his counsel telling everything in the Senate because he was frightened of getting raped if he went to jail. Sophocles could have explained it better than the constitutional scholars I read.

Maya went on a cross-country campaign to promote her new book. It started off in New York with an interview with Barbara Walters. Of course the interview focused on Maya's time as a prostitute and Maya smilingly strolled all over hapless Barbara. That turned out to be the best thing that could have happened. It cleared the air and, for the rest of her tour, interviewers avoided crossing swords with her on the subject. The reviews were good. I went on a little promotional jaunt myself travelling from west to east and enjoyed a couple of weeks of unfettered egotism without getting nominated for a Pulitzer.

I had watched a couple of Maya's appearances on prime-time talk shows and observed that her strategy was not to talk about the book she was promoting but to project herself as a figure of national importance. She presented an image and let the viewer make what they would of it. During her years of lecturing all over the country to every sort of audience, Maya had learned what key statements worked on audiences and how to give answers that would be remembered when the question was forgotten. The talk show host would say, 'Maya, this latest book deals with your difficult times growing up Black and poor, single with a young son . . .' she would interrupt without seeming to interrupt and say, 'A diamond is the result of extreme pressure. Less pressure and you have coal, less pressure than that and all you have is *dirt*!' The studio audience would burst into applause. It was very well done. Nixon had won re-election by a landslide by projecting not himself but his Presidency. Kennedy had been elected President by projecting himself as a person, not his scant achievements as a Senator. Eisenhower had been elected by voters who retained the indelible image of the newsreels, the victorious supreme commander who had defeated Nazi Germany, in rather the same way that the Duke of Wellington who had defeated Napoleon at Waterloo had become Prime Minister of Britain. Now there was a dab hand at the memorable short quote. Gad, Sir! What would the Iron Duke have done with television?

Her efforts bore fruit. She was invited on prime talk shows for who she *was*, not what she had written. It was a significant step up on 'young ambition's ladder' because literary hucksters are the lowest form of talk show life. They are the 'Tits and Feathers' acts, little time-fillers whose sent"ent"ious explanations are cut off by commercial breaks. Real celebrities are allowed to finish their statements and then the camera goes to the audience to show the wild applause.

Bill Moyers came to the Berkeley cottage to film a half-hour interview for his series *Moyers' Journal*. It was an important event. The imprimatur of a Moyers' interview positioned the interviewee as a celebrity with *the right stuff*. After all, Zsa Zsa Gabor is a major celebrity for talking in a funny accent and still having big pretty tits in her sunset years but that is *not* the right stuff. Bill Moyers was to Johnson much of what Clark Clifford had been to Truman: personal protégé and all-round adviser, whose influence overshadowed that of the other Texans. Like Clifford, Moyers' greatest contribution was in domestic affairs, where he was a major force in getting the ambitious programmes of the Great Society off the ground, as Dan Rather and Gary Paul Gates wrote in *The Palace Guard*. And, as they further wrote, 'Long before his Presidency came to an end, Johnson lost some of his most intimate aides: his prize pupil, Moyers, and even the hero-worshipping Valenti himself decided they were better off living and working outside of Lyndon Johnson's orbit. And those who escaped were the lucky ones. As Richard Rovers wrote in commenting on Hubert Humphrey's melancholy experience as LBJ's Vice-President: "For four melancholy years he was a slave to a master who destroys his slaves." ' But before the gods and the Viet Cong made Johnson mad, Moyers jumped ship and swam to respected safety as a TV journalist aboard PBS TV and Jack Valenti washed ashore at the American Film Institute.

A Bill Moyers' interview for the American Public Broadcasting Service was a videotape of record. The network talk shows, no matter how primely timed and widely viewed, were throwaways. PBS programmes were rebroadcast at intervals for ever.

It was an important event. The film crew arrived in Berkeley mid-morning on a grey California day. I showed the director through the house. There wasn't much to show. I made coffee and we sat in the twelve-foot by twelve-foot dining-room. I had never really noticed how small it was before. 'I didn't expect this place to be like this. We can't really shoot much inside,' he said.

'There's plenty of yard.'

'I see. We'll work with that.'

'Suppose it had been raining?' I asked. 'It often does at this time of year.'

'We'd have managed somehow. Lot of talking head shots. It's a bitch. Somehow I thought Maya Angelou would live in a bigger house. I don't know why.'

Later Bill Moyers arrived and I made more coffee and we chatted at the dining table while Maya was being made up. He was a good listener and a good journalist, I thought. He was a good interviewer as well. His interview with Maya still looks and sounds well years after the event. It is still shown on PBS all over the country.

But we needed a bigger dining-room. The trouble was that houses within our price range in Berkeley were either small or ramshackle. I planned to do some independent research on alternative places to live but meanwhile we were invited to spend a couple of days with an English friend of Maya's on his ranch in the Sonoma wine country.

The drive north was a feast for the eyes. After a few minutes on the freeway we were on the San Raphael Bridge crossing the bay and I sat up wide-eyed. It wound into the mist like an English country lane. Actually that was an optical illusion. The bridge was really two bridges in one. The first part ended in the middle of the bay and then the second part went on at an angle and set us ashore by San Quentin. The prison looked very fine in soft morning light, like a chateau in the Loire Valley. A few miles on, as we came over a hill, Frank Lloyd Wright's Marin County Jail climbed the hillside to our right, growing out of his Civic Center in the valley. The agglomeration of arch forms might have been inspired by a honeycomb or the hillside cave villages of southern Spain. Angela Davis had been the jail's most famous prisoner. Maya chuckled as we drove by. 'I visited Angela and asked her how she was enjoying the architecture. "Honey, jail is jail," is all she said.'

I was very impressed. I had heard Angela Davis speak a couple of times and never imagined she was capable of such succinctness. Angela Davis was a sweet and wonderful person but a mind-numbing bore when she got up on a podium.

After Marin the vistas opened out to low, smooth, rolling hills, green and straw gold. Fat, sleek cattle grazing in groups of two or three added a black-and-white accent to the soothing scene. In less than an hour we were in the Valley of the Moon, driving among vineyards and horse ranches and soon we were in the town centre. We parked in the town square and took a stroll to stretch our legs. It was something of a tourist town and the sights were signposted. The Old Sonoma Mission was just east off the square on the road to the Sebastiani Winery. General Vallejo's adobe and timber barracks was on the north side. It was closed for restoration. There were feed stores and farm equipment suppliers as well as pottery boutiques and smart little shops selling native American jewellery. It was a pleasant combination, a tourist town that worked, a working town that welcomed tourists. We paused by an attractive bar called Gino's on the east side of the square.

'What do you think of Sonoma?'

'Reminds me of St Paul de Vence some ways. I'll bet the old boys play bocce ball somewhere hereabouts. Gino probably stocks Ricard 45.'

'Let's find out.'

Maya was the only Black in the bar and so far as I had seen the only Black in town. Gino greeted us with uneffusive pleasantness as if we were old and valued customers. He did not stock Ricard. 'First time I've had a call for it. I have Pernod.'

'Close enough for rock and roll,' I agreed.

'Am I going to like David?' I asked Maya as we headed out of town towards the ranch.

'An interesting question. You two will either fall in love or despise each other on sight.' There was mischief in her eyes.

'What's the morning betting line?'

'Mmmm . . . four will get you five you'll like each other. Jessica had dreams of marrying me off to him at one time, for her own purely selfish reasons of course.'

'Of course, what other reason can she understand?'

'She and David fall out periodically and when that happens he takes her off the guest list to punish her. She hoped to get me installed as Châtelaine of the Bouverie estate so that I would give her free run of it. "Lapping up the luxury of it all", as she calls it.'

111

'I presume she's dropped her plans, or shelved them at least.'
'They're a dead letter. Shana Alexander is in hot pursuit these days.'
'What's the betting line on her?'
'Five to one against and lengthening.'
We turned off the road, unlatched a five-bar gate and started driving up a gravelled farm road. There was a small sign posted that showed a skull and crossbones.

DANGER.
BOUVERIE RANCH. RIFLE RANGE AHEAD. CROSSFIRE.
TRESPASSERS WILL BE VIOLATED.

Ahead on a knoll to the left among some trees was an attractive single-storey house. From a distance it looked rather small, but as we passed it I saw that there was more to it than met the eye at first approach.

'That's Mary Francis's house. She's the genius-in-residence . . . I say that in all seriousness. Have you read M. F. K. Fisher?' I had not. 'Then you have a treat in store. We'll meet her I'm sure. She and David are old friends of one sort or another and she usually pops in for tea to look over interesting new guests, and you qualify. She also evaluates new ladies in David's life. The gossip is that she and Shana don't hit it off.'

We drove uphill between vineyards that grew tight to the edges of the road. Beyond them the ground sloped up, rock-strewn pasture with cattle grazing off to the left. We parked in the cobbled courtyard. The east and south sides of the courtyard were enclosed by low rough-stone buildings linked into an 'L' by an arched passageway. A few yards beyond the north-west corner was a squat stone bell tower.

Following the boldly written instruction I pressed a buzzer on the wall beside the arch. A man in a crisp white shirt, open at the neck, with cuffs rolled up to the elbow, dark slacks and polished black shoes came striding out under the archway. He was African-Black and built like a light-heavyweight boxer fifteen pounds over fighting weight. He nodded pleasantly to me and headed for Maya, hand outstretched. 'Ms Angelou! Lovely to have you back!' They shook hands. 'How have you been, Maya?'

'Never better, thank you, Joseph.' She introduced us. His hand engulfed mine. She handed him the car keys. 'Where are we?'

'The main guest wing. Let me take your bags. Mr Bouverie will be with you momentarily. Perhaps you'd like to make yourselves comfortable on the terrace. Sherry, Scotch?' Maya nodded to Scotch and I chose sherry. Joseph raised his eyebrows enquiringly.

'Fino,' I said. He approved my choice with a quick smile and took our bags from the car. We went through the archway and turned right on to a stonewalled terrace that overlooked a large circular pool edged with field stone and a ten-foot-wide border of trim lawn hedged around by roses.

'Joseph is David's butler,' explained Maya with a quirky smile.

A man in a wide-brimmed straw hat, epauletted shirt, linen slacks and work boots emerged from the passageway and headed towards us. His gaze was fixed on Maya. Five feet away from her he stopped, legs astride, knees slightly bent, hips thrust forward. He planted the palms of his hands, fingers down, on the front of his hips, strained his shoulders back, craned his neck forward and opened his mouth in silent agony. Poor bastard! His back had gone out on him. I knew that one well. Just as I started forward to help him over to the stone wall so he could get some support he unfroze, shouted, 'Mayaaa!', stretched his arms out horizontally in the ten-to-the-hour, ten-past-the-hour position, let out an eerie, 'Wu uh ah ahhaaaha!' crescendoing bray and embraced her.

'Paul, know David Pleydell Bouverie,' said Maya after they had exchanged fond greetings.

We had lunch in the kitchen, served by the housekeeper, a sturdy middle-aged woman with the gritty determined look of farm-wife in the Oklahoma dust bowl days. She was pleasant enough to Maya and I, but it was clear that cooking and serving lunch was an unwelcome interruption in her day. The dessert had a very unusual flavour. David spat his first mouthful out. 'Good God, Phyllis! What have you done to this soufflé? Taste! Just taste it!'

'I cooked it. I don't want to taste it.' It was clear from her scornful tone that she considered soufflé eaters effete jerks. 'I followed the recipe you gave me.'

'Taste it! You put salt in it. You put salt instead of sugar!'

'Easy mistake to make. They look alike. Well, if you don't want it I'll clear the table and get on with my work.'

'Don't want! Don't want? Of course we don't want a soufflé with a pound of bloody salt in it.'

113

'Then I'll clear the table.' she said and proceeded to do so.

David's voice sank to a self-pitying whine as he headed for the living-room. 'That woman is becoming impossible. She's always been a truculent bully but lately she's started to be incompetent as well.'

He took me for a tour of the ranch buildings. I had to step out to keep up with him. He was very spry for a man in his sixties, lean and wiry, full of enthusiasm. He was a compulsive builder and not only showed me the additions made over the years but outlined his future projects. One that looked fun was a pyramid-roofed shed to accommodate four cars. I was looking over the sketch plan and asking a few questions when he said, 'Perhaps you'd like to come and build it for me?' It was an idea. 'Next time Maya's away on a lecture tour why don't you come up here and build it? Take about a week, don't you think?' I agreed. 'In return for your work I will stock your household with a season's supply of wine. How does that sound?'

I did a quick calculation. 'If a season is more than three months I think you'd be getting the short end of the deal. Have you any idea how much wine we drink?'

His knees sagged and he froze again in his odd posture and burst into another braying laugh. But this time I was ready for him. I asked him about house prices around Sonoma. It sounded as if we could afford quite a nice big house up there. David recommended a realtor in town if I wanted to proceed further.

Maya and I went down to Mary Francis's house for afternoon tea. She was a beauty of a certain age who had the knack of making flirtation a social grace. As we left she gave me a copy of her translation of Brillat Savarin's *Anatomie Gastronomic*, explaining that she was prouder of that than anything original she had written.

Maya privately disagreed as we walked back. 'M. F. K. Fisher is the best writer about food in America . . . bar none. She's one of the best writers about *anything*. She's of the Dorothy Parker, Algonquin Round Table generation and still writing as well as ever. What a beauty she was in those days, and a heartbreaker.'

During cocktails on the terrace David asked me to do him a favour and go to the bell tower and ring the curfew.

'That time already? I hadn't noticed the lowing herd winding o'er the lea yet.' He exploded in his strange braying laugh. Maya looked thoughtfully at the two of us.

114

When we were getting ready for bed I talked with Maya about looking at houses in Sonoma. She was enthusiastic. 'And I see that it was love at first sight between you two. Ringing the curfew is an honour.'

'Really? He's a funny man.'

'He's a genuine English eccentric.'

Among the pictures and curios in our guest quarters was a letter one of his ancestors had sent to George Washington congratulating him on leading the American Revolution and wishing him success. The sender's address was the House of Lords. David obviously came from a long line of English loonies.

Next day we visited the realtor and told him what we wanted and how much we could pay. Two weeks later he called to tell us that he had found two houses that fitted our needs. We drove up and bought one of them. The kitchen/dining-room was about thirty feet by thirty. There was a guest cottage, a serious swimming pool, mountain and meadow views, three acres of land, two huge oak trees, a creek with a bridge and the golf club (open to the public) was two minutes walk away.

CHAPTER SEVEN

WINE COUNTRY AND COWBOYS: THE SUMMER OF '75

Emeryville is a tiny thumbnail clipping of a city, pared out of Oakland's bay shoreline. Most of the four thousand or so souls who lived there were Blacks and blue collar. The oligarchic government was White, unpretentious and insouciantly corrupt. The city coffers were filled with tax revenues from the legal gambling rooms along San Pablo Avenue and emptied by police chief John La Costa and his City Hall cronies. La Costa was the son of a former mayor and boss of the town. He ran his fiefdom from the corner seat in a funky country and western bar on Doyle Street that was called the Towne House but generally referred to as the Town Hall. During the political turmoil of the Sixties, while the Black Panthers traumatised White conservative power brokers in Oakland and just a short bus ride away to the north, student revolutionaries confronted authority on the Berkeley campus, Emeryville went about its business and steadily built out into the San Francisco Bay on landfill and pilings. By 1973 a high-rise Holiday Inn, an impressive luxury apartment complex, a new city hall-cum-police station and some good comfortable restaurants had risen out of the bay.

Maya and I were about to move into our new home in Sonoma. She was out of town on a lecture tour to earn the money to pay for the new house but family and friends rallied round to help me move. With the help of Vivian and Liz, her shipmate friend, I had spent the day packing up the contents of our rented cottage in the Berkeley

117

Hills. By five o'clock our day's work was done and I proposed sunset cocktails and dinner at a location to be discussed over those cocktails. Soon enough the women were changed, dazzling in tailored suits, silk blouses and diamonds, and I was in my best suit. We had one for the road among the packing cases.

'Where are you taking us for cocktails, Paul?' asked Liz.

'I thought Charlie Brown's out on the water in Emeryville. Do you know it?'

'No, but it sounds fine. You go there a lot?'

'Never been there. Never been anywhere in Emeryville as a matter of fact but I'd like to try it.'

'Well, let's go. Good as *we* all look, baby, Charlie Brown's is in for a treat,' said Vivian.

It was busy enough in the bar but was not too crowded. We took a table with a view of the Golden Gate Bridge and the setting sun, and gave drink orders to a smiling waitress. I noticed that Vivian and Liz were the only two Blacks in the bar. They were also the snazziest, jazziest, best-looking women in the place. The waitress promptly brought our drinks, set them down with professional elegance and put the bill by my left hand. I gave it back to her. 'Why don't you run a tab for us?'

'Sure thing.'

'I'll be paying by cheque.'

'That'll be fine.'

After the third round of drinks the sun was down, the jokes flowing and we had decided where to dine. I called for the bill. The waitress was not smiling this time, her pretty face was unpretty with tension. In an effort to cheer her up the first thing I wrote on the cheque was the dollar amount in figures, showing a handsome tip.

'I'm sorry. I can't take your cheque.'

'What do you mean?'

'You'll have to talk to the manager.'

'I will. Ask him to come here please.'

The manager was about thirty, blond, athletic and getting ready to enjoy himself. As he came and stood at my shoulder he looked the women over with contempt. They looked at him with amusement and pity. Somewhere in their steady eyes was the message that if he wanted a pistol whipping right there and then they were ready to oblige him. I knew Vivian had her pistol with her and I'd lay money Liz was armed too. He dropped his eyes and his face tightened, he pointed at my chequebook.

'I won't accept that.'

'Why not? I told the waitress I'd be paying by cheque when we first ordered. She said okay.'

'She made a mistake. I'm the one who decides whose cheques I take.'

'*You* made a mistake. You take a cheque or nothing . . . boy.'

'Pay cash or I call the police and you go to jail.'

'I guess you know where your phone is.'

He turned on his heel and walked off. He didn't walk like Dirty Harry any more. Now he reminded me of Charlie Chaplin.

The distraught waitress sidled up to Liz. 'I'm sorry, he's like that. He likes to mess with . . .' she flicked her eyes around the table. 'You know . . .'

Liz's sweet smile never reached her eyes. 'With what, darling?' The waitress blushed and scuttered away. Liz lifted her purse on to the table and opened it and reached for the bill. 'I'm carrying plenty enough cash. Let me do it, Paul.'

I pushed her hand back. 'I'm holding a couple of bills myself. It's the principle.'

'What principle?' asked Vivian.

'I don't know . . . My mother's name was Mary Catherine Kelly. The pig-headed Irish principle, maybe.' She smiled and nodded with understanding.

'Well, do the right thing, baby.'

'As Hannibal said when he was crossing the Alps, "Fuck 'em!" '

Two police arrived. One was a taut, medium-sized White man about my age. His partner was a tall, fleshy young Hispanic. They stood ten feet off from our table. The Hispanic beckoned to me. Vivian and Liz gathered their purses and stood up.

'We'll go on to dinner, baby. I'll have my bail bondsman check on you first thing in the morning . . . and remember, baby, jails were built for people not for horses.'

I started laughing. 'Whatever that means I'll remember it.'

I went out between the policemen to their cruiser, bent forward over the hood, legs apart, was pat-searched and handcuffed behind my back. The handcuffs were painfully tight. I mentioned to the White cop that I'd like them adjusted.

'They're not supposed to be a lover's caress, *baby!*'

'They're supposed to be a restraint not a punishment. I'm not guilty yet.'

119

'Shut your fucking mouth, nigger lover.'

I was duly charged with 'attempting to defraud an innkeeper of his profit' and taken from Emeryville police station to Oakland jail. The young Hispanic watched as I gave up my belongings to the admissions officer. His eyebrows rose as the money in my wallet was counted out. I had close to the three hundred dollars that I had drawn from the bank that day for moving expenses.

'You had all that money and you wouldn't pay the bill?'

'Not at all. I offered a cheque.'

'And you were drinking with the good-looking Black ladies?'

'Yep.'

'Anglo cocksucker!'

'Me?'

'No, the manager. Emeryville has its own rules . . . You know how to make bail?' I nodded. He patted me on the shoulder and grinned. 'Okay, hombre. Take it easy.'

It was still early in the evening and there were only a couple of talkative winos in the holding cell. I eschewed conversation beyond common cellmate courtesy, folded my jacket into a pillow and stretched out for a nap on the upper bunk nearest the door. I was awakened around two o'clock. Guy had posted bail. Meanwhile the cell had filled to capacity and I had slept well. Vivian was right. Jails were built for people not for horses.

'Well, Paul, what would you like to do for the rest of the evening?' he asked as he drove across the bridge to San Francisco.

'I'd like to eat.'

He thought for a while. 'There's an all-night hamburger place called Clown's Alley. You know it?'

'No. But it sounds appropriate.'

Some of our Black friends had misgivings about our move to Sonoma. It was a 'lilywhite' town and they believed its inhabitants intended to keep it that way. Maya shrugged off their fears. 'We'll just have to educate them.'

I put on a brave face and agreed, but I was concerned. So far, in Berkeley, our inter-racial marriage had been no provocation to anyone because we always went to places where Maya was known and very welcome. It could be different in Sonoma.

Bigotry, when you are the object of it, is very irritating to say the least. It is also a distraction. Maya needed a safe, calm place to work and enjoy life. As I sat wolfing down hamburgers and fries I wondered what the jail was like in Sonoma. I hoped I would not find out. And I hoped we were not making a big mistake.

In the month while our house purchase was being finalised the town's gossip mills must have been grinding away on double shifts. Apparently just about every one of the town's six thousand inhabitants soon knew that a six-foot-tall Black woman writer was coming to live among them.

'Morning, Maya,' said the grinning young service station attendant the first time we pulled in for gas. She glanced at the name embroidered on his coveralls.

'Morning, Tom.' She gave him her biggest smile. I was surprised. One of the minor irritations for Blacks is being denied surnames and respect by Whites who would never have had the temerity to be familiar with their White elders and betters. I had often heard her squelch callow youths who addressed her, unbidden, by her first name: 'I'm Ms Angelou . . . and who are you?'

Her change of tactics was interesting to me. Secure in her burgeoning celebrity status, she now assumed respect from strangers without demanding its linguistic trappings. In a quantum leap she nodded agreement with Rabbie Burns that 'the rank is but the guinea stamp'.

When we went back to Gino's bar later that evening he greeted us again like old customers but this time by name.

'Usual Scotch and water, Maya?'

'I might just see what that tastes like, Gino. Thank you.'

'And this is for you, Paul.' He set a bottle of Ricard 45 on the bar and poured me a shot. He made no attempt to collect any money. Our next drinks came up without being ordered. 'These are with Joe there.' He pointed to an old man in a cowboy hat further along the bar. Joe smiled and touched his finger to his hat brim.

On our way home we decided we wanted another drink. I pulled into the parking lot of a brightly lit saloon just outside the city limits. As soon as I cut off the engine we could hear the twanging country music. 'Oh no,' said Maya. 'I don't want a drink that much.'

'Come on. We're exploring.'

Reluctantly she got out of the car. The saloon was packed with young men and women in cowboy boots and stetsons dancing and whooping it up. She was tense and dignified as we walked through the crowd to the busy bar. The barman was in front of us before we had climbed on our stools. 'Howdy folks, what can I bring you?' He filled

121

our order then hurried away to deal with other clamouring customers. After a couple of minutes there was a lull and he came back to us. 'Ms Angelou, let me welcome y'all to our saloon. And can I say how much I enjoyed that TV series you did on channel nine a few years ago? It was called *Blacks, Blues, Black.*'

Her eyes widened, she held her hand out across the bar. 'I'm Maya, and you are . . .?'

'Hank.' They shook hands.

As we left Hank called out, 'Don't be strangers now. Come back, y'hear!'

She stood by the car and looked back at the saloon lights beaconing out in the country-black night. 'Are we lost in the fucking twilight zone?'

It seemed as if the whole town had made a collective decision to show us what good old Western hospitality was.

Sam Floyd was on summer break and due out to be our first house guest. The guest house had been neglected by the previous owners, so I set about a quick fix-up. I went to the local building supplies stores and gave them my list of needs. I explained that I had no truck to haul the goods.

'We do,' said the laconic salesman. He made up the bill and I wrote out a cheque and slid my driver's licence across the counter for identification. The storeman smiled and pushed it back without looking at it. 'Well, now I know you can drive, Paul. When do you want this stuff delivered?'

'Let me give you the address.'

'I said "When?" not where.'

'Soon as you like.' I was beginning to get the hang of the Sonoma idiom.

'Be there in a couple of hours. That soon enough, buddy?'

'Yep.' An hour later it was delivered.

I picked Sam up from San Francisco airport and we got to Sonoma while there was still two or three hours of daylight left. After a quick drink to celebrate a successful journey he headed off to take a walk around the golf course. He reported that it was very beautiful and quite testing. He would be out playing first thing next morning. We started to talk about dinner plans but he begged to be excluded. He had met some people on the course and arranged to meet them in town for drinks.

We gave him the local map and the car keys and settled to enjoying a quiet evening at home together. The house and its location turned out to be ideal for entertaining long-term house guests. There were innumerable things for them to do to keep themselves entertained. It was a sort of Rorschach blot test. They could stay cocooned on the premises and find amusement, or adventure through Northern California. San Francisco was only a bus ride away, the Gold Rush country was a comfortable day trip. Skiing and gambling were within easy reach in Reno. They could be private or socialise with anyone in sight. Neighbours would wave them over for cocktails or respect their quietude. *Faites ce que vous voudriez* was the motto in Club Sonoma.

Sam was already on the golf course next morning when I went to buy hot baguettes from the French bakery in the town square. I parked across from Gino's and he spotted me as I was putting up my purchases.

'Where's Sam?' he called out. For a moment I missed the reference.

'Sam?'

'Yeah. Black Sam.'

'I missed him. He's already out playing golf.'

'Got time for a beer?'

'Nope. I got time for a Scotch.' I was starting to speak Sonoma pretty well. Gino opened up the bar for me.

I had a couple of Scotches while Gino told me Sam stories. He had been in the night before and entranced the company with his arrogant wit. Gino's favourite story of the evening was not new to me but I enjoyed hearing him retell it.

Sam swore that he had seen and heard it all himself. All the best stories are true stories even when they are lies. As a teenager in North Carolina, Sam had been waiting at the Greyhound bus station watching a miserable young White soldier who clutched his crotch in agony from time to time and kept visiting the rest-room. A sassy young Black woman came into the waiting-room and the soldier's face lit up in angry recognition. 'Bitch!' he shouted. 'You're the bitch who gave me a dose of clap!'

The crowd in the waiting-room was all ears. The woman looked him over with calm contempt. 'Soldier boy, I didn't *give* you the clap. I *sold* you the clap!'

123

We enjoyed laughing at the memory of Sam's elegant comic timing.
'I don't want to pry, and it's none of my business . . . but what does
Sam do?'

'It's no secret. He's a professor of literature in New York.'

'No kidding. I reckoned he had to be an entertainer.'

'That too, buddy.'

Maya's interview with Bill Moyers attracted very favourable attention
and columns of commentary around the country. Cause and effect
would be hard to pin down. She had attracted plenty of notice before
the interview, but the type of notice seemed to change after the Moyers
connection had been made. For example, when the government-funded
American Film Institute came under criticism for not encouraging
and developing women film-makers, they responded by setting up a
Women's Director course and inviting a blue riband class to initiate
it. The idea was to get the project off to a prestigious start by inviting
women with established reputations to participate. Carol Burnett,
Lee Grant, Ellen Burstein and Maya were among those invited to
participate. Maya was the only Black woman, as far as I recall. Jack
Valenti, who had been Bill Moyers' colleague in Lyndon Johnson's
kitchen cabinet, was the head of the American Film Institute. The
United States Information Agency, which is the media arm of the
CIA, commissioned Maya to develop and write a two-part educational
film on Blacks in the performing arts. The efficient woman producer
who came out to stay with us in Sonoma casually mentioned that she
had punched up Maya's computer file as well as read her books and
so they could put all that behind them and get on with the job in
hand. Maya's project for the Film Institute was a gem of a short film
called *All Day Long* starring Leslie Uggams, and her USIA film was
made in Washington as written and won a Golden Eagle Award. She
was invited to direct two TV plays for a public broadcasting series
called *Visions* in Los Angeles, and Gerald Ford invited her to join the
Presidential Commission for the Bicentennial.

Meanwhile I had bought a funky house on an acre or so of rough
grassland on the outskirts of Santa Rosa, half an hour north of our
home, and was remodelling it for a rental property. My neighbour
had sold me a three-quarter-ton pick-up truck that accelerated like a
Porsche. When Maya was tired of writing or cooking or tending our
garden she would help me with the remodelling. I showed her how

to lay bricks and she took to the trowel like a duck to water. We were just about finished with the remodelling and Maya was building two decorative brick piers at the sidewalk end of the front path to the house when a couple of Sonoma cowboys drove up in a flatbed truck hauling a backhoe on a trailer. As they saw Maya they slowed to a stop and then backed up till the truck cab was right opposite her. I was nearby stacking bricks. I felt Maya's fierce anger as she challenged their impertinent curiosity.

'Yeees? Can I help you?'

'Did you know the back field's on fire, Ma'am?' said the driver.

We turned and looked. The flames were ten feet high and the wind was whipping them. 'Better call the fire service.' I ran across and yelled to a neighbour to call 911. By the time I got back the cowboys had unhitched the backhoe and one of them reversed it off, then went full speed across the rough field towards the flames. The bulldozer was bucking and twisting like a Brahmin bull coming out of a rodeo chute. He lowered the front blade as he went and charged into the flames, already twenty-foot high, scooping and scattering dirt as he went. He swung through the flames, then reversed and charged in again scattering more dirt. Peddle down all the way. The man was a backhoe virtuoso and fearless. Within five minutes the brush fire that could have wiped us out was under control, and the fire engines were coming. He swung through the smouldering dirt then bumped back to the roadway.

'You're in good hands now, Ma'am.' He touched his stetson in salute and then they quickly reloaded the backhoe without another word. Just before they pulled off he looked at the brick piers for a moment. 'Nice brickwork, Ma'am. You have a good one.' Off they went.

'Who *was* that masked stranger?' I said as I watched them go.

'Goddam cowboys,' snarled Maya. 'Won't even let a poor southern Black girl hold on to her stereotypes. They try to take everything away from us.' We started to giggle and broke out the wine.

On the other side of the continent stereotypes were alive and well. Court-ordered integration of the Boston schools was being fought tooth and bloody nail in the birthplace of the country's freedom. The Black pupils from Roxbury were riding into Irish blue-collar south Boston, in a hail of insults, brickbats and gunfire. The Boston City School Board defied the federal courts. Mayor White waffled and President Ford washed his hands. It was on television news night after night but no

125

freedom marchers flocked to Massachussets. Of course I was not there either. The Vietnam war was lost and it seemed as if everyone wanted to *look away*.

Jimmy Baldwin came to visit with a twinkle in his eye and a new friend. I took special care to check that the guest house was well stocked with liquor and provisions and in every way a suitable bridal suite. It was a pleasure for us to return the hospitality we had enjoyed in St Paul de Vence. Unfortunately I forgot to set the thermostat for the heating.

Remembering that he was an early riser I took them coffee and rolls and orange juice at seven-thirty. Jimmy was already dressed, swaddled in a blanket and reading in the little living-room. His friend was still asleep.

'Is it cold in here or is my blood running thin?'

'It's chilly.' I turned the heater on. 'Sorry about that.'

'Don't worry. I was fine once I got a rug around me. I'm really not such a tender blossom as you seem to think. It was very nice. I watched dawn break, listened to the birds. A lot of birds. More than we hear in St Paul.'

'The French have eaten them all, that's why.'

He laughed. 'That is *very* true. Tireless hunters of sparrows and other tiny creatures.'

'It's nice and toasty over in our kitchen. Come on, let's give this place a chance to warm up.'

As we walked across the wooden bridge that spanned the creek, Sargi, our fox terrier, came yapping up to join us. I faked throwing a stick for her and off she charged.

'I was surprised to find you had a dog. Maya was terrified of dogs. What happened?'

'You know Mary Jane Hewitt in LA I think? Sargi was her dog. She turned up here one day for a visit and gave us the dog. She's off teaching in Honduras and we're dog-sitting.'

'And Maya loves Sargi. Interesting.'

'Maya also rides elevators and swims now. There may be a Freudian explanation. On the other hand maybe it just happened that way.'

When I offered him more coffee he seemed not to hear. 'I think I'm still on New York time.'

'You mean you're ready for an early pre-lunch drink?'

'I think that must be what I mean. Any Scotch left?'

'Sure. Do I get a story while we drink?'

'As a matter of fact you do. I have an idea for a story. I don't want to talk it into stillbirth but I want to talk about it. I always want to talk to you when I'm starting an affair of the heart. An American gospel/jazz singer on tour in Europe dies in mysterious circumstances. His brother goes to Europe some time after the death and starts to retrace his dead brother's steps. All is not as it seems. As the brother digs deeper he begins to reassess the dead man's life. They were friends but very different and very private from each other.'

I liked the story so far. 'Is it a whodunnit or a whathappened?'

'I don't know. It might turn out to be a *whowashe? whathappened? whodunnit?*'

'When Jimi Hendrix died there was a lot of speculation in the British papers about his last hours, where he was, with whom and why? Then some time later there were rumours about stolen tapes and missing tapes that had never been published and questions of copyright and ownership etc. . . . Two sets of questions about Hendrix's death, right? I always thought if you put those two sets of questions together you would have the makings of a good story . . .'

Jimmy nodded. He was staring out at Sargi who was yapping around pestering the horses in the meadow. Our conversation was not connecting.

At another time much later when he read me some of his draft of *Just Above My Head* I realised that *he* was the singer who died. He read me a scene in which the dead man's brother explains to his own children that their uncle had been a homosexual.

'Does it work?' he asked. I thought it did. It had the probing uncertainty that adults use when they explain to children things that probably worry the adults more than the children. 'But does it work for the children?' asked Jimmy.

'You mean if your brother was telling his children about their dead uncle, would they still love your memory?'

He laughed. 'For the sake of example, yes.'

'I think so. I had several aunts and uncles who were different from my father . . . and from one another. My father was fond of all of them. That was all I needed to know. I liked them all fine. I wish I could be more objective and more profound but it's not given to me.'

'It's a bitch of a book to write. Like all of them.'

'I'm sure. Unending meditation on the four last things, *death, judgement, heaven* or *hell*.'

'Not *quite* that grim.'

127

'Do you remember the end of Chaucer's *Troilus and Cresyde*?'

'Tell me.'

'Troilus has just been killed. His spirit floats up from earth and he is among the stars and hears the music of the spheres and then he looks down and sees his bleeding body lying there on earth . . . and he starts to laugh . . . he's done with the troubles of the world.'

'I'm looking forward to being done with the troubles of this book.'

But that morning in our kitchen I was too obtuse to get the point and Jimmy promptly changed the conversation to practical matters.

'I have no money, my dear Paul. I mean cash.'

'What do you need?'

'I have a bank draft for a thousand dollars. Will I need to go to San Francisco to cash that?'

'We can do it here in town. Anytime you like after ten o'clock. There's a bank five minutes ride away.'

'Would you go with Lawrence and do it? I don't feel like facing the world this morning and he's desperate to go shopping for clothes. What are the shops like here?'

'Shop. Good solid quality. Not the latest styles.'

'Please take him shopping anyway, he'll love an outing. Some days I feel very ancient and boring. I feel ancient and boring this morning.'

The clothes store was well stocked with Pemberton all-wool sweaters, Arrow shirts, Florsheim shoes in classic styles, 'Fruit of the Loom' underwear . . . hardly the place to inflame the imagination of a twenty-year-old dandy, I thought.

I introduced Lawrence to the storekeeper, who asked what he was looking for. Lawrence gave him a radiant smile and said, 'I'll know when I find it.' While I chatted with the storekeeper Lawrence went through the racks with the sharp-eyed concentration of an accomplished shopper. He pulled out a cardigan here, a scarf there, posing, and adjusting the clothes in front of the mirror. The storekeeper was intrigued. He excused himself and joined Lawrence. Soon they were deep in creative shopping, talking skin tones, accessories, mixing and matching and all the nuts and bolts of flair. I excused myself and went across the square to Gino's for an Irish coffee. Half an hour later Lawrence joined me with an armful of packages and a big grin on his face.

'Nice guy in that store. You'd be surprised how much he knows about clothes. He asked me if I'd ever done any modelling. What do *you* think?' I thought the storekeeper was a good salesman.

The waitress was eyeing Lawrence with unmistakably carnal interest.
He adjusted his sitting position to encourage her interest.

'Think about what?' I asked.

'Me modelling.'

'It's something to think about. Come on, put your packages in the
car and we'll take a walk round the town.'

We strolled and chatted and window-shopped in the tourist boutiques. I walked him through the Spanish Mission and the Old Barracks, showed him a statue commemorating the Bear Flag Party,
a gang of nineteenth-century Hell's Angels on horseback who had
extorted California from the Mexican governor at gunpoint one Sunday morning right there in Sonoma town square. If he was bored with
my tourist guide patter he was too well raised to show it. His lean
figure and milk chocolate brown good looks drew admiring glances. He
was a little more than six foot tall, with straight legs and high buttocks.
His broad flat torso would show clothes to advantage.

We stopped in a courtyard café for a soda. 'I'd give it a try if I were
you,' I said.

'You mean modelling?'

'Yep. But don't give up your day job.'

'I don't have a day job.' He laughed and licked his lips whorishly. 'I
do night work, mister.'

One of the things we enjoyed about having house guests was that
it gave us the excuse to throw parties for them. We planned a
full three-phase bash for Baldwin. Phase one would be a buffet
lunch for about twenty people who knew him or we thought he
would like to meet. Phase two was an outdoor party, two o'clock
till sundown, primarily for families with children. There was a kids'
barbecue with burgers and hotdogs out by the guest house, basketball,
ping-pong, and 'kids-only-in-the-pool' till five o'clock. Card tables
under the oak trees, outdoor bar by the pool and indoor bar in
the kitchen for those who liked the quiet life. We usually had a
hundred and fifty to two hundred guests for phase two, many of
them locals. Phase three was sundown till the end. Dancing, flirting,
lying, boasting, drinking, wheeling and dealing and another running
buffet.

We had refined the whole business and preparations were not too
stressful. I sometimes enjoyed the preparations more than the parties.

129

Lawrence was fascinated by the whole business and very curious. 'How many Black people?'

'Hard to say, About half and half.'

'How many young people?'

'Twenty or thirty kids. Sometimes more. And then there's Guy and a bunch of his friends who come later.'

'How old are they?'

'About thirty, average age.'

'You call that young?'

He had a point. 'It depends whether you're looking back or looking forward, I suppose.'

'Will any of them know how to dance?'

'They'll do old folk's dances like thirty-year-olds do.'

'What are you going to do for music?'

'We'll play records.'

'But you don't have a sound system.'

'We play them on the console.'

He shook his head. 'I don't get it. You have this big house, a swimming pool, built-in barbecue pits, a library . . . and you play music on the TV console . . . oh boy!'

'You're making me feel bad, kiddo. Let's go for a drive and you can help me with some grocery shopping. There'a lot to do before Saturday.'

I called Guy that evening and explained the impending youth short-age we were faced with, and asked him to go out into the highways and byways and bring in some twenty-year-olds to the party.

'Are you kidding? There's a generation gap, Paul. You must have heard of it. I don't know any twenty-year-olds . . . I'm glad to say.'

'Please, Guy, try and find some.'

'Okay. What's the preferred sexual orientation of these twits you want me to find?'

'I don't think it matters. *Young* is the keynote.'

'I'll see what I can do. Regards to Jimmy. See you Saturday.'

The party started well. Lunch seemed to be enjoyed by everyone, and I slipped away to check on arrangements without anyone noticing my absence. Phase two was always my busiest time. I felt like a chief steward on a cruise ship, making sure that food and drink supplies were kept up, directing newcomers and socialising with our central core of regular guests. Friction was rare and I tried to spot it early and head it off. The regulars always did the same things, drinkers even took up the same positions at the bars, flirters always flirted, parents with children enjoyed the company of other parents, sitters always sat and standers always stood.

I remembered from St Paul de Vence that Baldwin was a sitter. He was sitting by the pool being entertained by Jessica Mitford. Everyone else was doing what they usually did so I went off to look for a twelve-year-old to beat me at ping-pong. Don from the building supply store was in charge of the children's barbecue as usual. I accepted a Ballpark Frank from him. I had not tried the brand before but they looked good on television. However, taste did not match up to appearance and I made a mental note to go back to buying Hebrew National Franks.

'Great news about Maya,' said Don.

'Great. What news?'

'Being appointed to the Presidential Commission for the Bicentennial.'

'Oh. I didn't know the news was out. Where did you see it?'

'One of my customers clipped it from the paper. How many commissioners are there, for the whole country?'

'Twenty-five.'

'That's something. We have our own commissioner right here in sleepy little Sonoma.'

I shook my head and puffed on an imaginary cigar and did a quick Winston Churchill imitation. 'Not a commissionah for Sonomah . . . not for California . . . for *all* the people . . . a time for unity . . . a time for healing, a time for the *petty* lines that divide faction from faction, party from party; to be erased . . . to be eradicated . . . to be swept *forever* into the dusht of *hish*tory.'

Don was a World War Two buff and rabid Churchill fan who always enjoyed my imitations. A less modest person than myself might say that he was in awe of my talents. I never disillusioned him by explaining that among the two hundred and fifty boys I went to grammar school with, two hundred and forty-five of us did Churchill imitations. As they say in show business, 'If you can't get a new act, get a new audience.'

He was running low on hotdog buns. I circuited the party on my way back to the house for more stock. Lawrence was shooting baskets and coaching adoring twelve-year-olds in fancy new moves at the basketball hoop.

131

I paused under the oak trees for a moment beside Bob Chrisman, a light-skinned Black man about my age who published and edited *Black Scholar*. It was a small but nationally distributed magazine with astonishing longevity. The canard spread by jealous rivals was that the CIA funded him lavishly. Jealous rivals were probably saying the same thing about Maya now that she was working for Gerald Ford. I rather wished it was true. Jessica told me how she yearned for the 'Moscow gold' that was supposed to pour into the coffers of the American Communist Party during the McCarthy era. I understood the feeling; with a couple of hundred thousand from a covert slush fund we could have plunged into the Santa Rosa real estate market in a big way. It would have been a nice change from working ten hours a day fixing up clapboard houses in the boondocks.

Bob and I stood on the edge of a small crowd that was enjoying Jimmy and Maya doing a double act. He sat at a card table and fed her semi-straight lines. She was working the crowd flat out. Funny walks, dialects, the whole shtick. Everything was going along as usual.

'Catch you later, Bob.' I nodded goodbye and moved over towards the pool. There was a little knot of commotion on the far side of it. Jessica was hovering on the edge of the action. I raised my eyebrows at her. 'The lady thinks she has lost her purse,' she explained. I inserted myself into the knot. It was focused around a youngish Black woman in stetson, cowboy boots, unfashionably cut jeans and nondescript tee-shirt and a youngish White woman identically dressed. They were similarly slim and unadorned. I recognised the Black woman though I could not remember her name but her lover was a stranger to me.

'Whose purse is missing?' I asked.

'*They* took my purse,' said the White woman. 'We were sitting over there,' she pointed towards the shallow end of the pool, 'all the time since we got here and they took it. I've lost everything, my driving licence, credit cards . . .'

'Who's *they*?' I asked and raised my eyebrow at her Black companion to ask the unspoken 'What sort of shit is this racist White bitch talking and why is she here?' question. The Black woman dropped her eyes and the White woman flushed with anger. Obviously the investigation was being handled by Scotland Yard bunglers. My deductive powers were needed.

'Cast your mind back. You parked your car with the others in the field to the east. Then what did you do?'

'I told you, arsehole. We came over here and sat down by the pool.'

132

'You have a drink in your hand. There are no waiters here so either a fellow guest brought you drinks . . . most unlikely . . . or you went to one of the bars. Do you remember going to a bar?'

'Of course we went to the bar.' She pointed to the bar at the deep end of the pool.

'And *then* what exactly did you do?'

'We hung around for a bit and then sat on the end of the diving board and then some kids wanted to use it so we moved over here,' said the Black woman.

'Aha. The game's afoot, Jessica! Pray God we're not too late. Better bring your pistol with you. I detect Professor Moriarty's evil genius behind this.'

Her purse was under the diving board where she had left it. I handed it to her and asked her to check the contents in my presence. '*They* put it back,' she said. Not a word of thanks or apology.

'What's your name and who are you?' I asked.

'Who the fuck are you?' she replied.

'I *was* your host. Goodbye.'

'You can't tell me to leave. *I* came here to meet Maya Angelou.'

'Be grateful you didn't. She'd have slapped the water out of your flabby arse. Sling your hooks, ladies . . . that's English dockland slang for "hit the bricks".' They left. I glanced up to see if Grandpa Kelly who had worked and died on the Liverpool docks in another century was up there watching among the music of the spheres. Grandpa said I did the right thing.

'A brilliant solution to a knotty problem, Paul. Absolutely brill,' said Jessica.

'You know my methods. If you pen an account of our little exercise in deduction you might call it *The Case of the Unpurloined Purse.*'

Phase two faded into phase three as the lowing children wound slowly over the creek bridge and headed for the car park. Guy and friends arrived in a caravan of cars. I did not see any new young faces. One or two of the women could have passed for twenty-five in a soft light.

'I failed you,' said Guy. 'To tell the truth I didn't even try. What was I supposed to do? Sidle up to twenty-year-olds and say, "Wanna come to my stepfather's party in Sonoma next Saturday?" '

'Difficult, I agree. Well, thanks anyway for not trying. I think Lawrence will be fine. He seems to have been mixing in well all afternoon.'

133

Baldwin looked tiny as he sat in the high-backed chair watching the dancers. The contrast between him and the dancers was pointed up because most of the dancers were Guy's friends and while my stepson was neither a racist nor a sexist, he was something of a 'sizist' and chose his friends from the super-heavyweight division. Lawrence was flirting with the women in Guy's group and showing out on the dance floor. By ten o'clock I thought that Jimmy's avuncular smile was getting threadbare. At a break in the music Lawrence beckoned me away. I followed him out through the kitchen door to the carport.

'I've got to go to San Francisco,' he said. 'Let me borrow a car.'

'You want to go to San Francisco, *now*?'

'I've got to get some action going. You understand what I'm talking about. You were twenty, once!'

'Here's what you do. Walk to the end of the road as if you were going to the golf course, then turn left. Follow the road for about forty-five miles and you'll come to the Golden Gate Bridge. Once you're over the bridge you're in San Fran.'

He looked at me as if I had slapped him in the face. 'You won't lend me a car, man?'

'Nope. You're here because you're Jimmy's friend. You two play whatever games you like but not tonight. Not in our house at our party. I think it would be a good idea if you went back and paid some attention to your friend. Do some night work, mister.'

He went back and pouted by Jimmy's side until they retired to the guest house. I went to the kitchen and settled down to talk with Bob Chrisman. Over the months our end-of-party talks had grown into a sort of ritual between us.

That night, in bed, I told Maya about Lawrence's restlessness and how I had responded. She told me I was wasting my time trying to protect Jimmy. 'He doesn't need it. Jimmy has a will of iron. When he's ready Lawrence will be on his way back to Philadelphia or wherever he came from as fast as Jimmy can call a taxi to take him to the airport. Don't get involved. Jimmy will do whatever he feels like doing.'

I'm not at all sure she was right.

The next day we were all up early. Half a dozen had stayed over and everyone gathered in the dining-room improvising breakfasts according to individual tastes. I moved around in the kitchen area assisting and directing the production of food and drink and footnoting the events and personalities of the previous day — gossiping in other words. The phone started to ring as friends who, for one reason or another, had not been able to attend the party but wanted to visit with Jimmy, called to see if we were 'at home' to them. I invited everyone and by ten o'clock we had a list of about twenty-five. I suggested that my fellow footnoters plan simple fare for lunch and dinner for about fifty and work up a grocery list while I went for a swim. Cousin Doris took charge of answering the phone.

Maya and Jimmy were out by the pool sipping Scotches under a sunshade and I watched them from time to time as I swam a contemplative backstroke. Seeing them together it was hard to believe they were only four years apart in age. Maya, in jeans and tennis shoes, had the indolent skittishness of youth: when kids were playing around at the basketball hoop she would spring in, make a quick steal and leap for a sky hook as she passed by, or chase the dog and wrestle with her for sticks. Jimmy moved quickly, but with the physical uncertainty of an old man aware of brittle bones. I did not remember him like that in St Paul de Vence and wondered what he had been writing lately. It followed that if he transported himself into a time and place mentally when he was at the typewriter that would be reflected in his physical bearing. It seemed to happen that way with Maya. In Sonoma she had been writing about her youthful success as a dancer and high old times in her twenties touring Europe with the *Porgy and Bess* opera company. The title of the work in hand was *Singing and Swinging and Getting Merry Like Christmas*. That was actually a gentrification of her mother's phrase, 'Switching and Bitching and getting . . .'. I had asked Vivian exactly what it meant and she demonstrated by pouting out her rump and flicking it laterally as she strutted across the room.

'That's *switching*, baby.'

'And bitching is being bad tempered?'

'Maybe that's what White folks think. You've seen a female dog in heat? That's what *I* call *bitching*.'

By the time I got back from the store with a dozen bags of groceries the first new guests had arrived. They were all old friends who needed no help from me to make themselves at home, so Cousin Doris and I set to work cutting and cleaning the dozen fryer chickens I had bought. Doris and I had similar cooking styles and we worked well together. The first thing to do when you are frying chicken is to pour yourself a drink, so I did that and put a little tonic water on top of a quarter pint of vodka for Cousin.

135

Then we set four cast-iron skillets half full of cooking oil to heat on the stove and had a cigarette and talked about fried chickens we had eaten in the past. As we cut up the chickens the conversation moved on to the poor quality of collard greens currently available in the stores and from there to the superiority of a mixture of collard and mustard greens over turnip greens. That reminded Doris of a truly awful dish of greens she had recently eaten at a White woman's house. The White woman's husband was Black and there was little hope for the marriage. That reminded me of a joke.

'A Black Maoist revolutionary comes back from China after five years and there are reporters at the airport who want to know how he was treated. He tells them that China is a socialist Utopia and an earthly paradise. The reporters ask when he is going back.

"I'm not going back."

"But you said everything is wonderful there. Why would you not go back?"

"It's the food."

"Chinese food is bad?"

"Chinese food is wonderful. It's healthy, delicious, plentiful, it's the best food in the world."

"Then what's wrong with it?"

"You can't TALK about it, man!" '

Talking about food is a social art to which Blacks bring their own style, and I decided early on that I would do well to learn the rules of the game. When the food is already prepared and served, the first rule is to make a complimentary comment as you eat the first mouthful. 'H'm *m'm!* This chicken is *saying* something! (. . . is *booming* . . . . is *kicking!*).' From then on the conversational ball is rolling.

One evening I was at table with Willie Brown, who is the most powerful politician in California, bar none, and that includes the State Governor, and a middle-aged White couple who seemed to be rich, liberal and charming. The conversation was limping along. Willie Brown had little interest in me, I had little interest in State politics and neither of us knew anything about the nice White couple who seemed so nervous of saying anything that might inadvertently offend Willie Brown that they were virtually silent. We were at a dinner party given by Black TV anchorwoman/journalist Belva Davis, along with a couple of dozen other guests all seated at tables for four. I suspected that Belva or her husband had paired Willie and myself out of mischievous curiosity. He had a reputation for not suffering fools and they wanted to see what sort

136

of chopped liver he would make out of me. The same sense of mischief had prompted them to employ a young White man with blond hair to his shoulders and the shining spirituality of a pre-Raphaelite maiden, as a housekeeper/cook.

When the main course, some form of chicken, was served, I savoured the first mouthful and of course said, 'H'm *m'm*, this chicken is saying something!'

Willie Brown stared across the table at me. 'Are you out of your cotton-picking mind? I could cook better chicken than this blindfold and drunk.'

'I said it was saying *something*. I didn't say *what*.' I grinned at Willie and he threw his head back and roared with laughter. The White couple smiled politely.

'I could go down on the Tenderloin right now and find five Black winos in five minutes who could all cook better chicken than this. I'm going to have to speak to Belva.'

'Listen, my old mum could cook better chicken than this and she was Irish and *dangerous* in a kitchen.' Willie laughed again.

The nice white couple looked nervous. I think they were alarmed that I was stereotyping the Irish race as inferior cooks. Willie just enjoyed the laugh. From then on the dinner-table chat cracked along. Willie had followed rule number two for talking Black about food; your comments come from knowledge of how food is *prepared*, not just an opinion of a consumer. Rule three is that comments open up on to other avenues of conversations.

Doris and I left others to the potato salad and tossed green salad. The meat course is the star turn — I never heard anyone say a lettuce salad was booming.

We all enjoyed the after-party day, it was often the best time because everyone was at ease. Jimmy acted younger as the day went on. So much for my theory. Maybe he had just been a bit hungover. As I watched Maya teaching Cousin Doris how to swim and Baldwin playing with the dog I reflected once more what a pleasant place our Sonoma house was. Not least among its charms was the fact that it was fifty miles away from Oakland where Maya's brother Bailey hung out.

Bailey had been the adored elder brother in *Caged Bird* and when Maya, after a lecture, asked for questions from the audience, invariably one of the first would be 'What is Bailey doing now?' Her answer was evasive but accurate. 'Bailey is a success. He is as much a success in his chosen field as I am in mine.' And she would move briskly on to the next question.

137

It was an accurate answer because Bailey was undoubtedly a success. He had spent about half his adult life in prisons on both coasts without being broken in spirit or killed. He had been a drug addict (dope fiend was his self-description) all of his adult life without any noticeable physical damage and in his fifties sustained not only an enviable sex drive but the charm to find partners with whom he could enjoy it. Bailey was charming. Fifty miles away he was quite charming, five hundred miles away he would have been a delight. In her rare sentimental moments Maya would point out that her brother, whatever else he had done, was not a violent criminal. It was a point in his favour but a small point because he was small himself, at five foot five and about a hundred and twenty pounds he was not cut out to be a thug.

She was usually far from sentimental towards him. When we were first living in the Berkeley bungalow and I had not met Bailey I got an urgent phone call from him. He had to speak with his sister *that moment*. She was with her editor, working at the dining-room table and did not want to be disturbed. 'This is a matter of life and death!'

I gave her the phone. She listened for a minute or so, then said: 'Let me speak to him . . . You've got a gun up beside my brother's head and you're going to shoot him if I don't give you two hundred dollars? . . . Is the gun loaded? . . . You know how to cock it? . . . Then pull the fucking trigger and blow him away.' She put the phone down and turned to her editor with a sweet smile . . . 'Where were we?'

Bob Loomis who had listened to the phone conversation with close attention was not quite sure where he was. Maya reassured him that the matter was over and done with. 'That's a tired old scam. Bailey calls up to say he's burnt someone on a dope deal and is going to be killed if I don't make good. Bullshit! That's the last I'll hear of that.'

Sonoma was pleasantly distant from his mischief but links were never finally broken. Cousin Doris and Vivian and Bailey's children were go-betweens who informed brother and sister of each other's doings and there were occasional meetings on neutral ground, usually at Vivian's house in Stockton. He endeared himself to me at one party in Stockton. It was a barbecue to welcome him from his latest stay in Lompoc Prison. He looked well fed and healthy, confirming Maya's belief that the penal system had saved his life. Without the healthy years he had spent in jail his main-lining addiction to amphetamines would probably have killed him before he was forty. The idea of an outdoor party was to give him the feeling of freedom after his months in a cramped cell.

138

He did not seem in very high spirits. 'Not enjoying the sweet breath of freedom, Bail?'

'The truth is I'm sick and tired of barbecue. That's all I've been cooking for the last six months. Lompoc's one long fucking barbecue.'

'You mean you haven't been pacing a narrow cell gazing up at the little patch of blue you call the sky?'

He endeared himself to me by catching my quote immediately. 'No, Paul, the *Ballad of Lompoc Jail* doesn't run like that. We gaze out at a nine-hole golf course. Unless we're out playing on it, Lompoc is Club Fed. That's where the Watergate gang served their time.'

In one of my 'rare sentimental moments' I offered to buy him a car and a couple of outfits of clothes to assist in his re-entry into lawful society. Tom at the gas station had a beautiful ten-year-old Chevy Impala for sale for $400.

'That's your business, honey,' said Maya when I told her of my plan. 'My name ain't Lit, I ain't in that shit.'

We caught the attention of the clothes store salesman immediately. Bailey was wearing a short-sleeved shirt and the scars of a lifetime's needle tracks on his arms were impressive. He was dark-skinned and his West African genes were dominant enough for him to grow scar tissue on the surface of his skin the African way rather than under the skin in the Caucasian way. To kiloid in other words. We got a fairly formal suit and a sporty outfit, shoes and the rest of the necessary accessories. I felt a glow of admiration for my own generosity as I watched him drive away in the white Impala.

When Cousin Doris told me a month later that the car and clothes were gone and he was running around Oakland raggety-arse again. I felt a spasm of irritation. Silly of me.

After the party for Jimmy the next big event was Maya's first meeting as a Presidential Commissioner. I think I was more excited than she was. I organised my help on the house I was remodelling so that I could take a full week off without leaving them idle in the vineyard and I bought a new suit. Neither of us could really work out why she should have been selected, not that there was the slightest reason she should not have been, but most of the other commissioners were linked to national associations like the Boy Scouts of America or the Daughters of the American Revolution and Maya belonged to no organisations other than various writing and acting guilds her work required her to join. She shrugged aside the question with uncharacteristic modesty. 'Maybe they had an alphabetical list of Blacks and took the first and last. Angelou and Shabazz.'

It may well have been that she was chosen as a national representative of the Black constituency *because* she represented no faction or special interest. When she travelled the country lecturing there were groups with special grievances clamouring for her attention at every stop on the road. She would listen politely and wish them well in their struggle and remind them that there was ultimately only one issue — *fair play*. One idea that children playing ball in a school playground understood, one simple idea that embraced a myriad of issues and causes. Rosa Parks had sat on the front seat of the bus in Montgomery and been taken to jail. That was *not* fair play and the Civil Rights movement had been born.

After she had spoken at colleges there was often a follow-up invitation to come and teach for a while as a visiting professor. In most cases the secretary drafted a courteous refusal. Maya added her own touches and the matter was done with. Such an invitation came from Wichita State University in Kansas.

'Usual letter?' asked Ms Berkovitz.

'Let me think about it,' said Maya.

Professor George Rogers followed up with a phone call. Maya negotiated hard. 'I can stay with you and Emelyn in your home? . . . One month only? . . . The title is Distinguished Visiting Professor? . . . How many times have your daughters read my books? . . . The first Black ever to be a Distinguished Professor in Wichita? . . . There's racism in Kansas? . . . The Regents want to abolish the Department of Ethnic Studies? . . . Stay by the phone, I'll call you back.'

After the phone call we discussed the prospect of her teaching a month in Kansas. I sensed that she was already planning her wardrobe for the trip anyway, but one thing I had overheard puzzled me. 'He told you there was racism in Kansas? . . . That's news?' I assumed there was racism everywhere, one of life's 'givens'.

'No, I misheard. What he said was there was racism on *campus*.'

'Ah.'

'The best about it is that they are a lovely family. Emelyn has two lovely teenage daughters. I will enjoy those young ladies.'

After she had been there a couple of weeks I flew out to visit. George Rogers and I connected immediately at the small airport. He was an athletic-looking Black man, something under six foot tall with a gleaming shaven head and a trim beard. I liked him for not offering to carry my small suitcase to the car. Many of the Blacks I met on my travels were full of southern courtesy and, charming as it was, it could be cloying. George was a mid-westerner to the bone and we shared a cultural heritage in which men did not carry other men's bags unless they were servants, and there were no servants anyway.

I stood a moment in the car park and took my first look at Kansas. It was late March and there were traces of old snow on the ground. The air was chill and so clean that I felt it bite into my lungs. As I turned through 360 degrees I understood what 'big sky' and 'dome of blue' really meant. The sky met the flat horizon all around us and seemed to arch away into infinity above our heads.

'Incredible sky,' I said.

George smiled and nodded. 'It's something. This is flying country. Where they make the light aircraft . . . and fly them.'

'I can see why. Hell, you could land a plane just about anywhere for a hundred miles round here.'

We had hardly left the airport before we passed a sign that said we were entering the city of Wichita. The sign was the only evidence that we were in a city, the rest was flat fields, occasional farmhouses and blue sky.

'Did Maya tell you what happened when she first got here?'

'Nothing I remember. She said she had a good flight and that sort of thing.'

'Nothing else?' I shook my head and George grinned.

'There's a young woman who's president of the Black women's student union and something of a radical and she put up signs all over the union offices. "Sister Angelou talks Black and sleeps White" and "Did you know, sisters? Maya Angelou is married to a White man".'

'I'm sure Maya dealt with that.'

George smiled. 'You know she did. She explained that you do not gain freedom by denying it to others . . . Anything special you'd like to see or do while you're visiting?'

'I won't be here long enough but what I'd really like to do is learn to fly. I took a few lessons in England years ago but the weather there is unreliable and flying is very expensive. I never finished because it was raining when I had money and I was broke when the sun

141

shone. However, I do like to shoot pool and I haven't done that in
a while.'

'You're a cheap date. Are you good at pool?'

'Average bar player. Win when I'm lucky, lose when I'm not.'

'My brother-in-law's the man you need to play with.'

'You don't play?'

'Seriously, when I was in the army. For serious money. But, when I
stopped betting I lost interest. I'm too good for most people.' He said
it without a hint of braggadocio.

The family were a delight as Maya promised. The girls, thirteen and
fifteen years old, coltish and tall like their mother, stood still just
long enough to shake hands with me and then dashed off in different
directions to their different activities. They *did* promise to be at the
table at seven o'clock for dinner.

Maya had taken over the family cooking. Emelyn, who worked full
time, was glad of the help and George seemed fascinated that Maya
could find as much to do in a kitchen. His view of cooking was quite
simple. You took something out of the fridge and either boiled it in
water or grilled it or put it in the oven and then you ate it and got
on with what you were doing. His wife and daughters all felt the same
way.

'They didn't even have cloth napkins, Paul. Can you believe that?'
said Maya.

Of course I knew a lot of estimable people who did not sit down
to beautifully set tables with heavy crystal and linen napkins but that
was one of the bees in Maya's bonnet and I humoured her. 'It seems
like you got to Kansas just in time. The barbarians were at the gates.
Another month and it might have been too late and civilisation as we
know it . . . phhuttt!'

Maya had purchased crystal wine goblets, table linen and wine for
the adults. The wine cellars of Wichita are a well-kept secret and you
will not find them discussed in the gourmet magazines. Sale of alcohol
is a state monopoly in Kansas and in those days the stores sold two
sorts of wine, white and red. We drank the white.

Dinner the first evening was Boeuf Bourgignon with rice. Maya gave
a blessing to the table and then we started to eat. I was touched to see
the girls make every effort to enjoy the food. They scraped the sauce
off the strips of beef and then picked at the beef and picked at the rice.

George and Emelyn obviously hated wine. Maya seemed oblivious. I really could not understand what she was up to. Had this already been going on for two weeks? No wonder the girls looked lean and coltish. The poor dears were starving.

Next day was Saturday and George and I went off to a pool hall in the Black section of town. There were a dozen pool tables and perhaps twenty card tables set along two of the walls of the pleasantly airy room. About half the pool tables were in use and all the card tables. Dominoes was the most popular game and the betting looked hot and heavy. Several players greeted George as 'Dr Rogers'. He looked around carefully. 'Brother-in-law isn't here yet. Let me call him. Sometimes he has an emergency.'

'Is he a doctor?'

'No, he's a lawyer. He makes jail calls.'

But brother-in-law was on his way. I suggested a game of pool while we waited. George chose a table near a domino game and placed a bet while I racked up the balls. I gestured to him to come and break, he waved for me to go ahead and kept watching the dominoes. I made two balls on the break and George took my cue and without seeming to study the table sank the next six balls, then went back to the dominoes. I made three more and George came over and finished off the game in short order. He was very, very good indeed. Brother-in-law turned out to be perfectly matched with me and we lost ourselves in a dour struggle for the next three hours. George lost fifty dollars on dominoes and a good time was had by all.

As we drove home George was thoughtful. 'You always drink wine at home in California?'

'Usually with meals, often without meals.'

'What you get used to I suppose. What's your favourite?'

'Whisky.'

He slid his eyes across at me and gave me a big grin.

Dinner that evening was curried lamb with a five-boy curry. Maya explained that in India each separate curry sauce was served by a separate servant or 'boy'. She had been in the kitchen all afternoon and everyone did their best to enjoy the exotic food. After dinner George invited me into the living-room for some whisky.

'Jack Daniel's alright?'

'A lot of people think it's the best. That'll be lovely.'

'There's a young man coming over to meet you this evening. His name's Mitchell.'

143

'I look forward to that.'

'Let me rephrase. He's coming over. I want you to meet him.
Mitchell's a revolutionary and a bit of a firebrand. He's one of my
students. Nothing wrong with being young and fierce, you probably
were a handful yourself as a young man. I was. As I said, he's one
of my students and a lot of people would like to see him kicked out.
I want him to finish college. Sometimes a word from a stranger . . .'

'Gotcha, George.'

'He'll confront you . . . not too much, he's in my house and he's not
that goddam revolutionary . . . but I want to keep him in school.'

Mitchell arrived with his younger sister. He was about my height
and sturdy, with bold brave eyes. My French name interested him.
I explained that it was probably Huguenot and briefly outlined the
religious wars of sixteenth-century Europe and why I grew up not
speaking French.

'But you can speak French anyway?'

'M'm . . . bit rusty but I learnt it for a few years. I can read a
newspaper.'

'My sister's got a test next week, end of the week. She needs some
tutoring . . . Can you help?'

'What level is she at?'

'First year.'

'I'm sure I can help.' He brought his sister over and we arranged for
her to visit the next day with all her books. George watched us from
time to time out of the corner of his eye.

Next morning Maya was preparing a West African chicken dish for
dinner when they arrived. I had worked out that Maya was playing
out the role of Mrs Flowers in *Caged Bird*. She was the gracious older
lady introducing the gauche young girls to the finer things of life and
the Rogers girls would be enduring a rite of passage while Maya was
staying in their house.

Tutoring is rather like reading whodunnits; there are clues all over
the place hinting at why the student is having trouble learning. The
tutor is the detective who has to put the clues together and find just
where the blockage in the pipe is that's stopping the flow of knowledge.
The case was still under investigation when Mitchell came to collect his
sister. We set another date for the following day.

I volunteered for kitchen duty next day and cooked a London broil
with baked potatoes. It was an act of pure compassion on my part
because I felt the whole Rogers family had suffered enough and were

due one solid meat and potatoes meal. Dessert was apple pie (store bought).

Next day Emelyn told me that the girls had enjoyed the meal. 'Auntie Maya is very interesting about food, but Uncle Paul's the cook in the family', they had told her. I said, 'For God's sake, don't tell Maya that.'

By Thursday I had the Case of the Irregular French Verbs wrapped up and Mitchell's sister was ready for her test. Mitchell came over and invited me out for a game of pool. We went to the students' union and settled into a good long session. Mitchell was about as good as I was but his mind was on other things. He wanted to know about inter-racial marriage. How did the Black Panthers in Oakland react when Maya married me?

'I honestly don't know. They seemed to enjoy themselves at the wedding.'

'Black Panthers came to your wedding?' He was shocked.

'Just a couple, David du Bois and another guy, I can't remember his name.'

'You know I've been thinking about quitting school and going out to California.'

'From what I hear a lot of people would like to see you out of school . . . why give them the satisfaction. Fuck 'em. Graduate and fuck 'em all.'

Saturday the Black students' union was putting on a big-time fashion show. It was one of the major events on the social calendar with a dinner for the spectators and plenty of pizzazz. Maya was the guest of honour at the head table and I was beside her. The faculty, Black and White, were well represented.

The head table was opposite the curtained entrance way from which the models emerged. Then they paraded about sixty feet, bowed to the head table, pivoted, strutted back and exited. The MC called the names of the students who were modelling and the names of the local stores who had lent the clothes and did the usual chatter of description as they paraded. About halfway through the hour-long show the MC announced, 'And now for the men, a full-length fur coat by Apparel and the Man, modelled today by *Mitchell*!'

He stepped out on to the floor and a collective gasp went up from the room. The faculty at the head table stiffened and held their breath. Modelling was not Mitchell's usual style and everyone was ready for some outrageous demonstration in support of Black Power. He strutted

145

quickly towards the head table, his stare was icy cold, you could almost hear the music from *Shaft* throbbing in the background. He headed straight towards me and stopped a yard from the edge of the table, legs astride, hands on hips in a classic pose of confrontation. The room was silent. Then he grinned and stepped forward holding his hand out in the casual European way. I stood up and took it.

'How do I look, Paul?'

'Very tasty, Mitch.'

'By the way, my sister passed her test.'

'Knew she would.'

I sat back down. He bowed to Maya. 'Ms Angelou.'

She was laughing as she bowed. 'Mr Mitchell.'

He bowed and smiled at the rest of the table. 'Ladies . . . gentlemen . . .' then turned and strolled back as the students applauded him to the rafters. Just before he exited he turned and gave the clenched fist salute and grinned to the room.

Mitch had style. Some humour and some style.

The more I thought about it the more obvious it became to me that Maya was uniquely qualified to represent the *national* Black constituency. Every other nationally recognised Black I could think of, with the exception of Alex Haley, was tied to a region. They were involved in regional politics like Jesse Jackson in Chicago or in entertainment like Sidney Poitier in Los Angeles. Maya and Alex Haley had been travelling the length and breadth of America for years. She had lectured the Mormon Elders in Salt Lake City, librarians in Michigan, tobacco factory workers in North Carolina, and Baptists in Harlem. And everywhere she went she probably spent ten hours in face-to-face conversation for every hour she spent on the lecture stage. It was a hell of a way to acquire an overview. I just wondered who it was in Washington that had come to the same conclusion. Maybe it was a computer called Linda.

CHAPTER EIGHT

THE WHITE HOUSE: 1976

The WPA guidebook on Washington DC, published in 1941, says that 'Major Pierre Charles L'Enfant's plan for Washington is justly considered America's most notable achievement in municipal planning . . . In making use of the Renaissance *patte d'oie* (or goose's foot), whereby three streets radiating from a singular point would permit simultaneous vista along all three, L'Enfant laid the groundwork for Washington's numerous "traffic circles" which have been roundly berated by many a driver since the advent of the automobile.'

The guidebook was not lying. I got hopelessly confused by the 'traffic circles' and when I thought we should be at the Madison Hotel we were in the middle of a dimly lit, desperate slum. It reminded me of Baldwin's description of Harlem in his childhood years with wine-stained alleys reeking of urine. I did not actually get out of the car to scrutinise the sidewalks for wine stains or sniff the air for ammoniac odours but that was the impression I got.

'God, it's so depressing,' said Maya.

'I think I'd better stop and get directions.'

'You'd better do a fast U-turn and get us *out* of here.' She hunched down in the car seat and ignored the feral urban landscape around us. The blues did not leave her until we were settled in the hotel suite with cocktails. Then she took a deep breath, smiled broadly and raised her glass. 'Where are you going to take me for an absolutely spiffy dinner?'

'What about the Mayflower Room in the Statler Hilton Hotel?'

'What on earth made you suggest that?'

'It was where John Dean met Herb Kalmbach just after the Watergate break-in to plan the cover-up. Kalmbach had a suitcase full of hot cash in his room. It was the high point of Dean's testimony to the Senate committee. He said he met Kalmbach at the Mayflower Hotel. Senator Gurney, who was Nixon's man on the committee, produced hotel records that showed that Kalmbach was never there at the time Dean was talking about. For a long moment it seemed as if Dean, who had been claiming an exceptional memory and reeling off dates, times and names for hours, was a fraud. Gurney has Dean on the ropes. Then Dean corrects himself and says that he meant the Mayflower coffee shop in the Statler Hilton. The records showed that Kalmbach *was* staying in the Statler Hilton at the time. Dean had made a tiny slip of memory, but one that he convincingly corrected. He was off the ropes. Gurney had taken his best shot and hadn't shaken him. The audience applauded Dean. High drama! . . . But I see it doesn't catch your imagination. So let's eat here in the hotel.'

'Excellent choice and the sooner the better. I have work to do tonight.'

After dinner Paul Dankwa, Maya's Ghanaian friend, came to our suite and settled down with her to plan strategy for next day's inaugural meeting of the Bicentennial Commission. Paul was a lawyer by training and a senior official with the World Bank. He was familiar with the bureaucracy and Washington ways. He took Maya's briefing papers and studied them for half an hour then outlined the course of action he recommended. He suggested that she should make an immediate bid to be vice-chair of the Commission. She was surprised by his advice and wanted to hear the reasoning behind it. He explained that the Commission staffers who had recommended appointments and who would continually guide the Commission would certainly have had a chairperson in mind right at the beginning of their selection process and would have already contacted the prospective chair. Since Maya had not been contacted she was not the chosen one.

He was not sufficiently familiar with the other twenty-four commissioners to guess who it might be, but the character and political views of the chairperson were a weather vane that would point the direction of the Commission. The staffers would also have selected a majority of members sympathetic to the chair's views to ensure that things ran smoothly. The vice-chair would be a person of differing views and background so that there would be an appearance of balance. There was only one other Black on the Commission, Betty Shabbaz, Malcolm X's widow, so whatever the political stance of the chair either of the Black women would give a semblance of balance by virtue of race and probably by virtue of sex. He assumed that Betty Shabbaz would not compete with Maya. It was all very simple once he explained it.

'Move fast before the Commission forms cliques. Every committee is a train pulled by a locomotive. Three or four active members are the engine and the rest are freight-cars pulled along for the ride.'

'What happens if I don't get elected?'

'Toss of the coin. Maybe you won't, but look down the list of members . . . James Michener . . . a fellow writer, David Wolper, he's producing *Roots,* and then Ms Shabbaz . . .'

'Anna Chenault won't vote for me.'

'No, she'd rather vote for Genghis Khan but if the three others *do* and you split the rest, you're home.'

'I hate to lose.'

Paul smiled. 'I know. I believe you wrote a poem on the subject . . . "I *really* hate to lose something". However, in this case if you lose you will have established yourself as a player. You have declared yourself part of the engine pulling the train. Meanwhile prepare your election speech. Remember when you plan your speech that you must not assume that the other people know anything significant about you. They may have looked you up in reference books but your speech *there* at the meeting is the memory and impression they will carry with them for the rest of the year . . . Now three points. *One:* brevity is the soul of wit. *Two:* collaboration not confrontation is the business of a Commission. *Three:* your audience are all eminent in their different fields and will have high opinions of themselves. You speak as *primus inter pares.*'

'Prim*a* inter pares,' I murmured.

'I'm sorry, teacher. I promise to do better on my next Latin test. And now I'm ready for a drink.'

Maya went to the bedroom to work on her speech and we went to review the mini-bar that the Madison thoughtfully provides. It was very well stocked. Paul hummed and hawed and then asked for a glass of tawny port which was not there. But room service promptly obliged and we settled to enjoy a bottle like old-fashioned African and English gentlemen ready for some after-dinner gossip. We were both of an age and had attended London University during overlapping years in our salad days. As we puttered around down memory lane

I learned that he had been an actor for a while. We enjoyed passing the port and comparing recollections of West End plays we had seen. Then the conversation started to meander. 'Does Maya have political ambitions?'

'Serving on a Commission like this is not really politics, is it?'

'Everything in Washington is political.'

'I don't know what Maya wants out of this job. I'm sure she had never planned on going for vice-chair. I think it was more like an honorary degree or an award for her. We all like to come out and take a bow once in a while. It helps us soldier through the catcalls we have to put up with.'

'It might give her a taste for the "corridors of power", to use a phrase from our youth . . . or "Potomac Fever" as it's known here.'

'She talks about wanting to direct and produce movies and television and she is starting to do that. I think what she wants is "clout", any sort of clout that will get her a foothold in an industry that has not welcomed Blacks or women . . . to say the least. You should talk to her about it.'

'Maya likes control,' said Paul.

'Yes . . . a tamer of horses.'

There was a handful of spectators at the meeting next day. Two youngish women reporters sat side by side in the front row of the gallery. Staff people came and went with an air of importance. The meeting started promptly. David Wolper was proposed and approved as chairman pro-tem. So he was the one tapped by the bureaucrats. If Paul Dankwa's analysis was right a liberal chairman like Wolper should be balanced by a conservative vice-chair . . . or the counterbalance could be different race or different gender. The perfect counterbalance would be Anna Chenault, an ultra-conservative Chinese American female. Betty Shabbaz proposed Maya for vice-chair and Anna Chenault proposed the president of the Daughters of the American Revolution.

Maya's brief address was really one paragraph. She described how her grade school teacher had spelt American on the blackboard . . . 'AMER . . . I . . . CAN!'

It took the middle-aged commissioners back to the better, simpler days of their own childhoods. It flattered everyone as self-made successes, and established that Maya was one of them. There was some applause from round the table and some from the spectators. The journalists got the quote down. 'Very neat, Maya.'

The Daughter of the American Revolution spoke a little longer and was difficult to hear. She talked about the history that had brought them all together in that room at that time. Everyone round the table nodded and smiled when she sat down but there was no applause.

Maya caught the chair's eye and stood up. In a few gracious words she withdrew her nomination to forestall partisanship and to expedite the Commission's urgent task. All the members applauded this time. 'Very neat, Maya.' She had got aboard the engine without risking loss of face. She might be very good at politics. I caught her eye, gave her a congratulatory grin and went out to do some sightseeing.

The guidebook's chapter on 'The Negro In Washington' begins: 'The Negro from the start has exerted profound influence upon the city of Washington. Benjamin Banneker, a Negro mathematician, was appointed by George Washington to serve on Major L'Enfant's commission for surveying and laying out the city. The lot of Banneker's fellows, however, even in our times, has hardly been so auspicious.' That was written in 1940. I thought about the miserable slum I had misrouted us into the evening before and remembered an adage from my own schooldays: 'There is nothing new under the sun.'

I was back in good time to catch the bus that took the commissioners and their spouses to the reception at the White House that was to wind up the day's work. The bus drove through the White House perimeter gate and stopped near a canopied entrance. I was one of the first off the bus. The young marine on guard in the entrance ignored me as I strolled past him. Maya was a few steps behind, busy in conversation. I turned and waited for her to catch up. The marine stepped in front of her, blocking her way. Vicarious irritation knotted my stomach. I realised that I had both our invitations in my pocket. I fished them out as I went back and snarled at the guard, 'This is Maya Angelou, she is a presidential commissioner . . .' I had the invitation card in my hand.

The marine's vacant eyes gave no hint that he understood a word I said but his response was prompt. 'Oh, she's with you.' He stepped aside.

Maya was silent as we entered the White House. Then she drew a deep breath and exhaled her rage. 'Ain't *that* a blip! Black get back. You're White you're alright! They meant it when they called this the *White* House!'

151

I watched her out of the corner of my eye as she carefully erased the tautness and rage from her face and posture. For the rest of her time on public view that afternoon she wore the mask — she was her smiling, confident public self.

The reception was held in a high-ceilinged, rather unadorned rectangular room about sixty feet long by twenty-five feet wide. A bar of trestle tables was set up along the length. Four Black stewards in mess jackets stood half at attention and half at ease, ready to serve drinks. They were all of a height and build, in their fifties with short, greying hair and sharp eyes.

I saw that David Wolper was getting Maya a drink so I moved to the other end of the bar to get one for myself. The steward served me a rather small scotch and water with courteous indifference and I turned away to look for company. In the course of attending many such receptions I had come to enjoy the ease of being a nonentity spouse and never lacked enjoyable conversation among my fellow nonentities. Informative conversation too: everything I know about the economics of operating a two-well oil business in Wyoming, the impact of nineteenth-century canal building on the lumber trade in Wisconsin, and the cadaver turnover needed to break even in the funeral business in Montgomery, Alabama, I learnt at receptions for my wife. Of course it's a two-way street. In Tempe, Arizona, there is a high school football coach with a pretty clear understanding of the mechanics of batting against a slow bowler on a wet cricket pitch; a librarian in Richmond is now aware of the change in nesting habits of the crested blue jay as a result of clean air legislation passed in London in the 1950s; and a Black Muslim minister in Chicago knows that polygamous households and yashmak-wearing women could be found in remote Spanish villages hundreds of years after the end of the Moorish occupation.

I was discussing the correlation between high ceilings and gas-lit chandeliers in particular and the symbiotic relationship between technology and architectural design in general with a witty systems analyst from Connecticut when Maya and Betty Shabbaz joined us. She formally introduced me as her husband and by my full name. I introduced the systems analyst. A few feet away, the steward noted everything while he mechanically served drinks. We all chatted for a few moments and then they moved on. My companion's wine glass was empty so I took it and hovered behind other guests waiting at the bar. The steward looked blankly past the others in front of me and smiled. 'Dewar's and water, Mr du Feu?'

'Thank you, and a white wine, please.'

This time he poured me a hefty triple scotch. It is obviously impossible to wink without moving one's eyelid but I had the illusion that he achieved the impossible as he handed me our drinks.

'And would your wife care for a drink?'

I looked around and located Maya. Ice was rattling in her glass.

'I believe she would and some orange juice for Ms Shabbaz if you'd be so kind.'

As I passed our drinks back to my companion the neglected guests ahead of me squinted around trying to figure out who I might be to merit preferential treatment. I delivered the ladies' drinks and came back and collected my own. My companion grinned and looked me over. 'Do you come here often, Mr du Feu?'

'Only when I'm in the neighbourhood.'

President Ford soon joined the party with his secret service escort and aides. Drink in hand, he chatted easily with his guests. I watched him out of the corner of my eye and felt rather ashamed of myself for waiting for him to spill his drink, trip over a rug or contrive some other feat of clumsiness for my amusement. Deep in my heart I believed that Ford's much publicised pratfalls were a clever ploy devised by White House image-makers to project him as a lovable bungler who could be trusted. A political Valium pill to calm the nerves of a nation frazzled by Nefarious Nixon and Conniving Kissinger.

As I watched him talking and laughing with Maya and Betty Shabbaz he came across as a 'clubbable man', in Samuel Johnson's phrase, handsome enough, healthy enough, at ease with himself and unconcerned with spoils and stratagems. But why did so many people want to assassinate him? It was not really his fault that he was President. No one in 1972 would have guessed that both the President and Vice-President would have cut and run to escape criminal indictment. Why did no one shoot Agnew or Nixon? Probably the answer was that Ford was an easy target. He campaigned for the Republican nomination like the brave and decent man he seemed to be. He went out and shook hands and talked to people. That was the way he had won election to Congress in 1949 and the way he had won re-election ever since.

'What do you think of your President?' I asked Maya as we went back to the hotel.

She stiffened her lips and in a fair imitation of David Niven playing a British naval officer said: 'I like the cut of his jib. Sound chap.'

'Did you know that Squeaky Fromme, the Charlie Manson girl who tried to shoot Ford, used to live in the first house we bought in Santa Rosa?'

'You never told me!'

'Slipped my mind, I guess. Is Ronald Reagan a serious candidate for the Republican nomination?'

'He was a *serious* governor of California. As in serious illness. He let the best freeway system in the world go to hell in a handcart, closed down medical care homes and put thousands of people who couldn't cope and thousands who were crazy and dangerous out on the streets to fend for themselves . . . a most uncaring man. No, I take that back, he cares deeply about very rich White people. I'm sure he would like to be one of them . . . it's too depressing to think about.'

CHAPTER NINE

BROADWAY AGAIN, BY WAY OF CALIFORNIA: 1977

I had already bought the house in Santa Rosa before I learned that Squeaky Fromme and other members of Charlie Manson's extended family had been former occupants. The first day I started work clearing out raggety furniture and ripping out walls that were in the wrong places, a neighbour came over with a jug of lemonade and introduced himself. He said he had been glad to see the former occupants leave.

'You know who they were, don't you?'

'No idea.'

'They were the Manson Gang. You know, Charlie Manson?'

'Really?'

'Squeaky Fromme used to be here all the time. Remember her? She was in the papers all the time during the Manson trial. They had to strap her to a stretcher and carry her out of court one day. It was all in the papers. You don't remember?'

'No, but I will. Her name was Squeaky?'

'She had a little squeaky voice, and a big X scar she'd carved on her forehead.'

'How did you get on with them?'

'They were always polite enough. But you think.'

'What were they doing up in this part of the country? I thought they were a southern Californian gang. Mojave Desert and Los Angeles.'

'They moved here to be near the prisons. There's a lot of prisoner families live up here. Easy for visiting to Folsom, or San Quentin . . . or Vacaville.'

That was another piece of trivia I was not going to share with Maya. I had already decided not to mention about the Manson gang because she took that sort of thing to heart. Her fears were no chimera. About half her year was spent in public among strangers, lecturing, shaking hands and listening to whomsoever pushed their way forward to talk to her. Like anyone in the public eye she attracted her share of loonies and who could tell the good loonies from the bad? The bizarre illogic of revolution could lead loonies anywhere. Charles Manson, for example, had masterminded the slaughter of a houseful of rich Whites in the hope of putting the blame on Blacks and starting a race war. His dim-witted projection was that the Blacks would win and get control of America but lack the expertise to handle the day-to-day administration of the nation's affairs so they would, in the natural course of things, seek him out and make him emperor of all the Americas. You had to laugh unless you were Sharon Tate. No, I was not going to share my titbit of news with Maya.

Naturally, when Squeaky Fromme tried to shoot Gerald Ford at point-blank range with a .45 calibre hand-gun, I followed the news reports with a special interest. When Squeaky, on a receiving line, raised her arm to take Gerry's outstretched hand, she was holding a gun powerful enough to blow a fist-sized hole clean through his midriff. The only thing that prevented Nelson Rockefeller from becoming the third President to hold office in little more than a year was that there was no bullet in the chamber, although there were four in the magazine, and a sharp-reflexed bodyguard grabbed the gun and slammed her to the ground before she could slide a bullet into the chamber and get a shot off.

Surprising facts came to light. For example, the secret service had a list of forty-seven thousand potential presidential assassins that they kept under some sort of surveillance but Squeaky was not on the list. Apparently Big Brother was watching somebody else although Squeaky had gone on public record threatening to kill Ford because he was polluting the atmosphere. She had been arrested twelve times on charges ranging from murder to attempted murder, kidnapping, attempted poisoning, armed robbery and fraud. Just what, one wondered, did a girl have to do to make the secret service list? Probably she had to be a man. Until Squeaky broke through the sex barrier, presidential assassination had been an exclusively male preserve. No demographic breakdown of the secret service list was published as far as I could discover, but according to my understanding people made the list because they fitted a 'profile' developed from data gathered on past assassins.

Three weeks later Gerald Ford was back campaigning in California. California was Reagan country and he was putting in a special effort there. This time a woman called Sarah Moore tried to kill him. She got a shot off at forty-foot range but missed and a bystander wrestled her to the ground. Ms Moore was not on the suspect list either. But she had phoned the San Francisco police and given her name and told them she intended to 'test the security' around the President. The police chief warned the secret service who found Ms Moore and questioned her and let her go.

This time Congress decided to hold an enquiry to find out what the hell was happening. Incidentally, Sarah Moore was an FBI informant. Congress questioned Agent Yauger who had interviewed Sarah Moore and he explained his interrogation technique. She had been carrying a gun when he met her so he asked her why she was doing so. She explained that people were threatening her life. It made sense to him. As he told Congress, he had conducted five hundred previous interviews and many of the respondents carried guns for the same good reason. No problem there. Then he asked Sarah the pivotal question: 'Do you intend to shoot the President at Stanford University tomorrow?'

'No,' said Ms Moore.

End of interview.

Sarah pleaded guilty and at her trial explained why she had tried to murder Gerry. Apparently she was suffering from low self-esteem and felt alienated from her revolutionary friends who had grown cool and distant from her when they found out that she had been snitching on them to the FBI for years.

At that point I decided I had read enough and concentrated on remodelling the second rental house we had just bought. It was the former residence of an old Italian lady who had died in her sleep. I know, because I checked before I bought it.

About a year later Agent Yauger and his interrogation technique came to my mind again. *Ladies Home Journal* had named Maya Woman of the Year in communications. First Lady Betty Ford was selected as Woman of the Year pure and simple. Awards and honours were fairly showering on Maya these days and she accepted them all. The award ceremony was being held at a New York theatre and Gerry

Purcell and I kept Maya company through the afternoon rehearsals. She tried out her acceptance speech on us; without her stage presence to carry it over, it sounded just on the edge of phony humility and just an inch short of repugnant self-congratulation. A typical acceptance speech, composed of simple ingredients, but very difficult to bring off well, like cooking 'pommes de terre au gratin'. I was sure she would get it right when the time came.

After rehearsals we went backstage and Gerry, who loved to edit and direct, sat with Maya to coach her. They did not need any help from me so I poked around the mechanical marvels behind the scenes and chatted with the stage-hands who had plenty of spare time and were sociable types. It was a black-tie event and Gerry had sensibly brought his tux with him. I had to go back to the hotel to change. When it was time for me to leave the theatre was full of burly men in dark suits, some with German Shepherds on leashes. I asked one of the stage-hands what was going on. It was a secret service sweep to check the theatre for bombs before Betty Ford arrived. The theatre had been sealed and no one could leave or enter until a few minutes before the start of the show. 'Shit. I've got to get out of here and get changed.'

'*Tough* shit. This place is locked down, tight as a drum.'

'Really?'

I borrowed Gerry's comb and wet my hair down and got it looking a bit military. I was wearing a run-of-the-mill blue pinstripe suit. I inspected myself in front of the mirror, squared my shoulders and tried out a few facial expressions. I headed out into the theatre doing my best to look concerned, hurried and authoritative. As long as I did not have to say anything I reckoned I had a better than even chance of passing myself off as a secret service agent.

A real agent with two dogs on a leash was headed towards me as I went up the side aisle. As he opened his mouth to say something I waved him on briskly, he nodded and went past me. I got past two more by pointing and nodding. Now for the front door. The agent guarding it watched me uncertainly. I reached back behind me and gestured to an imaginary subordinate then brusquely waved to the guard to open up. I gave him a tight tough-guy smile. He opened the door and I was gone.

If my charade had been discovered I had planned on refusing to talk to anyone but Agent Yauger. As I walked back to the hotel I fantasised how the interview might have gone.

YAUGER: 'Are you planning on blowing the First Lady to smithereens this evening?'

ME: 'No sir, I am not.'

YAUGER: 'Hey, I don't like to ask these tough questions but it comes with the territory. You have a good one, buddy.'

Then perhaps he would have let his guard down for a moment and let me glimpse the vulnerable human being behind the robot-like façade. 'Man, this job is busting my derrière. Forty-seven thousand suspects to keep tabs on and we're not halfway through the list yet . . . the goddam show starts in two hours. What do they think we are? Infallible machines?'

Life in Sonoma was settled and contented. It was the first house Maya had ever owned and she enjoyed putting down roots. I enjoyed the rustic life more than I would have ever guessed I would. Of course there was always an excuse to get on a plane and fly somewhere if I caught a dose of rural *longueurs*. Knowing I *could* naturally prevented me from wanting to, most of the time.

Being settled in one time zone in a country place made one aware of the circles in life. The creek filled up in December and dried out in June and then filled up again in December. There was a time to reap and a time to sow and a time to reap again. It also alerted me to the circles in our personal lives. I had been going in circles all my life, like everyone else, I suppose. Sometimes the circles got closed out and sometimes that was a relief and sometimes a grief.

One circle closed off when I got a phone call from Germaine. She was lecturing at a nearby college and suggested that she come over to visit. I supposed she had got Maya's number from the publisher.

'No. I don't think that's a good idea.'

'Let me speak to Maya.'

'She's not here. And please don't call again.'

I had no intention of letting Germaine, with her penchant for psychodrama, anywhere near our happy home.

Another circle, one that was a joy and delight, rounded out when Maya filmed an interview with Baldwin in the Los Angeles home of Charles and Zeta Bloch who had produced *Look Away*, in what seemed half a lifetime ago.

WGBH, the public television channel in Boston, had asked Maya to do a series of interviews. It was an attractive offer because she chose her own subjects and her own format. Of course the budget was tight, it's axiomatic that budgets are always tight but especially so in public television. She skimped on some of the interviews so that she could shoot her wad on Baldwin. The two ways to skimp on a taped interview are personnel and time. You use one camera and setting and film it all in as close to real time as possible. With this in mind Maya chose experienced performers who would not be confused by *reverses* which are necessary when only one camera is used. The camera focuses on the interviewee and then when it's done it sets up again and focuses on the interviewer who asks the questions all over again. In spite of the technical restraints the first three interviews had come off well. Baldwin was the fourth.

Charles and Zeta lived in a large and charming house in Coldwater Canyon and agreed to lend it for a location. If the interview was filmed in Los Angeles there was, in theory at least, a limitless supply of highly-skilled technicians available, without any travelling expense being incurred. The Blochs' house had a beautiful courtyard garden and the plan was to film Maya and Jimmy having a conversation over lunch outdoors. The opening shot would be Maya in the kitchen finishing off her cooking. Cooking was becoming Maya's signature. Whenever a journalist came to interview her she would provide lunch and start the interview while she was cooking. It was a photo opportunity no photographer could resist — a shrewd ploy. It showed her public that she was 'just plain folks' and the exotic nature of the dishes she prepared went against the watermelon and fried chicken-eating stereotypical view of Blacks that the larger public held. She was fascinated by food anyway. Every couple of months I would build another shelf or two to hold her mushrooming library of cook-books. And as far as I could tell she had a standing purchase order with every used bookseller in Northern California for any books by, or about, Blacks, and between the Black library and the food library we would soon have to add on to the house. That would be fun. Construction was my signature.

Jimmy was in New York on business and the filming was set up around his schedule. Two days before the shooting he called to say he was sick and could not come. Maya took a deep breath and a stiff drink. I took a stiff drink too and quoted Kipling:

If you can look on triumph and disaster
And treat those two impostors just the same,
Yours is the world and everything that's in it.

Maya nodded. 'And what is more you'll be a woman, my daughter. Very apposite. Have you seen my phone book?'

She called Leo Maitland, a doctor friend in New York who was a friend of Jimmy's too, and explained the situation. Leo promised to do his best to work a miracle of medicine and, if at all possible, get Jimmy on a plane west the next day. The young woman producer had already learned of Jimmy's illness and was ringing every half-hour in total panic.

Maya and I started a hand of gin rummy. I quoted Kipling again:

If you can keep your head
When those about you
Are losing theirs and blaming it on you.

Maya nodded. 'Kipling got it right, didn't he?'

A few hours later Leo Maitland called to say Baldwin was going to be able to travel and that he would personally accompany him to the airport.

When I met him off the plane next morning Jimmy looked disoriented, as if he had never flown into Los Angeles or any other airport before. He started off right as all the other passengers turned left. I ran after him and grabbed him. He gave me a huge grateful grin of recognition and kissed me on the cheek. I realised that this was the first time that I had ever seen him alone in a public place. He seemed puzzled without a companion. I also realised that he was shaky after his flight and not in the best of health, whatever miracles Leo had worked.

'Take my arm, Jimmy. We'll stroll through this like a couple of gentlemen taking a walk in the sun. Or . . . as they say in Chicago, "take it easy, greasy, got a long way to slide".' He smiled politely at my feeble attempts at sick-bed humour. I sympathised with him. Travelling when you're under the weather is a cruel ordeal. I knew that the walk from the plane to the luggage carousel would seem like crossing the Sahara.

Once we got out of the airport I pulled into a huge filling station/restaurant complex to get gas. Jimmy perked up and looked around with bright-eyed interest. Everything was on a vast scale and looked as if it had just been built last week. The landscaping was green and every shrub was identical in size. A tall young man with long, wind-blown, sun-bleached hair and superb teeth smiled and said, 'Fill it?'

I nodded and popped the hood. 'Check the radiator please.'

Jimmy watched and listened with full attention. The pump jockey set the pump in the gas tank and checked the radiator and washed the windscreen while gas pumped.

'How does he know when it's full?' asked Jimmy.

'It cuts off automatically.'

I paid and tipped a dollar.

'Is that the usual tip?'

'Well . . . depends on the smile you get. Anyway I'm driving a celebrity so we have to keep a front up.' Jimmy chuckled and punched me playfully on the shoulder.'Did you eat on the plane or do you want to do brunch?'

'Where?'

I pointed to the huge Spanish mission-style restaurant beyond a few acres of car park. 'Right over there.'

'Let's do brunch.'

We waited for our hostess to seat us, as the notice by the cash desk requested us to do. The hostess was there in a moment and led us to a window booth, gave us large menus, told us our waitress would be right with us and wished us a pleasant meal.

Our pretty, plump, middle-aged waitress was right with us. 'What would you boys like this sunny morning?' We ordered breakfasts and I asked our waitress to send the cocktail waitress over. When we had ordered drinks I went to phone Maya and assure her that Jimmy had arrived.

A Black waitress stopped me on my way back to the table. 'Excuse me, but is the man with you who I think he is?'

'If you think he wrote *Go Tell It On The Mountain*, the answer is yes.'

'He *is* James Baldwin! Would he mind if I came over and spoke with him?'

'I'm sure he would be charmed but he's just off a plane and hungry and thirsty. It would be nice to let him get something to eat and have a drink first.'

'Of course. You have a nice day.'

Jimmy was delighted with the food, the service, the ambience, the cheerful efficiency of it all. He did not drive cars himself and I guessed that most people who drove him, except me, had the good sense to fill up the tank before starting out, so this was a rare experience for him. He was looking healthier by the minute. The truck-stop life suited him.

When the table was cleared we asked the waitress for another round of drinks. She said she would let the cocktail waitress know. The Black

162

waitress brought our drinks. 'The Scotch is for you, Mr Baldwin?' Jimmy's face opened up in surprise and he gave her a big smile. 'Could I ask you for an autograph?' She set a crisp sheet of paper beside him and gave him a pen. He asked her name and wrote her a short note and signed it with a large autograph. She was trembling with excitement as she picked it up and thanked him. I knew how she felt. I had once shaken hands and exchanged a few words with Muhammed Ali in his home in Hancock Park. He addressed me as Paul a couple of times. That's all I remember of the conversation, I was too excited to listen to him and too nervous to remember what *I* said.

As we drove to our motel I told him about the interviews so far. The idea was not so much for Maya to conduct interviews as to record conversations. They had all been completely different. Bill Russell, the 1960 Olympic high jump champion and, in the opinion of many people, the greatest basketball player who ever lived, had been wry and terse. He had defied Maya to lure him out of his macho shell. He had been the first Black national league basketball coach and later a TV commentator, both occupations that require a readiness with words. Certainly when I had been around him before he seemed as talkative as everyone else, but when the camera was on him he played a game with Maya. They were contemporaries and Bill had been going to school in Oakland while Maya was in school across the bridge in San Francisco. Their conversation had the flavour of two fifteen-year-olds teasing and flirting in the school yard, a conversation-that-might-have-been, if they had met in those school days.

Actress Valerie Harper had been eloquent and persuasive about sexism in Hollywood. Most people knew her as Mary Tyler Moore's sidekick in TV sit-coms, and it was interesting to see her step aside from her TV persona in her conversation with Maya.

Ray Bradbury had asked to do the show in the Magic Castle, an illusionists' club in Los Angeles. He was a hobby illusionist himself and a storehouse of information on the subject. Maya just gave him his head and off he went.

Baldwin listened and grew gloomy. 'I was in a funk all the way out here on the plane. I don't want to let Maya down. The truth is that I'm not really well. I know this means a lot to Maya. She told me how everything depended on me . . . I didn't realise. I thought it was just another "go in the studio and get a mike pinned to your jacket and speak eternal verities". If not me, then anyone. I really didn't know how much hinged on it.'

'*You* were right. All you can do is sit down and talk. There's producers and camera people and editors and all the rest of them to worry about everything else. So just eat well, take your medicine, get a good night's sleep. Why don't you ask me about where we're all staying?'

'Where are we all staying?'

'The Del Capri Motel.'

'It sounds romantic . . . and a little risqué.'

'It is. Lana Turner's mafioso gigolo boyfriend was stabbed to death there some years back. The story is that her fifteen-year-old daughter offed him . . . maybe . . . maybe not. The day manager is an old buddy called Noah. He is eagerly awaiting your arrival and I undertook to promise that you would sign his first edition of *Giovanni's Room*. Actually it's a very nice place indeed, forty or so units arranged on two storeys around a large swimming-pool. The rooms have little kitchenettes. You get good coffee and Danish pastries for breakfast and the *LA Times*.'

'Just where is this earthly paradise?'

'Way out west on Wiltshire Boulevard hidden among corporate high rises. You'll enjoy it.'

The temperature had dropped fifteen degrees overnight and a gusty wind was coming in off the ocean when we got to Charles and Zeta's next morning. It was not outdoor living weather but the cameras and mikes and props were already being set up in the garden. At least a dozen technicians were tripping over one another. I retreated into the living-room with Zeta for coffee and a bit of a gossip. Taping started around noon. Charles came in early from work about four o'clock and was surprised to find taping still in progress. Maya, in a light silk pant suit, was still chatting over lunch to Jimmy, shivering in a blazer and sport shirt. The sky was overcast and dusk was coming in, the wind was getting stronger than ever, and as I watched on the monitor screens in the mobile control room parked out on the driveway sometimes a gust of wind would sway and shake the trees and bushes in the background while Maya and Jimmy leaned into the gale like Captains Courageous butting up the Channel in the teeth of a nor'easter. As the light faded the camera crews started to set up lights.

'They're going into extra innings,' said Charles with the bemused smile I remembered from Broadway days.

'It's all the producer's fault,' I said.

'That goes without saying,' said Charles with a smile.

The producer *had* lost it. She seemed to be everywhere, darting and hovering like a humming bird in a state of high anxiety. Every syllable was repeated and every shot re-shot.

. Maya and Jimmy rose at five-thirty from the windswept lunch table. 'Ladies and gentlemen, thank you all for your efforts . . . That's a wrap,' said Maya. The two of them strolled into the living-room to join us for cocktails. The producer came in dithering. Baldwin stopped her dead with a cold smile.

'The weather forecast says that the wind will blow out before midnight,' Charles told me. 'We're going out to the beach house tomorrow if the sun shines. Why don't you join us and play some volleyball on the beach? A good sweat will do wonders for you.' I liked the idea.

Next day at the beach was clear, sunny and hot. I had never played volleyball before but had watched enough to understand the general pattern of the game. The other players were as middle-aged as myself or older and played a finesse game. A bunch of panty-waists with low pain thresholds in my opinion — which I kept to myself. I did quite well and improved as play went on. The only problem was that sometimes I forgot what game I was playing and when the ball was hanging in the air near the net I thought I was back twenty-five years on a soccer field defending desperately against a floating corner kick and went in charging, elbowing and leaping to claim it. The second time I was amnesiac I took down one player on my team and two of the opposition and the net. But we made the point. As I helped re-rig the net the opposition players were slow getting up. My team-mate was complaining about a clash of heads. I thought it had been more like a lover's nudge.

'Why did you do that, Paul?' asked Charles, perplexed. I explained about my absent-mindedness, and the urgency to claim what looked like a soccer ball in territory I regarded as mine . . . if we had been playing soccer. 'I always thought soccer was a non-contact game.'

'Don't you ever read Andy Capp comic strips?'

'All the time. And now I understand them better.'

The producer called from Boston a couple of days later when we were back in Sonoma. Ms Berkovitz, the secretary, came running out to catch me just as I was driving off with a truckload of bricks.

'Paul! Maya's producer's on the phone from Boston.'

'Hallelujah! Maya's around somewhere. It is a far, far better thing I go to do . . .'

'She specifically wants to talk to you.'

The producer was still in a panic. She had reviewed the tapes and wanted to shoot the whole thing over again. 'There's no continuity. I can't make a show out of it. What do you think Maya would say?'

I felt sorry for the young woman. It was her first major producing assignment and she had been out of her depth. Maya was still furious at the sorry botch-up and Jimmy was back in New York.

'Maya will ask for another producer . . . and she'll get one. Why don't you forget about the tapes for a few days, get on with the next interview . . . Here's an idea. You must have three or four hours of tapes so have them transcribed then go through them and *create* a continuity. Take a highlight pen and piece together half an hour of talk. It doesn't have to be *that* continuous. Then you go through the film with the transcript in front of you and red pencil out all the talk that's in the bad shots. Then you're narrowing it down . . .'

'Are you telling me how to do my job?'

'No. I'm trying to help you *keep* your job.'

'Sorry. Thanks. I'll call you in a couple of weeks.'

It turned out fine. But perhaps those hours of tapes are still in a storeroom at WGBH. I would like to see them one day.

One of the by-products of Maya's popularity in Sonoma was that strangers could find out where she lived simply by walking into a store in town and asking. One afternoon I got back from Santa Rosa and while I was having an after-work cocktail Maya said she had had a big disappointment that morning. 'A big, black stretch limousine pulled into the driveway and a smart young Black lady in a cap and chauffeur's uniform came to the door. I thought you had a surprise for me. Maybe a tour of the Napa wineries.'

'That would be a nice idea one day. Sorry I didn't think of it. Wrong address?'

'No, she came to see me. She had just finished a job in Vallejo and saw a sign to Sonoma, remembered reading in *People* magazine that we lived here so she came to town and asked around . . .'

'Did you have a nice visit?'

'She was here on business. She wanted to sell me her limo. She's buying a new one and thought we might like to buy her old one. Something to sui. our lifestyle.'

'You see what happens when you get yourself photographed posing like a glamour girl by your swimming pool on your country estate in the heart of California wine country? I'm surprised you didn't buy it.'

'I was tempted.'

'I can imagine.'

Maya loved to drive, as fast as possible in the biggest car available, and I could easily picture her bombing down the interstate at ninety miles an hour in a stretched Cadillac. Wearing a snappy chauffeurette's cap of course. One of her teenage ambitions had been to work as a chauffeurette and I suspected that she had not entirely given up on it. Vivian loved to drive big cars very fast too, but lately she had become preoccupied with eighteen-wheeler big rigs. Her plan was to retire from the merchant marine, go to truck driver's school and start a new career as a teamster. Maya did not encourage the idea. Her joke was that she did not want people calling her mum the mothertrucker, but under the flippancy was a concern that Vivian would not be able to sustain the rigours of transcontinental hauling. Vivian unblinkingly ignored the passing years but they *were* passing. Exactly how many years had passed her was a secret she shared with no one, but simple arithmetic added up to about sixty-five . . . and that was a low-side estimate. When her attempts to lobby Maya to support her new ambition failed she turned her attention to me. We spent some happy times studying brochures extolling the virtues of the latest truck models. Her heart was set on a Peterbilt, the Rolls Royce of tractors. I had no trouble at all joining the dream. I would go to driving school myself and once in a while we would team up for a cross-country haul. Big wheels rolling, CB chatter over the country and western music wailing out of the stereo speakers. Swing into a mid-western truck stop, climb slowly from the huge cab and swagger across the truck park for a gigantic high cholesterol breakfast in the company of our peers. We would be wearing Eisenhower jackets and cowboy boots, of course. Vivian would wear a rhinestoned cowboy hat and I would have a baseball cap, Oakland A's probably. The main impediment to the dream's fulfilment was that Peterbilts cost about $60,000 and our steady acquisition of real estate had fairly well cleaned out the cash drawer for a while.

After a few months she set the dream aside and asked to borrow Maya's birth certificate for a few days. Her only explanation was that she was taking a trip to Michigan and might be doing some business while she was there. Maya was immediately suspicious. The only need for a birth certificate she could imagine was that Vivian was planning on getting married.

'Dammit, mother, you are planning on committing bigamy for me by proxy. That's not fair. I get the guilt without the pleasure.'

Vivian shrugged and dismissed the matter without comment but her irritated glance fully expressed her impatience with her daughter's piffling preoccupation with petty technicalities. She promptly drove off to Michigan anyway.

A few days later she was back with a new husband.

He was a retired Pullman car porter, slim, unbelievably dapper and he looked as if he was not enjoying California for one minute. Vivian was already having second thoughts. She confided in me that he slept in a snood, a string net that kept his hair in place. 'Nothing wrong with that but it still takes him half an hour to fix his hair in the morning. And then it takes him another hour to get dressed. I can't stand men who spend half their lives getting dressed, women either. I can get up, shower, make up, dress and be out the door and getting to stepping in fifteen minutes . . . and looking *good*.'

Next weekend we had a small party for them. Guy and his friends and twenty or so of ours. The new husband sat and watched in stony discomfort and the newly-weds left after a couple of hours. Vivian called Bob Treuhaft next day and retained him to get her a divorce. It turned out that as soon as they had started to drive away from the party the new husband had started to tremble in a paroxysm of rage and had launched into a harangue about the vileness of being forced to associate socially with Whites and Asians and the sickening spectacle of inter-racial dancing. Vivian had pulled off the road and proceeded to deal with bigotry as directly and decisively as she dealt with everything else.

'I told him to step out of the car because we were going to jar the ground.' She illustrated her point by taking up a boxer's stance.

'What does "jar the ground" mean?'

'Fight to a knockdown.'

'Ah.' I knew Vivian was a fast draw and a crack pistol shot but I had not realised she was a fistfighter as well. 'Did he accept the challenge?'

'Of course he didn't. He may be stupid but he's not crazy. I'd have beaten him until he gave up his arse and shat through his ribs.'

'I never realised you were a fistfighter.'

'How could I be anything else, growing up with three brothers who boxed? I used to love to spar. A lot of boxers used to stay at our house when they came through St Louis. I used to spar with them too.' She smiled at the happy memories. 'Henry Armstrong was always my special favourite.'

My mouth dropped open. '*The* Henry Armstrong? The only man to hold world titles in three weight divisions simultaneously? Welter, middle and cruiser weight?'

'He was good. He was about a middleweight, more or less your build . . . longer reach.'

'There's an old English vaudeville song that goes, "I danced with the boy who danced with the girl who danced with the Prince of Wales" . . . so get your dukes up. I want to be able to tell my grandchildren that I sparred with the girl who sparred with the boy who held three world titles simultaneously.' We settled into our fighting stances and she drove me back with a couple of left jabs, then back again with a couple more. Damn, but she had quick hands. I threw in the towel.

'Now make Momma nice drink.'

As she sipped reflectively she said, 'The man has to be a fool. What did he think I was going to do when he started to talk that silliness, with a White granddaughter-in-law and a White son-in-law?'

'Not to mention your memory of your own White mother.'

She bared her teeth in a huge smile. 'You got that *damn* right, baby.'

Bob Treuhaft decided they should go for annulment of the marriage instead of divorce. 'What grounds?' I asked.

Vivian gazed at me in wide-eyed innocence. 'Non-consummation, of course.'

Bob found a friendly judge and pulled it off. But after the judge gave his decision he looked down imploringly at Vivian and said, 'But please, Mrs Baxter, never come before me again in similar circumstances. Please.'

One day a stranger in a wheelchair rolled up to the front door. Ms Berkovitz answered the door and came to find me where I was laying cobbled walkways. I had a new house purchase in escrow and was improving the shining hour by doing some landscaping at home while I waited for the deal to close. 'There's a young lady wants to see Maya. She doesn't have an appointment.'

'Well, Maya's swimming her morning laps in the pool. Invite the woman in and give her a cup of coffee or whatever else we've got that she cares for . . . show her some Weshton hoshpitality. Ain't no way we turn shtrangers away hongray or thirsty, lessen they deserve it of course . . . for Christ's sake, Sal! Lighten up! I may not be funny but I'm trying. Give me a bloody smile.'

Ms Berkovitz looked at me as if I was poison oak and she was barefoot. 'She can't come in. She's in a wheelchair and there's a step at the front door.'

'Then show her round to the back door. There is no step there.'

Sal was in a sour mood in those days. She had been attending a class in Women's Studies and Feminist Sensitivity at Santa Rosa Community College. At some point in the course women who had relationships with men were encouraged to bring their partners into the class. Sal had invited her husband of many years to participate. He was an intelligent man and after listening to the persuasive arguments had decided that their marriage had no future. Their children were grown and self-supporting, he was semi-retired and recovering from major heart surgery. He was prepared to settle generously with her. He was hearing 'death's winged chariot drawing near'.

'Am I wrong, Paul?' he had asked me.

'Of course you're wrong, boy. Your wife wanted to redecorate you, not terminate the lease.'

'Was I wrong, Paul?' asked Sal.

''Course you were, Sal. As my old Irish mum used to say, "You can take a horse to the water but you can't make him drink".'

'What does that mean?'

'It means that you can have all sorts of schemes to adjust people's attitudes but people can be stubborn to death. Take it easy, greasy. Where was it all those Jews threw themselves off the rock face? Forty of them, at Massada? Rather than have their attitudes adjusted by the Roman soldiers?'

Naturally I had not made friends of the Berkovitz family.

'Invite the woman in the wheelchair in and give her a coffee. I have four square yards of cobblestones to set before the sun goes down. Excuse me.'

Maya dealt with it effortlessly. The young woman wanted her support. She wanted all the public facilities in town to be accessible to the disabled. She went on a drive with Maya and pointed out that she could not cross the town square, she could not go into City Hall, she could not use the library or get a drink of water at the fountain in the square. I helped her out of the car as she got back. We had a cup of tea.

'Why me?' asked Maya.

'You wrote a poem, *Just give me a cool drink of water 'fore I Diiiie.*
I thought you would understand about not being able to get to a water
fountain.'

Maya reached her hand across the table. 'Use me.'

For the next month the young woman in a wheelchair was a regular
visitor. I was amused by the way she sweetly bullied Maya. The two of
them were rather alike really, both had the knack of involving those
around them in their own preoccupations. Maya was a good sport
for a while but soon got impatient with playing second fiddle. The
relationship was cooling by the time Maya addressed a town public
meeting to advocate access for the disabled. I was otherwise engaged
that evening but my friend Don at the hardware store gave me a full
account. Maya had made a reasoned plea for fairness and equal access
for all taxpayers to the public facilities their money supported and then
she had turned on her oratorial after-burners and brought tears to her
listeners' eyes. The city fathers had promised there and then to make
all the public places accessible to wheelchairs. They promised to write
an ordinance that would be a model for the county.

Not long after that I bought a handsome three-storey Victorian in
the best part of downtown Santa Rosa with the idea of converting
it to professional offices with living accommodation over. I took my
blueprints to the county planner's office. The planner looked them over
and shook his head. 'A year ago these would have been fine, Paul,
but they won't fly now. There are new ordinances and all offices have
to be accessible to wheelchairs, special rest-rooms, ramps or elevators
. . . you haven't got enough floor space to even make it worth while
. . . Sorry. You see what happened was a Black woman writer down
in Sonoma got everybody fired up and the laws got changed.'

'I heard about her.'

'A good thing really. It's only fair when you think about it.'

'Very true.'

Ron Stacker Thompson, the young director of the Oakland Ensemble
Theater, came up to Sonoma with a proposal for Maya. He wanted her
to update *Hand on the Plough* for the company. Ron was a witty young
man and they discussed the idea over a lighthearted and bibulous lunch
under the oak trees. Maya was not looking for work at the time. As
lunch wound down I watched her reach around for a pleasant and

polite way to turn him down. She talked about other local writers who would do a splendid job, she questioned her own qualifications; she hummed and hawed over her ability to commit to a deadline because of existing assignments . . . Then Ron got to the subject of *money*.

When he named the fee OET was offering I watched her lips twitch. She looked off for a moment across the meadow where our dog was kibitzing the horses as usual. I knew she was seduced. The money had got her. She reached across the table. 'Shake on it. We have a deal.' They shook hands. 'When do you want it delivered?' We did not know it at the time but our course for the next two years was set. There, that afternoon, under the oak trees.

The scene between the two of them reminded me, not altogether inconsequentially, of my favourite scene in *The Magnificent Seven* when Yul Brynner is watching an argument on Boot Hill. The issue is whether or not a Black man's encoffined body should be buried in the cemetery. The mob says 'no'. Whites only in consecrated ground. A few timid souls say that justice requires the man should have a proper burial, but there's no one ready to drive the hearse to the graveyard for fear of being lynched. Yul Brynner, the professional gunfighter in black who up till then has had only the mildest interest in the proceedings, perks up and says, 'Hell, if that's all it's about, *I'll* drive the wagon.'

Ron had offered Maya one hundred dollars to rewrite the show. Her average fee for a speaking engagement was two thousand dollars. *Noblesse oblige,* movie gunfighters and artists alike.

Hand on the Plough was originally an off, or perhaps off-off Broadway show devised, produced and performed about twenty years earlier by Roscoe Lee Browne and a group of actor friends. As I listened to Ron and Maya discuss the updated version I sensed that Maya wanted to take it away from the original format which was essentially a dramatic recitation of Black poetry. It had been a showcase for professional actors who came and went according to the ebb and flow of other acting jobs. The Oakland Ensemble Theater was a semi-professional company and their strength was ensemble playing. Maya changed the title to *And Still I Rise*. By the end of rehearsals it was a full-blown musical with dance, comedy, dramatic recitation, songs and big production numbers.

Gerry came out for the opening which was a roaring success. The reviews were excellent and the show was a hot ticket for its two-week run. On opening night Gerry took a dozen of the company to dinner. I had asked around for advice and booked the Hungry

Farmer restaurant in Oakland's Jack London Square. Gerry was quiet and smiled paternally at his guests who were all flying ten feet above the ground with the adrenalin rush of conspicuous success.

'There was only one White in the company?' said Gerry.

'Yes, Cleo. Down at the end of the table. She's married to Ron Stacker.'

'And ninety-five per cent of the audience was Black?'

'I guess that's the way things go. Oakland is the home of the Black Panthers. White folks don't come downtown after sunset.'

'But it's not really an exclusively Black show? Is it?'

'No. Take it to Berkeley or San Francisco, I'm sure it would do well with different audiences. Oakland is just that way.'

Gerry was sampling his dessert cautiously. 'Is this the best restaurant in Oakland?'

'I asked around. This was the best one that fitted the needs, opens late enough, near the theatre and big enough to accommodate our party . . . safe parking.'

'Maybe we should open Paparazzi West.'

'In Oakland? That's not one of your best ideas, Gerry.'

I knew it was not a serious suggestion but I sensed he was ready for a project.

A month later he told Maya that he wanted to produce *And Still I Rise* on Broadway. It was only half-serious at first, and we enjoyed acting out old showbiz movies and planning our wardrobes for all those out-of-town openings. I fancied a straw boater on the back of my head like Dan Dailey. I would amble around exuding loose-limbed tipsy charm. Maya was going to go furs and diamonds all the way.

It soon turned fully serious. The production at OET had freely borrowed other people's published works without worrying about copyright or royalty arrangements. It was a non-profit-making company and a two-week run, so what? But a Broadway show would be different. Gerry wanted Maya to rewrite the show so that everything in it, words and music, was her own original material. That was when it got serious.

We had just bought another house in Santa Rosa and by the time I was driving off to work at seven o'clock, Maya was already at our slightly out-of-tune piano searching out melodies with the first and third fingers of her right hand.

173

Gerry had acquired control of a rundown country club in New Jersey, and I had just settled in to my remodelling project in Santa Rosa when I got an anguished call from him.

'These scumbag contractors in Jersey are trying to bleed me white, Paul. I kid you not.'

'You already are White, Gerry.'

'I'll be a lot fucking whiter next time you see me. I'll be bloodless. How busy are you right now?' I told him. 'How soon can you come out to New York? I need a presence in Jersey. You understand what I mean? These fucking sharks are trying to eat me alive. I need you here to protect my interest. When can you get out here?'

'I was planning on going with Maya or as soon as I've got this new house finished.'

'Can you come sooner?'

'I'll do my best.'

I replanned my work and settled for a cosmetic spruce-up instead of a full remodelling job. Meanwhile, Maya was plunking at the piano and filling up the yellow pages at a steady clip. One afternoon when I was nearly finished in Santa Rosa I came in from work and she was sitting at the dining-room table leaning over a tiny microphone attached to what looked like the first portable tape recorder that Sony ever made. She waved me to silence as she sang. For the next half-hour she continued to sing and I narrated.

The songs had a sweet blues flavour. They reminded me of our first times together in London. One evening she had asked me to sing an Irish song. I sang *Danny Boy* in my best light tenor, then she sang it as a blues. Absolutely astonishing.

'Done.' She switched off the tape recorder with a flourish. 'Now I deserve a drink!' We sipped and replayed the tape. The whole show was there, words and music. Absolutely astonishing, again! She mailed off the tape and two weeks later the Sonoma house was closed up for the duration. Tony, a footloose young carpenter who sometimes worked for me, was driving our car and the dog across the country and we were playing gin rummy aboard the overnight flight to New York.

CHAPTER TEN

GOODBYE BROADWAY, FAREWELL JERSEY SHORE: 1977

We set up housekeeping in the Alcott Hotel, half a block from Central Park and a few doors down from the Dakotas on West 72nd Street. There was a tiny alcove kitchen and a slightly out-of-tune piano. Maya started having meetings with the Schubert Organisation bosses who were going to co-produce the show. That seemed like an auspicious start, for they were the landlords of Broadway and owned more than eighty per cent of the theatres, and you cannot put on a show without a theatre. I started renovating the Knowle Country Club, a Great Gatsby relic built just before the Wall Street crash of '29.

My days started with a pre-dawn breakfast at a coffee shop on Columbus Avenue and a fifty-mile drive to mid-state New Jersey and ended mid-evening in Manhattan. It soon became apparent that bringing a musical to the New York stage involved temper tantrums, chicanery, compromise, extortion, bullying, hard work, weaseling, humility, long hours and a cast of dozens. Remodelling the Knowle was about the same thing writ small.

At first we took advantage of excellent complimentary tickets from the Schubert people and enjoyed an orgy of theatre-going. When we had seen all the shows we cared to, we started exploring New York restaurants with friends but after a while our tourist curiosity faded. Maya was getting bored and depressed. Her music was being picked to pieces by arrangers and her delicate bluesy melodies were being reknitted into elevator music. A demonstration tape was made at vast expense by an orchestra of session musicians and a choir of journeyperson singers. It did not have that swing and it did not mean a thang to me. Maya complained about feeling 'unreal'. I understood what she meant. She was losing her sense of self and her feeling of being in control of events. Ego and control were the fuel mix that powered her creative motor. She faced the depressing fear that her psychological eco-system was being destroyed by the endless frustrations, humiliations and delays. Negotiations over contracts and venues took on the timelessness of glacial erosion. Availability of theatres is a constantly changing factor and everything was renegotiated every month. As the seasons changed my concern over the way the show was sounding gave way to doubt over whether it would ever be heard at all.

Gerry Purcell asked me to meet him alone for dinner at his restaurant. I ordered veal piccata and a glass of Valpolicella and waited for him to get to the business of the evening, which he did without delay.

'I had to borrow on this restaurant to pay our fucking taxes. You understand what I'm saying? I took out a loan on *this*!' He reached forward and tapped his palms down on the table to emphasise his point. '*This* restaurant.'

I chewed my veal and nodded and waited.

'Paul, I kid you not, my back is up against the wall.'

I nodded and he jerked himself back from the table and pressed against the wall behind him, arms outstretched in Christ-like suffering. A waiter rushed forward anxiously. 'Something wrong, Mr Purcell?'

Gerry waved him away and leant forward over the table. 'I am up against the wall.' This time he just turned and patted the wall.

'I'm familiar with the metaphor, Gerry.'

'You've got to sell some of that real estate in California.'

'Okay.'

'Are you going to be able to sell it easily?'

'I don't know. It was easy enough to buy it.'

'Why don't you fly back next weekend and put it on the block?'

'What's the tab? How much are we in the hole?'

'One hundred and ninety-two thousand dollars!'

'No kidding. I didn't know there was that much money in the world. Must have been a helluva party. Too bad I can't remember it.'

Next Sunday I took the bus from San Francisco to Sonoma. The house seemed like an abandoned stage set from another life. I walked around without nostalgia. I knew we would never live there again. I thought about going to Gino's for drinks to kill the evening but decided I had nothing to say to anyone. I watched television for a while and was in bed by nine. Next morning I listed our four rental houses with a Santa Rosa realtor. The California property market had heated up while we were gone and I was pleasantly surprised at the prices he suggested. Not that it really made much difference, every last cent would vanish into the black hole on Broadway.

I was late getting my seat reservation on the flight back to New York so there were no window seats left. I was disappointed because the weather forecast was clear skies most of the way and looking out the window was my favourite way to pass a journey. My travelling companion who *did* have the window seat was a middle-aged businessman ritually fumbling through papers from his briefcase on his lap. Once we got to cruising altitude he decided to talk to me and launched into a whining lament about racial discrimination by the Federal Small Business Administration who, according to him, would only make government-insured, low-interest loans to undeserving Black-owned businesses. The third time he used the word 'nigger' I decided I did not want to hear any more of that shit.

'Let me buy you a drink, boy, and I'll ask the cabin attendant to have the captain arrange for an ambulance to meet the plane at the next suitable airport along our flight plan.'

'What's wrong?'

'My wife is Black, my stepson is Black, and *his* son is Black. You keep talking that shit and one of us is going off this plane to an ambulance. I'm not saying *which* of us . . . I'm saying *one* of us. Black people have a saying, "Fuck with the cook, fuck with the baker but fuck with the family and you fuck with the undertaker".' He turned very red, shut his briefcase and pushed past me. I took the window seat.

My work at the country club was winding up and I took to coming home mid-afternoon. Maya was usually playing solitaire and drinking when I got in. One such afternoon just as I got in the phone rang. Maya snatched it up. 'I told you to hold my calls, dammit! . . . Yes . . . yes . . . exactly right . . . put her on the line . . .' For the next five minutes she listened and nodded and made occasional comments. Finally she said, 'I accept,' adding 'Go and buy that young woman at the switchboard a large expensive bunch of flowers, *please*. Right now.'

The call that the operator had insisted on putting through was from Midge Costanza, special assistant to President Carter, inviting Maya to join the President's Commission for International Women's Year.

The appointment came at a crucial time. It was a recognition that she was 'real' and had something important to say and it was an opportunity for her to explore her changing feelings about the Women's Movement. Until her miserable sojourn in New York she had been lukewarm to the cause and regarded women's rights as part and parcel of human rights in general. As she wryly noted, Black women, whatever else they were denied, had always had the right to work, often at two jobs. They would have loved the economic freedom to stay home and enjoy looking after their children. However, the offhand treatment and patronising indifference that White males in New York had meted out to her as she bumped her head against the 'glass ceiling' that allowed her to see success but blocked her from climbing up to it, had sensitised her.

She cheered up immediately, convinced herself that it was all a roll of the dice and that she would not let it bother her if the play never went on. James Baldwin came into town in an exuberant mood and for a few days they had a boisterous reunion.

It was winding down when the three of us went to dinner at a Cuban restaurant round the corner from the hotel. We got our favourite window table in the covered sidewalk section and settled to enjoying a bottle of inky-red wine when I noticed two flamboyantly dressed Black hermaphrodites swishing slowly along the sidewalk. They were almost level with our table when one of them caught my gaze and pulled at his companion's lace sleeve. Their smiles were radiant as they came over to the window. Maya and Jimmy became aware of them and, seasoned celebrities that they were, they both put on their 'meeting our fans' expressions. The hermaphrodites ignored them and waved at me. Then the more voluptuous of the pair pursed his lips and leaned towards the glass as if to kiss it, but instead he carefully mouthed the question: 'Where's the dog?' I pointed in the direction of the hotel, closed my eyes and mimed sleep. They nodded understanding, waved again and continued swishing and mincing uptown. Maya and Jimmy stared after them.

'Friends of yours?' asked Maya.

'Not really friends but I see them regularly.'

'Tell, tell!' chortled Jimmy.

'They're usually cruising Central Park around midnight when I take the dog for a walk . . . we're all part of what I call the West Gate Set.'

Maya grinned. 'Who else is in the West Gate Set?'

'There are a couple of muggers. I presume they are muggers although I have never actually seen them at work and may be falling into the trap of stereotypical perception. For all I *actually* know they may be biology students studying nocturnal fauna. But they look like muggers. There's a bearded roller-skater who wears red hot-pants in all weathers, a couple of women whores who propositioned me a. few times when I first started visiting . . . derelicts come and go, temporary members, so to speak . . . we're an informal little group . . . Oh, and sometimes I run into Lauren Bacall.'

'In the park?' asked Jimmy.

'No, on my way to the park. She walks her dog from the Dakotas west towards Columbus Avenue and we nod as we pass. Dog walkers greet each other in the street. I think we're the only strangers in New York who do.'

Jimmy shook his head. 'You really walk through Central Park at midnight. Child, you are a CRAZY mo'fucker.'

'I can't think what else to do. Sargi's family crest bears the motto RUN FREE OR DIE, so I let her run free in Central Park.'

'No,' said Maya. 'Forgive me, but I must correct you. That's her *mother's* crest. Her *father's* crest says "GIVE ME MOTOR CARS OR GIVE ME DEATH!" '

'You're right. Thank you for the correction. That's why I can't take her to work with me in Jersey. She'd hop the first golf cart smoking and we'd never see her again. Anyone with anything on wheels could steal Sargi.'

'No,' said Maya. 'Forgive me, but I must correct you again. Anyone with car *keys* can steal Sargi.'

'Sweet Sargi,' said Baldwin with a smile. 'I used to love watching her fuss with the horses in the field behind your house. I've no idea why I enjoyed that so much. I've never been very interested in dogs really.'

'I was terrified of dogs until I met Sargi. She's a great proselytiser for the canine cause.'

'True. She's the darling of our set.'

'Are you going back to California soon?' asked Baldwin.

'Maybe the day after tomorrow,' said Maya.

About that time the lights went out. Dim, battery-operated emergency lights kicked in after a moment. Women picked up their purses and set them on their laps, waiters patrolled their tables. The room

179

went quiet as everyone waited to see what would happen next. Like a vast orchestra cued by an invisible conductor, a thousand motorists on Columbus Avenue started honking their horns. The traffic signs were out, the low buildings across the street were dark shapes illuminated by car headlights. Diners from the interior of the restaurant crowded over to the sidewalk windows.

'I told the mayor to pay the light bill when he got the final notice,' said a wag. It was not the best one-liner but his timing and delivery were first class and he got the laugh he deserved. Baldwin, who was usually frazzled by life's minor practicalities like buying shoes or calling taxis, was relaxed, smiling and alert. Maya's response to the mysterious darkness was constructive and prompt.

'Let's get another bottle of wine.'

'Two more,' said Jimmy. 'We're going to have company . . . and cigarettes.'

'Three,' I suggested. 'We may be in for the long haul.'

I found our waiter in the crowd. Wine was no problem but the cigarette machine was powerless and no one had the key to open it up. Across the street candles started to flicker in a store front window and then the metal shutter over the door was rolled up. By the time I crossed the avenues, a line of customers already tailed out on to the sidewalk. If a nuclear bomb is ever dropped on New York there will be street vendors at every intersection selling anti-radiation pills before the mushroom cloud has finished forming.

I joined the line and bought cigarettes for two dollars a pack, candles for three dollars and a couple of two-dollar flashlights for ten dollars, batteries included. When I came out of the store the traffic was moving smoothly under the direction of a well-dressed executive type who was performing point duty with the brio of a Roman traffic cop. While I waited for him to beckon me across the street I searched the four points of the compass for any sign of electricity but it was dark in all directions. As I passed the amateur traffic cop he looked radiant. Like Sir Gawain gazing on the Holy Grail or a man with a childhood dream fulfilled.

The diners had settled back to their tables. Jimmy's brother and a friend had joined ours. My news that Manhattan was blacked out as far as I could see was already stale. News coming through on radios was that all Manhattan and parts of the boroughs were dark.

'How about Jersey?' I asked.

180

'So far Jersey's okay.'

'What do you mean, so far? Is there a domino effect?'

The waiter's voice throbbed with civic pride. 'I don't know. But it is BIG!' the Big Apple would show the rest of the world how to have a BIG foul-up.

The Baldwins went off to check on mother Baldwin who lived close by. I touched wine glasses with Maya. 'Win or lose, we'll have some booze.'

Her eyes were twinkling. Nothing like a bit of an adventure to get the juices flowing. 'Want me to do some night work, mister?' she said.

We went back to the hotel and climbed the pitch-black staircase to our suite and spent a romantic night by candlelight. Next morning we drove to Jersey and settled into a guest suite at the country club like Renaissance nobles escaping the plague-ridden city.

When the lights came on again after two or three days everything else started to fall into place. Suddenly auditions were scheduled, an opening date at the Ford Theater in Washington was set and memoranda of agreements were drawn up between everyone's lawyers. It was all turning out just like the old-fashioned showbiz movies. 'Hey kids, let's do a show!' Next thing we would be riding on the Starlight Express from Washington to Philadelphia to Chicago to Boston. I could picture the destination boards flopping over as the train pulled into the stations. Time to buy my straw boater and maybe a jazzy bow tie. I went to the rehearsals half expecting to see Vera Ellen or Ann Miller or Mitzi Gaynor. They did not show up but talented young people turned up in hundreds. The first call was a general call for singers who could dance and dancers who could sing. Talent came in every size, shape and skin colour. The idea was to have a spectrum chorus. After the first auditions came the call-backs and eventually the show was cast and the performers put on two-week retainers.

Maya was in high spirits. At last she had something to say when asked the inevitable question, 'How's the show coming?' She went off one afternoon to be interviewed by a magazine journalist at the Café des Artistes downtown by the park and left me in charge of the beans simmering on the stove in our tiny kitchen. Just before six I remembered that I had to pick up a pair of slacks that I had bought in a clothes store in the next block. I turned down the fire under the beans and headed for the store. I guess I was daydreaming and not looking where I was going because I bumped headlong into a sturdy Black man. We both stepped back and started to apologise, then stepped forward and started hugging each other. Bob Chrisman was a sight for sore eyes.

Once we got over our surprise I invited him to dinner and he walked along with me to the clothes store. He was telling me about his visit to New York to address a subcommittee of the United Nations as I nudged him into the store.

A lean Hispanic just inside the door shoved what looked like a sawn-off shotgun partly concealed in a *Daily News* into my ribs and ordered us to keep moving to the rear of the store. Off to the left another young Hispanic was emptying the cash register. We were prodded left and then right to the doorway of a tiny storeroom about six feet by eight. Three young White men were prone, handcuffed together on the far side of the room, a plump dark man lay prone with handcuffed wrists above his head against the near wall and near him a small elderly woman with Jewish features sat, knees drawn up, back to a radiator, clutching her purse under her chin. Another young Hispanic deftly handcuffed Bob and pushed him gently down between the three men who were hitched together and the plump man. His bulk overflowed the floor space.

'Now you,' he said as he closed a handcuff over my left wrist. He pushed me down on top of the plump man. I lay on my right side and watched him out of the corner of my eye as he snapped the other cuff over the stem of the radiator control knob. 'Face down. Don't look at me!'

'I can't, I've got a bad back,' I said. A purposeless lie, a reflex attempt to score a debating point and retain some illusion of control. He smoothly produced a small chrome-plated automatic pistol and touched it to my ears. 'Maybe I can manage,' I said. I buried my face between the plump man's shoulder blades. I heard our captors leave. The small woman was muttering and vibrant with anger. The rest of us lay still and silent.

Footsteps returning. My wallet was removed and my pockets searched. The others were similarly robbed. I saw a brown hand reach for the woman's purse and noted the liver spots on the backs of her hands as she clutched it defiantly. 'Give it to me.'

'No.'

The brown hand drew back. 'Give.' The hand made a beckoning gesture then clenched into a fist. He wanted to finish the job but he hesitated to lay hands on an old lady. After a moment he said, 'You open it then.' I found myself rather liking him.

She opened it and snatched out a silvery disk and held it away from him. 'You're not going to have this.' The lady had balls. It was an old-fashioned powder compact.

'Give it to me!'

'No!'

The robber was getting dangerously agitated.

'Give it to him lady. I'll buy you a new one at Tiffany's tomorrow.'

Another moment and she handed it over along with her purse.

'Thanks,' said the robber and patted me on the shoulder.

'You're staying too long,' I told him. 'You tripped the silent alarm when you lifted the cash draw to get the big bills. That rings direct to the precinct house, right? Response time in Central Manhattan during peak traffic is eight to ten minutes. Time's up. You'd better get the fuck out of here, man.'

I sensed him straighten and step back to the doorway. 'Nobody open this door for ten minutes. You understand?'

The door closed and we all started to rearrange ourselves. I reached and slipped the handcuff up over the radiator control knob, stood up and stretched. I could smell my sweat. The three young White men were stumbling to their feet like a slapstick comedy team. Although still handcuffed to his buddies, the one in the middle managed to reach down the front of his pants and pull out a huge revolver that looked like Wyatt Earp's original peacekeeper. I recognised him. He was the store manager who had sold me the pants. A small man about five foot three and fine-boned. The pistol looked enormous in his tiny hand. The three of them started to stumble towards the door. I shook my head at them. 'No way.' They paused. 'Too many of us here could get shot in the crossfire.' They looked relieved and nodded agreement. We waited for a couple of minutes then went cautiously into the empty store. The police arrived almost immediately.

Bob Chrisman looked very thoughtful. 'We were about three minutes away from being hostages.'

'That crossed my mind, kiddo.'

'You talked a pretty good game.'

'I guessed pretty well. I used to write a monthly column about how to be a crook, so I can fake that talk and fake that walk. Ten minutes was a pretty damn good guess.'

We were all in the precinct house going through mug shots when I remembered the beans on the stove. I explained my problem to a sympathetic cop.

'You burnt dinner? Oh boy! Now you're *really* in trouble. Hit the phone.' I called Maya at the Café des Artisans.

'You're at the Precinct House? . . . with Bob Chrisman? . . . What's bail?'

I laughed. 'We're going to walk . . . own recognizances . . . but maybe you could take the beans off the stove. Bob's coming to dinner.'

Bob and I were walking back to the hotel when it occurred to me that Bob had not finished telling me about his speech to United Nations.

'I'm supporting independence for Puerto Rica.' He grimaced. 'I'm having second thoughts. Those bastards got more than two hundred bucks off me.'

It was all coming right down to the wire. In less than a week contracts would have to be signed with the cast and everyone else, but the lawyers for the Schubert Organisation had still not come up with any final agreement spelling out the terms of the production partnership. I found myself sitting next to Vinette Carroll at a dinner party and took the opportunity to ask her a question that no one seemed to have answered so far. 'When a show starts out of town, in Washington for example, does it make money?'

'No.' Vinette had been producing Broadway shows for fifteen years. Her latest show, *Arms Too Short To Box With God*, had just closed after a successful Broadway run.

'What's the timetable from starting out of town to opening on Broadway?'

'Whatever the White lords of creation decide, whatever suits them. *Arms* was a year in Chicago while three or four White shows went into New York after a few weeks. And the contracts got rewritten and rewritten. You want to see how a successful Black producer operates? Come and have lunch with me at my office. We'll have salami sandwiches and deli coffee in my low-rent, walk-up executive headquarters.'

'Why do you do it?'

'You know the answer to that. Black folks like us got to keep moving on, inch by inch. Can't give up, chile.'

I nodded. 'It's a handsome offer. I'll have my people get with your people and we'll set it up to do lunch.'

The final agreement was delivered less than twenty-four hours before the deadline for signing. It was substantially different from the memoranda. Maya would give up virtually all rights and control if she signed it. The deal was busted.

Maya was crying when I took her to the airport. When I called her in California at a friend's house in Los Angeles she told me she had cried all the way across the continent. I knew those were not tears of self-pity, they were tears of rage. I closed up the hotel apartment, delivered our car into Sam Floyd's charge, boarded out Sargi and flew out to join her a few days later. It occurred to me just before I left that all my identification had gone with my wallet. While I was looking for my passport I came across an invitation to Mr and Mrs du Feu to have tea with Mr and Mrs Jimmy Carter at the White House. For no particular reason I slipped it inside my passport.

We stayed in Los Angeles with Mary Jane Hewitt and her new husband Ed. Maya was outwardly cheerful but I did not want to guess how thin the veneer was. After a couple of weeks Maya went to Washington for the first meeting of the Commission for International Women's Year. I left her at a friend's house and went on to New York to collect the car and drive it back to California.

CHAPTER ELEVEN

MONTGOMERY, ALABAMA, BY WAY OF STAMPS, ARKANSAS: 1978

I came to think of it as 'Non-incident at Bud's Diner'. And maybe the reason it went down the way it *did* go down was the haircut I got three days earlier.

I rose early, eager to be on my way. I was ready to follow the legendary trail, light out for the Territories like Huck Finn, follow the sun like Davy Crockett, get my kicks on Route 66 like Chuck Berry. I was headed West like Kentucky Shannon, but first I needed a haircut. I walked out on Dupont Circle and started to explore the neighbourhood. A few blocks away an elderly Black barber sat alone in his shop reading the newspaper. The sign said OPEN.

'Can I help you?'

'Yes, I'd like a haircut.' He nodded, carefully folded his paper and gestured me into the chair beside him. I had never had my hair cut by a Black barber but I knew that Blacks had to prove proficiency in cutting White hair before they passed the state licencing exam, although Whites were not tested cutting Black hair. Just another amusing/irritating road bump Blacks have to slow for on life's highway. Amusing because every Black I had ever known would give up his last pair of shoes before he let a White anywhere near him with a pair of barber's shears, and irritating because they were compelled to learn a useless skill since Whites never went near Black barbers anyway.

'Just trim it up and make it neat, please.' He showed no sign of

187

hearing my request, picked up his electric clippers and started shearing with the insouciance of a drunken Australian sheep shearer. I resigned myself and avoided looking in the mirror. The flyblown price tariff caught my eye. A shave was $1.50, a haircut $2.50. My last haircut in Manhattan had cost twenty-five dollars. It was the worst haircut I have ever had in my life.

Our elegant and beautiful host was making breakfast when I got back to the house. She took one look and said, 'My God! What happened to you?'

'I went for a haircut.'

'Poor baby! Who did this to you? Let me get my gun!' She grabbed me by the shirtfront and peered up into my face snarling ferociously, 'A name! Just give me a name! And tonight he sleeps with the fishes, paisano.' Eleanor was a drama teacher with a tendency to be boisterous early in the day.

'Just a local barber, across from Safeway. I didn't get the name.'

'A Black barber?' I nodded. She started laughing again. 'Honey, he got his revenge on you. Three centuries of slavery avenged in three minutes . . . or less. God! You look like a vicious and unspeakably depraved twelve-year-old. The pre-teen from Hell.' She went to the other side of the kitchen and scrutinised me again. 'On the other hand from another angle when the light falls on you in a certain way you look more like a psychotically criminal fugitive from a Georgia chain gang. Well, at least this will set Maya's mind at rest. We were talking about you last night and she was worried about you travelling alone across the Deep South for the first time . . . given that you never made the dean's list for tact or patience. But no need to worry about you now. Ain't nobody goin' to mess with a crazy-looking mu'fucker like you. White, Black or Brown, they all have enough sense to leave a mad dog alone.'

Maya started laughing as soon as she saw me. I had a bone to pick with her. 'You told me Black barbers had to learn to cut White hair to get a licence.'

'They do. How old was the barber?'

'In his sixties.'

She started to giggle. 'He probably hasn't had much practice in the last forty years.'

I drove south and west along the new and improved Route 66. The countryside was still green and the landscapes were restful to the eye. Holding to the *in latrina veritas* theory of anthropology I studied rest-room graffiti along the way. It seemed that southern wall writers had a single unifying theme: 'Niggers suck shit!' Spelling varied. I searched in vain for humour or prurience on the tiled walls. It made me wonder about the 'good ole boys'. Had racial bigotry supplanted procreation as their biological imperative? And if so how were the 'good ole girls' getting along? What was Burt Reynolds *really* doing in those truck-stop johns? Was there a dramatic decline in the birth rate of 'good ole babies' these days?

It was late afternoon when I crossed the Mississippi into Arkansas. By the time I turned south off Interstate 40 towards Pine Bluff it was a moonless night with sharp flurries of rain. The last two hours' driving left me tense and gritty-eyed. I was glad to pull into a motel's parking lot on the edge of Pine Bluff.

The motel clerk hardly glanced at me. He was watching an evangelist on a compact TV.

'I'd like a room for the night.'

'That's what we're here for.' His attention was still on the TV and the Lord's messenger.

'Where can I get a drink around here?'

'Try Texas.'

'I asked for a fucking drink, not a smart answer.'

In a trice his attention switched from the hereafter to the there and then. He looked at my haircut. I stared him down with my gritty bloodshot-eyed stare.

'I intended no offence, sir. It's Arkansas State law. No liquor is sold on the Lord's Day.'

'You mean Sunday?'

'That's the Lord's Day.'

'Not if you're Jewish.'

'Yessir. That's very true. May I show you a room?'

'Just give me the register to sign and the key. How much is it?'

'Eight dollars, sir, single occupancy.'

My purpose in Pine Bluff was to visit Maya's great-uncle Lindsay and attempt to unravel some family business in Stamps, Arkansas. She had told me that her great-uncle was 'a very *southern* gentleman'. After more than fifty years of marriage he and his wife still addressed each other in public as Mr and Mrs Johnson. In short, he was a man who stood on ceremony. With that in mind I unpacked my most formal suit, a three-piece dark blue chalk stripe, and hung it for the creases to fall out overnight.

It still needed pressing the next morning. The same clerk was on duty and eagerly arranged to have it pressed for me within half an hour. He also directed me to a car wash. He was just glad I was leaving.

I pulled into the Johnson driveway at one minute to ten, on time, nattily suited and driving a squeaky clean car. Maya would have been proud of me.

Uncle Lindsay was a trimly built man of a little less than average height, elegant in a well-cut tweed country suit. His greeting was pleasant but uneffusive. It was as if we had been meeting each other regularly for years. He led the way to a comfortable study and waved me to a seat at the desk, set a thin sheaf of typewritten sheets in front of me. 'You may want to look these over while I say goodbye to Mrs Johnson. She's not feeling very well this morning so I won't introduce you.'

I looked over the year's accounts of the three small properties in Stamps and read two attorneys' letters. Everything was orderly and clear. I looked around the study, an old, tinted photograph caught my eye. It was a young Black woman with tightly braided hair gazing squarely into the camera. It was hung in the place of honour.

'Is that Maya's grandmother?' I asked when Uncle Lindsay returned.

'No, that's my mother. Kentucky Shannon.'

Maya had told me the story of her great-grandmother who had walked out of slavery as a teenager and started a family in Arkansas. I nodded. 'Did she come from Kentucky?'

'I don't know. I don't remember that any of us talked about the past. I suppose we should have cared more about our roots . . . perhaps . . . but in those days we just wanted to get on with the future. Well, I'm ready. Will you drive?'

We were soon out of the city limits and headed south-west on a two-lane highway that raised on a low embankment above the surrounding marshy fields. I drove at a steady fifty-five miles an hour. 'Is this a six-cylinder engine?' asked Uncle Lindsay.

'No, it's a small V-8.'

'Should be fast. This is an excellent road for the next twenty miles.'

'I don't want a speeding ticket.'

'There's nowhere the police can get on or off this road. If you don't see them behind you or in front they aren't there. When I'm in a fast car on a good road I like to *travel*.'

'Okay.'

190

He watched the speedometer needle get past eighty-five and then settled back with a contented sigh. We rode in silence for a quarter of an hour, his eyelids drooping, then he sat up, alert.

'The road's all bends from now on.' I slowed to fifty miles an hour. He pointed to a dirt track ahead on the right. 'There's where the old road used to run. I had my first gas station . . . just about *there*.'

'When was that?'

'1932. It was just one hand-cranked pump and a roadside stand really. But I was very proud of it.'

'In 1932! I can imagine. There can't have been many gas stations back then.'

'Or many roads or many cars. But I believed in the future.'

I concentrated on travelling as fast as I could through the bends.

'I have a minor diabetic condition. It's little more than an inconvenience but I do need to eat lightly at regular times.' I awaited further instructions. 'There's a good place for lunch coming up soon on the left. It's called Bud's Diner but it's not easy to see from the road so drive slowly or you'll run past it.'

The diner was set off from the road behind a screen of stubby pine trees. Most of the cars in the gravelled parking lot were late model compacts. 'Most of the customers work for Lafayette County. In the offices. It's a twelve-mile round trip but it's a good lunch.'

We took the only free table, which was near the kitchen door. For five minutes the only waitress passed by our table maybe twenty times without acknowledging our existence. Uncle Lindsay, the only Black customer, was unperturbed. I tried to beckon her attention. Finally I spoke loud and clear. 'Come here, miss!' She hesitated. 'Now!' The buzz of conversation faded. 'Bring my uncle a glass of cold milk . . . and some crackers on a plate. Now. Then we'll order.' No pin dropped, but if it had, I would have heard it. Uncle Lindsay remained as imperturbable as ever. The waitress's thin-lipped mouth snapped shut like a sprung mousetrap. She turned on her heel and marched back into the kitchen. After that service was prompt — unsmiling, but impeccable.

When I went to pay the bill at the cash desk I reached over and took the phone, simply saying, 'I need to make a phone call.' The man behind the desk said nothing and concentrated on some paperwork. I got through to Stamps and gave my name. 'Just tell Attorney Lofton that we'll be there in half an hour. He knows what it's about.' Uncle Lindsay strolled up as I put the phone back. As we left there was a loud stage whisper in the background, '. . . FBI . . . he's FBI.'

191

He was smiling as we walked to the car. 'You heard what they said?'

'Yes, must be my Yankee-style suit.'

'Or maybe their guilty consciences.' He stopped and started to laugh. 'Of course, it may be your haircut.' He set his snap-brimmed tweed hat at a jaunty angle on his shining bald pate, then patted me on the shoulder sympathetically. 'Never mind, at least you still *have* hair. Let's go and see what this lawyer has to say for himself.'

He started to grin again as we drove. 'I feel we know each other better now, Paul, so I trust you'll pardon an older man's impertinence, but may I lend you a cap to wear on the rest of your journey to California?' We both started laughing. 'Do you recall what the Duke of Wellington said when he was inspecting some newly recruited soldiers?' he asked.

I knew that one. 'The scum of the earth enlisted for drink.'

'The Iron Duke did say that, didn't he? But I was thinking of another occasion when he said, "I know not what they will do to the enemy but by Gad, sir, they terrify me".'

'What brought that to mind?' I teased.

'My first sight of your haircut this morning.'

The attorney was a hokey, drawling good old boy who wore cowboy boots and a shoestring tie. He called me 'Paaawl' every time he spoke to me, and Uncle Lindsay he called Dr Lindsaaay Jaaahnson. He expressed himself succinctly, made sense to Uncle Lindsay and myself and we were out of the office in less than half an hour.

'Let's go and look at the properties. What would you like to see first?'

'The store. Maya's grandmother's store.'

We were soon in the old Black section of Stamps. I drove slowly down a narrow dirt road bordered by clapboard houses. Some were well kept and others patched with tar-paper and cardboard and looked as if they would not survive the next strong wind. All of them were small, four hundred to six hundred square feet living space, I guessed. The store was a two-storey wood frame building on the corner where the two main dirt roads intersected. Old sheet-metal soft drink advertising signs were nailed to the upper part of the front wall. It was overdue a coat of paint like the rest of the town but looked solid enough. The door was chained and padlocked. I parked among the weeds in the gravelled front yard. Uncle Lindsay asked if I wanted to go inside. I did, because Maya had asked me to bring away any letters or photos or mementoes of past times. 'You won't find much,' said Uncle Lindsay as he unpadlocked the door. 'Willie's sister-in-law cleared it out after Lizzie was killed. It needed to be cleared out.'

I found a couple of ledgers in the back of a counter drawer. Slipped inside them were some newspaper clippings from the Twenties and Thirties about oil and natural gas discoveries in Arkansas and East Texas. Some clippings were reports of church events. As to the rest, the store was dusty and empty. I asked if it would be alright to take the old advertising signs. There was precious little else to take back to California.

'I'll see if I can find someone with a ladder and a crowbar.'

'Don't worry,' I said. 'I'll just move the car over and stand on the roof. I can pry them off with a lug wrench.' He seemed pleased with my improvisation. Half-a-dozen bystanders gathered to watch me. When I had the signs stowed in the car trunk Uncle Lindsay introduced me to the tenants of the houses that Maya's family owned.

'Anything else you'd like to see while we're here?'

'Maya asked me to look at her grandmother's church. I mean the one her grandmother used to go to. Maya was thinking of making some addition or improvement for the church as a memorial to Mrs Ann Henderson.' Uncle Lindsay nodded. He was not cheering.

The small church was clean and tidy but the foundation posts and entrance steps were rotting out. 'This was her church?'

'At one time or another. She changed according to how she was getting along with the ministers. Anyway, it's the only church that's in use now. They all share it, I believe. So in a way it *is* Big Sister's church one way or another.'

'What do you think about this? A new reinforced concrete foundation, some new steps and then a brick apron about two feet high all around the exterior base?'

'I suggest you give it some serious thought before you make a decision.'

Later, as we drove back to Pine Bluff, we reviewed the day.

'Have you checked the ownership of the land the church is on?'

'No. I presumed the church owns it.'

'Probably not. You should check. No point in spending two or three thousand dollars as a gift to some White landlord. Big Sister wouldn't have done that. She was very close with money.' He chuckled. 'We used to say she was so tight she squeaked when she walked. It's your wife's money, but I think it would be better spent endowing a scholarship to help some young person get an education and a chance in life. That's what I'm doing with my money. If you give someone money they spend it. If you give them an education they can earn their own money . . . I learnt that many years ago. I was . . . fifteen, sixteen. I left home and went to live with a Jewish couple. I was the houseboy. Servant. I worked hard and made myself agreeable and they treated me like a son. I know that's not a popular thing for Black people to say today but *I* thought I was treated like a son. They encouraged me to study, they helped pay my way through school at Pine Bluff Agricultural and Mechanical College as it was then. That changed my life. I could almost say that education is my religion. Years ago I was the first Black superintendent of Negro schools in Lafayette County. The pay wasn't very good and I didn't need the job, my businesses kept me occupied. But you know why I took that job? I wanted to make sure it was done right! I wanted no one to have the excuse to take the job away from Blacks again. You see there was a belief that Blacks couldn't be trusted around money. From the start every request I made for pencils or . . . books . . . everything, the White folks were looking over my shoulder. So for the first six months I just took my county pay cheques and folded them in my wallet. I had enough income from the auto business for my needs. One day I got a call to see the county treasurer. He was in a tizzy because the books wouldn't balance. He wanted to know what had happened to my salary cheques. He said the whole thing was a mystery. I pulled out my wallet and put the uncashed cheques on his desk. "How have you been living, Mr Johnson?" he said. I told him, "The same way I was living before I took the job. But if it will make *your* job easier I'll go down to the bank right now and cash them . . . there is enough money in the account, I hope?" They left me alone after that.'

There was something on my mind. 'You know Maya is sure that her grandmother owned more property than just the store and the three houses . . .'

'I think it's very probable that she did, but you read the letters from the attorney. He's had Lafayette and adjacent counties' tax rolls searched. There's nothing showing there now.'

'What do you think happened?'

'We'll probably never know. How long ago was it that Big Sister talked to your wife about this?'

'About thirty-five years ago. From what I understand.'

'Time doesn't stand still. It could be the deeds were never recorded. Big Sister was very careful to keep . . . er, what they call a "low

194

profile" nowadays. It could have been dangerous for a Black person to be known to record a lot of property deeds. The Whites didn't like that. She could have hidden them under different names . . . straw men. And then again they could have been sold over the years or swindled away. You'd have to be a pretty good detective to find out what really happened. I don't think we'll ever know.'

When we got back to Pine Bluff he told me to park in the University Service Station right across from the main entrance to the campus. He gave instructions to the attendant to clean the car inside and out, fill the tank and check the tyres and hood. 'Leave it in my driveway and drop the keys in my mailslot. We'll need it in about half an hour.' The attendant went to work with a will although the service station was buzzing with activity. The Exxon station thirty yards away on the opposite corner was deserted. I mentioned the difference to Uncle Lindsay. He nodded. 'Business looks slow. It used to do very well when I owned it. I sold it to Exxon and built this one, and our house behind it.'

'Unusual. When you sell a business there's usually a clause in the sale contract prohibiting the seller from opening up a competing business within so many years and so many miles radius.'

He smiled. 'I believe that's not uncommon. But that's not the way my contract read. I suppose they didn't bother. They thought I was a nice old coloured gentleman ready to sit in my rocking chair and let the world go by.'

Cars kept coming right out of the campus and right up to his pumps. 'Tell me, Uncle Lindsay, do you have to prove you buy your gas here to graduate from Pine Bluff U?'

He chuckled. 'Of course not, Paul. I endow the university with what little money I can afford and the faculty and students find my gas station convenient. It works out very well for everyone.'

'Except Exxon.'

'They should have kept on their toes, shouldn't they?'

I was introduced to Mrs Johnson who was rheumy and congested with a heavy cold. I invited them both to dinner but she sweetly declined and insisted that Mr Johnson and I go on without her. He recommended the Plantation Embers for dinner.

'Interesting name,' I said. Maya would have starved rather than eat in a place with a name like that.

The pragmatic Dr Johnson smiled urbanely and said, 'What's in a name? It's a fine restaurant.'

195

After dinner he presented me with a navy blue waterproof cap, without comment. We exchanged warm goodbyes and I drove north to Little Rock to look for a convenient motel so that I could get on the road early next day. As I saw the city lights ahead of me I felt too tired to bother with a big unknown metropolis so I swung west and checked into a motel a few miles along on Interstate 40.

'Where's the best place for a drink around here?'

'There's a place about ten miles west just over the county line. It's pretty lively.'

'Over the county line?'

'Yessir. Conway County is dry.'

A piece of trivia surfaced in my mind. 'I'm in Conway County? Did the singer Conway Twitty take his name from this county?'

'Sure did. You like country music?'

'Sure do.' When in Rome . . . hell, I wanted a drink and I had just had a seminar in pragmatism from Dr Johnson.

The motel clerk produced a thick short glass tumbler and filled it with clear liquid. 'Not planning on driving anymore this evening?'

'Nope. And so to bed.'

'This is White Lightning. Sip it. When it strikes you'll sleep well.'

I thanked him and gave him five dollars. He was right. It struck and I slept like a babe.

Next day I drove across the Texas Panhandle and into New Mexico. I stopped for the night in Albuquerque and phoned Maya in Washington. She sounded terrible. She was in Houston for a big women's rights conference and she was in a blind funk.

'I'm scared stupid. I have a terrible feeling something terrible is going to happen. Meet me in Houston, *please*. I don't want to die alone.'

I had never heard her in a panic like that. Houston was more than a day's drive south. It was too late to call our travel agent and have him book me on a flight and I did not have enough cash to buy my own ticket. I promised to call her first thing next morning and spent a quiet evening drinking beer in a Tex-Mex bar.

To my surprise she sounded full of beans next morning. After we had talked she had spent the evening with Coretta King. They had a fine time, '. . . and, honey, Coretta does not move anywhere without help, you follow me? I'll stay right beside her and I'll be fine. You go on back to California, I'll see you in a few days.'

I drove on west with a light heart. I was most of the way across

196

Arizona, pedal to the metal and making good time when the flashing red light and siren came up behind me out of nowhere.

'Spread your hands on the hood of the car, legs apart, lean forward.' The state trooper pat-searched me. 'You were doing ninety-five miles an hour. That's reckless driving in this state. You go to jail.'

Hey ho, there you go. I had about fifty dollars in my pocket. Not enough.

'Let's see your driver's licence.'

'I don't have a licence. I did but it was stolen just before I left New York. I have a passport in the briefcase there on the passenger seat.'

He unclipped the flap on his pistol holster. I realised that with my three-day stubble, sweaty tee-shirt and travel-stained jeans I was not making a very good impression. I could at least have worn Uncle Lindsay's cap.

'Reach in and get it, slow and steady please.' I had no problem with that. 'Now open it and bring out your passport between the thumb and finger of your right hand.'

He looked at my photograph and squinted at me doubtfully. 'It says here you're a journalist.' I knew that. He started to leaf through the back of the passport and found the White House invitation. He stared at it and turned it over. Then he compared the spellings of my name for a while. 'You must be a very important person, Mr du Feu.'

'On the contrary. My wife is an important person.'

'Oh. What does she do?'

'She writes books. Under her own name.'

'Would I have heard of her? I read a lot.'

'Her name is Maya Angelou.'

His eyes popped wide open and he stepped back and stood legs astride like a movie gunfighter. For an alarming moment I had the fantasy that he was going to draw his pistol and gun me down like a dog. 'Maya Angelou is your wife?'

'Yes.'

'Well . . . well . . . well.' He grinned and handed me my passport.

'*I Know Why The Caged Bird Sings.* You know, I was raised in Arkansas. Just outside of Stuttgart.'

'Wild rice capital of the world. I was in Stamps a couple of days ago. Let me show you something in the trunk.' I showed him the tin signs from Mrs Henderson's general store. He patted them reverently. 'This is history, buddy. You know when my daughter read that book she said, "Was it really like that for Black people in those days, daddy?"

197

You know what I told her. "It was worse." ' He started writing. 'I'm still going to give you a ticket, Mr du Feu.' I nodded.

'We live in a nation governed by laws,' I agreed.

'Sixty-five miles an hour sound okay? You pay by the mile. There's a tariff on the ticket. Mail your cheque when you get back home.'

My most pressing concern when I got back to Los Angeles was to find us a house and get settled while we knitted up the unravelled skeins of our lives. We wanted somewhere out of the very worst of the smog belt and Maya wanted a swimming pool, a basic amenity in Southern California. I found a house in the Pacific Palisades. It was a three-bedroom, ranch-style house with a forty-foot swimming pool and an unusual leasing arrangement. The owner, a middle-aged divorcee named Mrs Green, would live in the garage while we lived in the house and she would have sole use of the pool from dawn till eight a.m. We took a six-month lease at nine hundred dollars a month, paid a hefty damage deposit and moved in. Maya was not altogether at ease around Mrs Green. The warning signal was that the landlady, obviously very nervous around a six-foot-tall Black woman, went out of her way to explain that she was not racially prejudiced and could *not* be prejudiced because she was Jewish herself. A non sequitur.

The house had a hillside yard covered in scrub and Mrs Green had stored the contents of the house in plastic bags in the cover of the hillside vegetation. All day long she moved around the hillside like a macquillarde checking that we had not plundered her *lates* and *penates* under the cover of darkness. Mrs Green was a sad case. Her story was that her husband had been part of the research team who had invented the laser but he had divorced her and left her nothing but the house. I felt sorry for her. The house was entered by a secured gate between the house and garage. Visitors rang an outside bell and waited to be admitted to the internal courtyard. We had a steady stream of nocturnal visitors, some of them arriving as late as ten o'clock and most of them Black. Mrs Green was a shadowy figure peeking at them from the garage. I was sorry for her but Maya was getting impatient.

Most of the working days I was out looking for a house to buy and fix up so that we could turn a quick buck on a resale. Cash flow was down to a trickle and finding a fixer-upper for little or no money down in the Palisades was testing my skills at creative financing.

Maya was putting together a volume of poetry from the ruins of *And*

198

Still I Rise and like most creative people she spent a good part of the working day staring out the window. The sight of Mrs Green lurking in the bushes irritated the hell out of her. One morning I was sitting in a realtor's office trying to nail down a deal when a secretary said my wife was on the phone. Maya was succinct. 'Get this crazy broad out of my face. Today! Just fucking do it! She started spying on me while I'm trying to write.'

'Gotcha.'

I put my negotiations on hold and excused myself pleading urgent family business. I walked out into the bright sunshine and kicked a near-bald tyre on the Plymouth. I had not the faintest idea what I was going to do about Mrs Green. Physical intimidation, a useful bargaining chip, was out of the question. The du Feus and the Kellys did not make war on women. I got in behind the wheel and realised that I did not even know where I was going to drive. I let my mind float and let the automatic pilot take over. I dropped down out of the Palisades hills to the Pacific coast highway and headed south to Santa Monica, cut off east and climbed up to Santa Monica Boulevard. I was in Raymond Chandler country.

Santa Monica was 'in transition' as realtors say. In other words it was just starting to be modern and expensive. But at road's end it was still sun-bright and dusty with absurd tall palm trees and funky little pawnshops and dry cleaners and shadowy little bars and the ocean at the end of it all. Philip Marlowe would have got a drink. I parked by a bar and blinked into darkness. The barman had a couple of scars he wore like battle ribbons. Along the bar a brunette, who must have been a beautiful cheerleader before her skin dried out, was rattling ice in the bottom of her glass. I called for a boilermaker and bought the company a drink. There were only three of us. I explained enough of my problems to the bartender.

'You need a lawyer,' said the ex-cheerleader.

That was the truth. Bob Treuhaft was five hundred miles away north. Gerry Purcell was three thousand miles and two time zones away. It was all becoming clear. 'Give me the yellow pages and the phone.'

I found an attorney within two blocks. He had an Irish surname and an answer service. An hour later I sat in his office.

'How did you come to call me?' asked the attorney.

'You're in a low-rent building. You're Irish. That means you're cheap and I trust you'll fight.'

'I'm a criminal lawyer. You do armed robbery?'

199

'You want me to? I'll start with you. Turn out your pockets.'

'Funny guy.'

'Here's the substance of the matter. By the terms of our lease we are entitled to the full and free enjoyment of the premises known as blah blah. That includes the garage and pool. However, we have verbally agreed to allow the landlady to occupy the garage and use the pool. *Verbal* is the key word. Nothing in the lease. No such thing as a verbal contract in real estate. Write an eviction notice and I will serve it today. How much money do you need?'

'Seventy-five dollars.'

'Here's a bill. Get it done.'

He took the hundred dollar bill and went to the typewriter. It turned out beautifully and by week's end we were out with all our money back and into a rather grand town house. Maya went to work as a producer for Twentieth Century Fox.

CHAPTER TWELVE

MONTCLAIR PINES, OAKLAND, CALIFORNIA.
A CIRCLE CLOSES: 1980

Circles continued to complete themselves. Maya and I went back to Arkansas, together for the first time there. We flew into Little Rock and there was a small reception committee to meet her at the airport. Charles Bussey, the city's Black vice-mayor, headed it up. He was visible and extrovert in the manner of all politicians but beside him was a woman, small, rather frail and quiet. When I was introduced to her I was tongue-tied and awe-struck. Her name was Daisy Bates and I had last seen her on newsreels twenty years earlier leading nine children into a Little Rock high school protected by a thousand paratroopers and ten thousand Federal National Guards as she ran a gauntlet of screaming, snarling White men and women who hurled stones and hatred. It was their third attempt to enter the school. On 4 September 1957 they had been turned away by National Guardsmen and attacked by the White mob. On 23 September they had gone into the school but retreated again when a thousand-strong mob threatened to break into the school and lynch them. Daisy Bates demanded an assurance from President Eisenhower that the children would be protected and two days later he sent in the army. She described that day. 'The streets were blocked off. The soldiers closed ranks. Neighbours came out and looked. The street was full, up and down. Oh! It was beautiful. And the attitude of the children at that moment: the respect they had. I could hear them saying, "For the first time in my life I truly feel like

an American." I could see it in their faces: somebody cares for me —
America cares!'

And twenty years later I was shaking hands with and bowing my
head to Daisy Bates. A real hero . . . not Gary Cooper or John
Wayne acting out cowboy fiction on a Hollywood back lot, but a small,
sweet-voiced lady who had walked alone in defiance of a murderous
mob. I did not trust myself to say anything coherent so I went off to
find our baggage. I hurried along the airport corridor and a tall Black
man loped along beside me. 'I'm Smiley,' he said and held out a hand
the size of a dinner plate.

'Why don't you stay with the party? We've only got two small bags
and I'll handle them easily.'

'Oh no, Paul. I go where you go.'

'Ah.' I understood. Smiley was my bodyguard.

We all drove in a convoy of cars to Hot Springs, a small resort spa where
next day Maya was going to be honoured at a luncheon by the Poets'
Round Table of Arkansas. The first Black to be so honoured.

It was dark and raining when we checked into the hotel where the
lunch would be held next day. Smiley and his wife checked into the
room across the passageway. It was a low-ceilinged room, barely eight
feet high. Maya looked up in gloomy distaste. 'Everything presses
down on me in Arkansas. I feel claustrophobic.' She stared out the
window at the rain that was sheeting down in a vertical torrent. 'Even
the damn rain is wetter in Arkansas.'

Next morning was sweet after the rain. We took a leisurely breakfast
with Smiley and his wife and around eleven Uncle Lindsay arrived
from Pine Bluff. He greeted Maya pleasantly and excused himself. 'I
have business to discuss with Paul.'

We found a quiet corner to sit and talk and he looked me over.
'I'm happy to see your hair grew back.' We started chuckling. He
got some papers out of his briefcase and went through the accounts
of the little rental houses in Stamps. There was something over a
thousand dollars in hand. 'Did you think any more about repairing
the church?'

'Not really. That's on hold.'

'Then I'll make out a cheque for the cash in hand. You see there that
I have retained a small fund for repairs and contingencies. I trust that is
agreeable to you.'

'Absolutely.' Business was done in a few minutes and we spent a pleasant half-hour discussing the success of Pine Bluff University football team. They had been having a good year and Uncle Lindsay had travelled to every game.

A middle-aged White woman with a name tag pinned to her blouse deferentially beckoned me away. 'I've just learned that Ms Angelou's uncle, Dr Johnson, is here.'

'I was talking with him.'

'We would be honoured if Reverend Johnson would give the invocation at luncheon.'

'Why don't you ask him? But he's not a reverend. He's a Dean Emeritus. However, I think all the Johnsons can preach a bit. Come and ask him.'

Uncle Lindsay accepted her invitation without being in the least overwhelmed. He went off alone to gather his thoughts.

Lunch was served in a medium-sized room with a head table set up at one end and three lines of trestle tables, pushed together refectory-fashion, leading off from it at right angles. I took a place in the middle of the room as diners started to trickle in. Half-a-dozen Whites had taken places at the middle bank of tables. There were no Blacks to be seen. Then there was a stirring at the far end of the room and a dozen large, smiling Blacks walked up the middle of the room in a phalanx. They were a mix of age and gender but they all had big smiles and burly physiques. They simply asked the Whites to excuse them and occupied the centre aisle. They explained that their cousin was the guest of honour. I shook my head when they asked me to move and stayed put. 'I'm a cousin too.'

An old man smiled and then grinned and held out his hand. 'Well, you must be Paul du Feu?'

Introductions all around. The noise was cheerful and the room had come alive.

Uncle Lindsay rose to give the invocation. He looked over the room like a practised orator. 'As I look over the company assembled here I'm reminded of some lines written by a Black poet, Langston Hughes, *I Too, Sing America . . .*'

> *I am the darker brother*
> *They send me to eat in the kitchen*
> *When company comes,*
> *But I laugh,*

And eat well,
And grow strong.

Tomorrow,
I'll be at the table
When company comes.
Nobody'll dare
Say to me,
'Eat in the kitchen,'
Then.

Besides
They'll see how beautiful I am
And be ashamed —

I, too, am America.

The Black cooks and kitchen hands in their aprons were crowded in the kitchen doorway listening with fierce attention. When Uncle Lindsay finished the poem he sat down without further comment.

My table was busy eating and drinking and talking. The Johnson clan had turned the occasion into a family reunion. Old men were reminiscing about the Twenties when they had ridden the rails to go to the Negro Colleges. I was struck by the fact that apparently a great many of Maya's relatives had gone to college, I was also struck by the fact that she had a great many relatives. I had always had the impression that her family was small. It was an impression she propagated.

'How are things in New Orleans then, Paul?' asked a man at my left.

'I don't know, that's one town I've never been to.'

'But du Feu is a Creole name, isn't it?'

'It's a French name.'

'Yes, Creole. I've always enjoyed New Orleans.' He took a healthy swig of his bourbon and water. 'I see you're drinking white wine. How is it?'

'Not bad.' I pushed my glass towards him. 'Try it.'

He took a sip. 'H'm. Alright I suppose . . . if you ice it down well so you can't taste it.'

As the luncheon broke up and we all drifted out to the car park a couple of the cousins asked me to remember them to the folks in New Orleans when I got back there.

'What was that all about?' said Maya as we watched them drive off.

'Your Arkansas family has decided I'm Creole.' She started to giggle. 'I tried to explain that I had never even been in the state of Louisiana but they wouldn't listen.'

That evening we went back to Little Rock and took a couple of suites at the Red Carpet Inn for a private party. The hotel was a franchise operation owned by Mr and Mrs Bates. He had been publisher of the town's Black newspaper during the civil rights protests, not exactly a cushy berth. His wife Daisy had suffered a mild stroke that left her speech slightly slurred, but they were a ceaselessly amused and amusing couple. I mostly stood back and watched them and tried to imagine the patience and courage that had enabled them to endure so much for so long. The hotel was clean but starting to look run down. Mr Bates explained that although the franchise had a central reservation system, would-be guests were constantly diverted to nearby White-owned hotels. He tested constantly by having callers ask for reservations. They were usually told that his hotel was full. They were still enduring. In what should have been a pleasant retirement they were struggling . . . once again.

It was a lively crowd with healthy appetites and I called down to the kitchen and ordered up some more trays of cold cuts. They were short-staffed and busy with a Saturday night disco session so I arranged to go down and collect the food myself. On my way to the kitchen I had to pass through the dance crowd. I was the only White in the room. As I smiled and threaded my way through the dancers young men glanced at me and dropped their eyes. I was not used to Black men doing that. They certainly did not do that in Oakland. I think that if I had been Black like them I would have found some way to catch the bus out of Arkansas. I agreed with Maya. Arkansas could make you feel claustrophobic.

Diahann Carroll in chorister's robes was looking small and demure on the choir stand in Old Ship church. The pianist played a few bars of introduction and Diahann started to sing. 'Nobody knows the trouble I've seen, nobody knows my sorrow . . .' Her voice was true and clear and thin. Her diction sounded English to my English ears. I shut my eyes and checked. Yes, I could have been in Westminster Abbey.

Beside me, Maya grunted, slouched in the pew and muttered, 'No, no, no, it's all wrong.'

IN GOOD COMPANY

I had a quick unpleasant memory of the first time we listened to the expensively produced tapes of the score of *And Still I Rise* in New York a year earlier. I left the church and smoked a cigarette in the chill Alabama morning. It was the third day's filming of *Sister Sister* in Montgomery and production was already behind schedule and thousands of dollars over budget. Diahann Carroll was the star, John Berry was director, and Maya was writer and co-producer. Star and director had lost most of the first day's shooting in sulky tantrums over Ms Carroll's hair-do. Her personal hairdresser, who travelled as part of her entourage, had primped and brushed while the crew stomped their feet to keep warm, drank coffee, ate doughnuts and watched the autumnal light change and fade. The first day's shooting was done on the second day and now the second day's schedule was going down the tubes on the third day. None of my business, but I felt like a jinx. I went back to the Holiday Inn and mooched about the room for a while until the business day started in California, then called our travel agent and asked him to arrange for me to go back to Los Angeles the next day. I had come out to Montgomery for a sort of vacation and to share the excitement of Maya's debut as a producer.

When I joined her a couple of days before filming started the hotel car park was already half full of eighteen-wheeler rigs and more kept arriving from California with all the material for location shooting. It was a magic and exciting time, watching the manuscript she had written on yellow legal pads at the dining-room table in our apartment bloom into a logistical wonder. A blueprint becoming tower cranes and scaffolding, a battle plan becoming an army on the move. Then filming started and the magic vanished in arguments about coiffure disturbed by the autumn breeze. I knew that was the nature of film-making but it was depressing because Maya and I would be quarrelsome, wretched and sour together while things went wrong. Nothing I could think to do about that except leave. And I *did* feel like a jinx. Everything had been going wrong since we went to New York.

Maya came back to the hotel early afternoon in a surly mood. We scarcely spoke and she poured herself a big drink and doodled over a crossword puzzle while I watched a TV talk show. After a while she brought me a drink and sat down to talk. 'It's all wrong. Diahann's supposed to be a passionate, repressed, forty-year-old unmarried woman in love with a Black Baptist minister who's caught in a loveless marriage. He's there, right next to her in the church, and his wife is sitting up in the pew in front of them . . . and she's singing a *blues* to him. She's

206

pouring out her love and anguish; it's a sexual thing. He has force and charisma, he's a politician running for state office and he's going to win. He's going to win, she's going to help him and when he wins he's never going to leave his wife. The church scene is the opening scene. It's full of *stuff* and it's sounding and looking like . . .'

'Westminster Abbey choir.'

'Something like that. But it's going to change. Do me a favour and find Bobby Jones. Get a number where he can be reached the rest of the day.'

'Anything else if he asks?'

'Ask him to be ready to come to Montgomery with some of his choir, four or five, and sing his buns off and save this fucking film.' She grinned for the first time that day. 'Express it in terms suitable to his religious calling. I'm off to talk budget and schedule.'

I grinned for the first time that day. 'It'll be lovely to see Reverend Bobby again.'

Maya had first heard Bobby Jones and his choir, New Life, while she was lecturing in Memphis earlier that year. When her Aunt Leah (Vivian Baxter's sister) had been ordained a Pentecostal minister in a late-life career change, she asked Maya to do a benefit concert to raise funds so she could establish a church. Maya had the idea of bringing Bobby Jones and twenty or so of his choir to Los Angeles to head the bill. It was not one of her very best ideas and she soon handed over the petty details of implementing the concept to me.

I got hold of Tony (the footloose carpenter who had driven our car to New York in another time) and the two of us tracked all over south Los Angeles distributing posters and flyers, arranging adverts on Black radio channels, setting up ticket outlets at record stores and canvassing Black churches for support. Aunt Leah arranged to borrow a church for the venue in a poor Black neighbourhood which had a well-deserved reputation for being dangerous. The crime of choice that year was holding up car drivers at gunpoint when they stopped at red lights on Imperial Way. It was midsummer and Tony and I dressed for our work in close-fitting jeans and tee-shirts that revealed on cursory inspection that we were unarmed. That was important because everywhere we went the local response to us was initially stereotypical. Two fairly muscular White men in the Black ghetto must be cops looking for someone. However, after a few days making the rounds of wig shops, liquor stores, churches, bars and fried fish shops, we were affectionately recognised as a couple of eccentrics on an incomprehensible mission from God.

When Bobby and company arrived we hired half-a-dozen cars and engaged students from the UCLA Black students union as drivers. They got lost all over Los Angeles on a regular basis. Funds were running out and we had to lodge the singers three-to-a-room in downtown hotels. Through it all Bobby and New Life remained cheerful and patient.

It was a terrific show, with guest appearances by Roscoe Lee Browne, Raymond St Jaque, Abbey Lincoln and Maya of course. We took about two thousand dollars at the box office and handed it over to Aunt Leah for her church. Maya was about six thousand dollars out on production costs. But that sort of thing forms a bond and I was eager to see Bobby again, especially since Twentieth Century Fox would be footing the bill this time.

After calling around for half an hour I tracked him down at a radio station and outlined the situation. What was needed was an élite commando squad of foot-stomping Baptist heaven-raisers to perk up the staid African Methodist Espiscopalian congregation of Old Ship church. I explained Maya would deal with money and terms later but he dismissed the matter as a bagatelle.

He started singing over the phone: 'Lean on me, when you're not strong . . . you may have a problem, I might understand . . .' Dammit, the man could sing! He did Bill Withers as well as Bill Withers. When Maya talked with him an hour later he had already gathered up his team and they were packing in preparation for a start at first light next day. They should make Montgomery by late afternoon. I cancelled my flight reservation.

With the advantage of hindsight it was easy enough to understand why things were going wrong. Of course, as usually happens, everything started out wonderfully. Irv Wilson, who was an independent producer, and Peter Andrews, who worked for NBC, suggested to Maya that she write a made-for-TV movie loosely based on Chekhov's *Three Sisters*. Irv and Peter were another odd couple. Irv was a funny man in the Mel Brooks mould who lived in a perpetual state of high anxiety as he plunged through a maelstrom of unravelling relationships, financial disaster and collapsing deals. Peter was a calm, youngish Black man who was pleasantly taciturn and always seemed to be thinking a year ahead. His home life was tranquil and obviously very satisfying. His favourite way to spend the evening after a busy Hollywood day was at home with his unflashily beautiful wife and happy, well-behaved children.

Their suggestion hit a chord in Maya's imagination. The characters walked into the dining-room and sat down and talked as she filled the yellow pads. I am not saying that the writing was easy, but some ideas work better than others and this one worked very well. She soon had a draft of the screenplay. Diahann Carroll had coincidentally just finished playing Vivian Baxter in a TV movie of *I Know Why The Caged Bird Sings* and liked the part of the unmarried schoolteacher sister in Maya's script. She came and visited for a few afternoons at our rather swanky town house apartment in the Pacific Palisades. Her Rolls Royce outside our front door added a nice touch of glamour to the neighbourhood.

An expatriot film director named John Berry had directed her in a movie two or three years earlier and he agreed to come over from France and direct her again. Rosalind Cash was signed up to play Diahann's thirty-year-old sister, and a rising newcomer, Irene Cara, was cast as the twenty-year-old. Paul Winfield and Dick Anthony Williams were cast as the male leads. It was a very strong cast. Long on experience and long on talent.

There was not much work in television drama for Blacks at that time. The Blaxploitation films of the early Seventies had come and gone. *Sounder* and *The Autobiography of Miss Jane Pitman* had made Cicely Tyson a generally recognised star, and *Roots* had featured dozens of Black film actors, including Maya, but just then there was a lull. And for Black actors a lull is a drought. I doubted if a similar movie about White characters could have attracted such depth of talent on a modest budget of three-quarters of a million. Maya was going to co-produce. At last her wooden horse was inside the walls of Hollywood.

John Berry and his demure young French wife arrived and settled into a motel on the west side. For the next two months they would come over to the apartment, John working with Maya on the shooting version of the script. Occasionally I would overhear the ponderous discussions. It seemed that every syllable of dialogue had to be picked over. A line like 'I'll see you later' was good for an afternoon's conference. Should it be 'I'll see you later' or 'See you later' or 'See you'? Or again, on the other hand, should it be in the script in the first place? But perhaps it should be preceded by another phrase . . . or *succeeded* by another line.

I had no way of knowing if screenplays were always edited like that but the time-consuming process reminded me of the depressing days in New York when the musical arrangers pecked Maya's melodies to death in our hotel room.

No bonds were formed between John Berry and me. He was full of 'gravitas' — an admirable quality, no doubt, but it bored me to death. Irv Wilson, on the other hand, never bored me for a minute. Sometimes he would come by and spirit me away in his unreliable, unkempt Mercedes for sundowner drinks in one of the beach-front bars.

One afternoon, while we were enjoying Margharitas and a bucketfull of clams and waiting for the sudden magic of the sun vanishing below the ocean rim, Irv let fall that *Sister Sister* had a good chance of being the first night-time soap with a Black cast.

'What's a night-time soap?'

'*Dallas* is a night-time soap.'

'Does Maya know that's the idea?'

'It's in the back of everyone's mind.' Irv sounded vague and quickly changed the subject.

I did not raise the subject with Maya because her patience was wearing thin during the long days with John Berry and if she hadn't been brought into the plan her annoyance might spark an explosion. I supposed that a good movie would be a good pilot and it probably did not make much difference from the creative point of view. However, it would make a lot of difference from the financial point of view. Authorship of a series would be like ownership of a gold-mine. Very interesting.

When Irv returned from Montgomery, where the advance team had been scouting locations, he could not wait to show me pictures of the church they had found. Old Ship church was magnificent. A wood-framed building had been towed a mile up the hill to its present site by newly freed slaves at the beginning of reconstruction and lovingly preserved and enhanced ever since. He showed me pictures of the fine old house they had rented for the Sisters' family home. There were going to be some good production values.

'I knew you'd love the house,' said Irv. 'Maya told me how much you like fixing up old houses.'

'The only reason I fix up old houses is that we can't afford to build new ones.'

'Stick with me, kid, and we'll be building shopping centres. The minister at the church was a trip. He wheeled and dealed us into the ground before he agreed to let us use the church. I'm Jewish and I think I can do that stuff pretty well . . . but he was tougher than my rabbi. He read the script and asked questions, he specified the fee, we had to hire the congregation as extras and we had to hire the choir.'

'What does the choir sound like?'

'Terrific.'

'You heard them?'

'No, but they're Black.'

African Methodists worship differently from Baptists and that difference in style persists outside the church. Maya had set her play in a Baptist background and the mortar that held the bricks of the plot together was the interplay of caste and class distinction in a Southern Black community, so the sociological and behavioural details had to be just right.

The church choir was not right.

Bobby Jones and four choir members arrived next afternoon. I fussed over them like a mother hen, not because the hardy and self-sufficient crew needed my ministration but simply because I was delighted to see them again. Maya was up in Diahann's suite when they gathered back in our room after unpacking and settling in. I called up to Maya and put Bobby on the phone. Maya put Diahann on the phone. In a minute they were talking music and in another minute he was singing it. Five minutes later they were all off to meet Miss Carroll. I sat back, poured myself a drink and glowed with vicarious pride.

When they came back an hour later I suggested we all go down to the restaurant for dinner. They pleaded work to do and asked if I knew where they could order take-out barbecued rib dinners. I went down to the modest bar where Dick Anthony Williams was having a drink and looking like a Baptist minister. With him was Paul Winfield, who was looking like a night-club owner. There were only a couple of other solitary drinkers in the bar. I accepted the offer of a drink from Dick.

'Lovely. Hope you won't mind if I drink and run this time?'

'Out for the evening?'

'No, I'm on a barbecue run.' They both licked their lips and I took two more orders.

I took the barman's recommendation for a rib joint and asked him to call me a taxi.

'No need for a cab. My car's outside. I'll take you there.' One of the solitary drinkers had moved over beside me. I turned and looked at him. He was a thick-set, dark-skinned man about my height. In his forties, I guessed, and starting to run to fat.

'Let me see that phone,' he said to the barman in a courteous, soft voice. As he started to dial I noticed that he had an impressive ring on each impressively powerful hand. He got the number of the rib joint and started to dial it. 'Order ahead. That way you'll have time to enjoy your drink. What's your order?' He ordered for me. We introduced ourselves and I introduced him to the actors. He was pleased to meet them but not overwhelmed.

His car was a late model Lincoln Continental. He put a tape into the dashboard deck and played some soft jazz as we drove off.

'You're here with the movie?' I explained that I was visiting my wife who was producing. 'I watched them filming downtown the other day. I watched for about half an hour but I couldn't make sense of what was happening. Do you understand when you watch?'

'I know where the scene fits into the story.'

'And you watch the filming every day?'

'I'll try to see all the main actors at least once. After that I'll probably have had enough. It gets to be like watching a bricklayer build a wall. If you're interested come and keep me company one day.'

'Are you going to watch tomorrow?'

'Sure. Come and have breakfast with me at the hotel. Eight-thirty okay?'

'Eight-thirty will be just fine.'

The rib dinners were a great success. Maya told me that the meeting between Diahann and the gang had been a love fest. She was sure everything was going to go fine from now on. 'It was just opening-night nerves,' she said. I could understand that. Film acting was a high-wire act if ever there was one. Dick Anthony Williams had arrived the day before acting his first scene. He had to step into the pulpit the next day and be a young, sexy, ambitious Baptist minister right off. No accumulation of bits and pieces of a part like a stage actor accrues over weeks of rehearsal. On an ambitious but tightly budgeted film like *Sister Sister* the pressure must be tremendous. I suppose everyone else already knew that but it struck me for the first time when I watched Diahann blow away a few thousand dollars on the first day. Another actor would be getting short-changed somewhere later in the film as corners were cut to make up for those first-day losses. I hoped Maya had got things set on course. I dared not be optimistic. Murphy's law was my credo in those days.

212

Next morning Henry came to breakfast wearing a beautifully tailored blazer, dark slacks and expensive-looking brogues. Whatever he did for a living appeared to pay well. He asked me what the scene he had watched downtown was about. It came early in the story.

The minister has embezzled church funds to keep his political campaign going. An audit has been called for and he asks Diahann, his lover, to lend him money to cover his tracks. She takes a family heirloom, an antique silver tea service, to a jeweller's to sell or pawn it. The White woman in the shop assumes she is a maid who has stolen her employer's valuables. Diahann is angry and embarrassed and leaves the shop. Apart from that scene there was very little interplay between the races. It was the story of three sisters and their relationships with one another. The male characters were sketchily drawn. They were really plot devices to move the action along. The minister was ambitious and horny and plausible. The club owner, played by Paul Winfield, was a rough diamond with a good heart, and the youngest sister's boyfriend was a juvenile male chauvinist who served as a whetstone for her to sharpen her feminist awareness on and little more. It was a matter of budget as much as artistry. The money was being spent on the *Sisters*.

We slipped into a back pew. The choir scene was being shot again. Maya spotted me and gave me the high sign. I beckoned her over and introduced her to Henry. She was in high spirits. 'Stick around,' she told Henry. 'You're in for a treat. Diahann is really singing this morning.'

Bobby and company were strategically mingled in the choir and miked for volume. They started the scene again. It was different. Diahann's voice was full and rich and she was sexy and sad at the same time. I watched Bobby Jones singing full voice and flat out and noticed that a camera was focusing on the New Life singers in turn. After an hour I sensed that Henry had seen enough and I certainly had. We waved to Maya and strolled back to the car.

'You seem to be pretty friendly with Maya Angelou?'

'I try to be. We're married and it isn't always easy. I'm sure you know how that goes.' His cool was shaken for the first time.

'You! You're married to her? Honestly?'

'Honestly.'

He started to laugh. 'You told me you were married to one of the producers and of course I thought . . .'

'. . . my wife was White . . . of course . . .'

'I saw her sing in Chicago, years ago.'

213

'How was she?'

'She was making it. She was singing in the White clubs. That was making it in those days. Still is. And you're married to her . . . that explains something that's been puzzling me.'

'What's that?'

'The way you got in the car and went for a ride with me. No questions, and you didn't seem nervous. A White American wouldn't have done that. Not a southerner anyway. He'd have smiled and joked and made some excuse. I thought maybe it was because you were a foreigner. But of course you're around Black folks all the time. Well, what would you like to do now?'

'Could we go and see Martin Luther King's church? Then if you know a nice bar I'll buy you a drink.'

'I think I can arrange that. Let me make a stop on the way.'

He drove towards the outskirts of town. The general look was suburban bordering on rural. He turned into a complex of single-storey buildings with open land around and beyond it. A sign said EVER-GREEN MORTUARY AND CHAPEL OF REST. Henry parked in a reserved parking space. 'Come on. I'll show you around my place.' It was my turn to be surprised.

'You! You're a mortician? Honestly?'

'Honestly.'

We went in through the reception office where two young men in dark suits looked very alert and willing to please. They hardly looked old enough to have graduated from high school. Henry spent a few moments with them checking on messages and business details and then led me off for a tour. He apologised for the lack of a cadaver that would have shown his state-of-the-art cold storage facility off to its best advantage. 'I'm not getting my share of business in this town.'

'Is this a profitable business?' I asked.

'Not for me. I'm losing money every week. But they won't break me.'

'What does it take to make it profitable?'

'You have to be in business for fifty years. A hundred years is even better. I'm a Johnny-come-lately and the other morticians are shutting me out. But I won't give up. If I got a fair share of cadavers I would be doing fine, but . . .'

'How long can you keep going?'

'Forever. I have another business in Chicago. I own three cocktail lounges on the Southside. They're all very profitable.'

'What made you choose Montgomery? We're a long way from Chicago.'

'I grew up here. I was a dark-complexioned kid from the wrong side of the tracks. I didn't talk like the aristocrats. My first job was sweeping up and running errands at one of the old-established Black funeral homes. I was hard-working, I knew I was smart and honest but they let me know I had no future. My hair was too nappy and skin was too dark . . . As soon as I was old enough I got the train to Chicago. Now I commute between here and there. I'm going to make it. Come back and see me in ten years.'

As we rode to Martin Luther King's church on Dexter Avenue I thought about the Paul Winfield character in the film. The tough boy from the wrong side of the tracks in love with the middle sister but forbidden from seeing her because her Pullman-porter father despises him as a social inferior. Too nappy-haired and too dark-skinned.

After visiting the church we went for a drink. Henry was cool and gracious again, his ferocity had gone back under cover. I did my best to answer his questions about film-making and the story.

'You know something I noticed,' he said. 'All the actors are Black but all the technical crew is White.'

'Hard to get into that side of the business. Like breaking into the undertaking business, I guess.'

'But your wife is a producer. So it can be done.'

When Maya came back to Los Angeles after the location work was finished she was in good spirits. Filming the rest of the movie at Twentieth Century seemed to be a breeze. I suppose that is why location work is done first while everybody is energetic and sane.

The finished film looked good. It could have been better, of course, but it was done within budget and on time. I particularly liked the performances of Paul Winfield and Irene Cara. Rosalind Cash, who played the tough and sexy middle sister, did not come off right for me on the screen, but other people thought she was fine.

Our lease was up and Maya was anxious to start work on her next book and homesick for Northern California. The Sonoma house was sold so we packed our furniture, put it in storage and went to stay with Bob and Jessica.

After a couple of days' hectic reunion Jessica started looking through the newspaper ads to find us a house. We had no money to speak of so the plan was to find something we could lease with an option to buy when cash flow picked up. Maya and Jessica went out to look at a house on Christmas Eve morning and then sent Bob and I to check it out that afternoon. It was an Art Deco monster high up in the Oakland Hills with huge rooms, a maid's apartment and grand views. I thought it was wonderful. There was no way we could afford it, but I enjoyed walking round it. Bob insisted on talking to the real estate broker anyway so we went on to the office. We had planned for him to do the talking and break off when I gave him a signal. I would put my hand to my forehead and say I wanted to walk outside for a smoke. At that point we would leave and regroup.

Bob started hard-nosed negotiation before I realised what was happening. He started to dicker about down payments and carrying back loans and I put my hand to my forehead and said I wanted to smoke. I was ignored. The tough broker started drafting up a purchase contract. I coughed and banged my hand to my forehead and demanded to go outside for a cigarette. He noticed eventually and we went out to the sidewalk.

'We've almost got a deal! Let's get back in there.'

'You're talking about twenty thousand dollars cash down payment, Bob, for Christ's sake. We're busted, don't you understand? Like Janis Joplin and Bobby McGee.' I sang for him, 'Busted flat in Baton Rouge, waiting for a train, our spirits near as faded as our jeans . . .'

'I've got twenty thousand dollars lying around somewhere I can lend you. Let's get back and do the deal while it's hot.'

The deal was done that day and papers signed during a Christmas party at their house. I thanked Bob for his generous loan.

'Nothing generous about it,' muttered Bob. 'Only way I could get my damned spare room back.'

We stood out on the terrace of our new house admiring the San Francisco Bay and the clear, starry night.

'We're up the hill again. Little bit higher this time. And still you rise.' I held my champagne glass up to toast her. 'Mud in your eye, babe.'

Maya clinked glasses. 'Looking at you, kid.'

The bad news was that the network premiere of Sister Sister had been postponed because John Berry was demanding credit for co-authorship. The dispute was going to arbitration with the Writers'

Guild. So *that* was what he was setting up during those afternoons of tedium he had inflicted on Maya. Co-authorship of a night-time soap could be like co-ownership of a little gold-mine.

'Pompous little weasel!' was my comment.

'Why do you say that? You got something against weasels?'

Like most of us, I imagine, I have my private pantheon of heroes. Men and women whose existence cheers me up when the naughty world is giving me the blues. Dr Heimlich is one of them and Chester Himes another. Dr Heimlich's elegantly simple method for preventing people from choking to death saves lives every day and Chester Himes's elegantly direct prose and dovetailed plotting has been giving me pleasure for thirty years.

I learnt the 'manoeuvre' as soon as I read about it because a friend of mine choked to death about the same time I first read *Cotton Comes To Harlem*. Not long after that another friend *nearly* choked to death but he was able to get up from the dinner table, point soundlessly to his open mouth and signal that he needed to be thumped on the back. I obliged but nothing happened and he signalled for more. For thirty seconds I slammed him round the restaurant like Jake LaMotta going for the knockout and eventually shook loose the ort of meat lodged in his windpipe. Our bout enlivened dinner-hour for the other customers and left my friend with bruised ribs but otherwise none the worse for wear. However, it was a close-run thing and the memory stayed with me, so I promptly mastered the 'Heimlich'. It has a perfection for me. It's simple to do, it saves life, doesn't cost a penny and its modest inventor has not parlayed his achievement into fatuous celebrity.

Our first guests in our new home were Lesley and Chester Himes. It was an unplanned visit, originally they were lodged in an uncomfortable room behind Ishmael Reed's studio and publishing warehouse down on the rough and tumble Berkeley Waterfront.

Ishmael is not everyone's cup of tea. He spends more time than seems useful railing against Black women writers who sell more books than he does. Alice Walker, author of *The Color Purple,* is the queen bee in his bonnet and he regularly sounds off about her degrading portrayals of Black men but he has shots in his locker for any of the Black feminists who cross his sights. Besides publishing he writes novels, plays, dabbles in journalism, teaches at Berkeley University and spreads himself thin in all directions. I rather like Ishmael. His novels are sloppy, picaresque romps that crackle with energy, and his plays are peopled with venomous caricatures of whoever happens to be pissing him off that year. The last play of his I saw portrayed a vain Oakland mayor (Black), teetering on senility while he sold out the city to White property tycoons. Mrs Mayor is a White snob who detests 'niggers' and ignores the fact that her youngest son is a crack cocaine wholesaler under his father's protection. It got mixed revues; it was generally praised for verisimilitude but criticised for lack of 'stage carpentry'. It played in Oakland.

In the course of a vinous conversation I once compared his work to the writings of eighteenth-century English novelists and satirists. With the impeccable vanity of the true artist, he was perfectly comfortable in the company of Fielding and Pope and simply expressed a glum wish that his critics were as perceptive as myself. Later, he suggested he could arrange a fellowship for me to write a thesis on his eighteenth-century roots. He felt I was the person to do it because so far I was the only person who had dug them up. Ishmael actually reminds me of that splendid literary journeyman, William Hazlitt, who quarrelled with everyone he ever met and whose dying words were, 'I have had a happy life'.

Ishmael had invited the Himes over from Spain for a writers conference he was organising and had invited Maya and me to meet them at an informal lunch. The Berkeley Waterfront was not Maya's favourite neighbourhood and Ishmael was not an uncritical admirer, but the prospect of meeting Chester Himes got her through the door. Lunch was sparse but the Himes were a delight. At seventy he was knowing and quizzical, exactly what I had imagined from his books; even in his wheelchair there was no mistaking his level-eyed toughness.

I hit it off immediately with Lesley, his English wife. They lived in southern Spain where I had not been since General Franco's death and her descriptions of the amazing changes since Franco's time engrossed me. I was so caught up in our conversation that I almost missed noticing that Chester was choking. I got him out of the chair and did a 'Heimlich'. He was frailer than I realised and I was heavier-handed than I meant to be. His dentures popped out of his mouth along with whatever had closed off his windpipe. He caught his breath for a moment while he realised what had happened, then nodded and smiled. 'Thanks for that,' he whispered. I nodded and recovered his false teeth. A perfect moment when one of my heroes came to the aid of another in his hour of need.

We arranged for them to move in with us and I rigged up ramps to make the house wheelchair-accessible. We enjoyed their company for a couple of weeks. They were a self-sufficient pair with plenty to talk about and between both of them they didn't seem to have two clichés to rub together. It was an auspicious debut for our new home.

The house had been designed and built in the early Forties for a childless couple who obviously liked to entertain on a generous scale. A huge living-room with bay views 'flowed' into a large and fully equipped bar. We bought it from a divorcing couple who had spent a year renovating and restoring it to the original Art Deco style but had never moved in because their marriage had not survived the stress of remodelling. Perhaps, with hindsight, we should have been warned by the house's history. Our marriage didn't survive the house either.

Actually it was grand to look at but not really very comfortable. Maya started writing her fourth volume of autobiography but couldn't find a cosy spot to work in so she drove every day down to Solomon Grundy's, a large bar restaurant on the Berkeley Marina, and settled to a seven a.m. till noon stint sitting at a bay-view table in the bar. It seemed to be working for her but it was a change of style. She had always worked at home before and in seclusion, but now she seemed to enjoy the added element of public performance.

Our home life became more and more a public performance, too. I was working in Arlene Slaughter's real estate office nine hours a day and six days a week and was usually work-weary by dinner-time. Maya on the other hand was usually in the mood for company. She soon gathered a platoon of admirers around her. I served drinks, smiled a lot and closed my ears to familiar conversations.

Our marriage began to seem like one of those that feminist writers had been describing during the previous decade except that in our case it was the husband, not the wife, who felt constrained and unfulfilled. Around this time I started to identify with Sheila Balantyne's heroine *Norma Jean the Termite Queen* and ponder whether shopping for groceries, serving drinks and watching Maya sing, recite and perform for an adoring audience was really all there was to middle-aged existence.

Her determination to take centre stage was nothing new to me, after all she had done exactly that the first day I met her and had continued to do it ever since, but she seemed to demand more applause now. Her psyche, the *I, Me of Me, Maya*, as she described it sometimes, had taken a bruising in the previous five years. Her months of effort to bring her musical *And Still I Rise* to the Broadway stage had

219

come to nothing in one sudden moment of collapse, and she had quit New York in the blink of an eyelid. Then her film script for *I Know Why The Caged Bird Sings* had been rejected and she had angrily refused to consider rewriting it. Now months of work writing and co-producing *Sister Sister* was cans of film gathering dust and the project was mired down in credit disputes. Her right to a producing credit and sole authorship was being challenged in union arbitration and the excitement had fizzled. Oakland was the safe place she had come back to to lick her wounds and be comforted by old friends and admirers. I sympathised, but her need to see her celebrity and success reflected in the eyes of those around her fed on itself, guests who were less than adulatory dropped by the wayside and her company became her adoring chorus. There was a lot to adore but the *I, Me of Me, Paul* happened to like the spice of contention as an occasional seasoning to the pabulum of unalloyed approval.

Another factor that was beginning to distance us was that her fourth volume of autobiography involved the disillusionment of collapsed marriages. When I met her first in London she was writing about her girlish adventures on the wild side, scuffling in San Francisco's *demi-monde*. She had been sassy and devil-may-care. When we lived in Sonoma she had written about touring Europe as a fancy-free dancer and she had been mostly fancy-free. In Oakland, while she wrote *Heart of a Woman*, the sadness of her subject matter crept into the substance of our life.

My bedroom failures and omissions certainly did nothing to help our situation. Maya left me in no doubt that sexual pleasure was hers by right to receive and mine by duty to deliver. In theory I agreed with her but in practice it often didn't work out that way. At her stern request I visited doctors for exhaustive check-ups that proved beyond doubt that I wasn't as young as I used to be. I started seeing a woman therapist in Berkeley and spent four unstimulating and outrageously expensive hours engaged in conversations, the purpose of which totally escaped me.

Then a letter came from England that put all our marital problems on hold. Peter, my younger son whom I had not seen since he was a toddler, wrote and proposed a year-long visit. I was dizzy with excitement when I saw him coming through Customs at San Francisco airport, miraculously grown to six-foot-three-tall, handsome enough and curly-haired like his mother. We stopped off at Solomon Grundy's on our way to Oakland. For some reason it seemed appropriate because it was the first place in California Maya and I had sat together, sipped wine and gazed at the Golden Gate Bridge. The leather armchairs and thick carpets had grown worn and shabby in the intervening decade, rather like our marriage. I mentioned to Peter that Maya wrote there in the mornings at a bay-view table. He raised his eyebrows, 'Is that normal?'

'As normal as anything else writers do. Thomas Heywood wrote his plays in taverns on the backs of menus. It's a grand tradition.'

'Who's Tom Heywood?'

'A Jacobean playwright . . . *A Woman Killed With Kindness* . . . ring a bell?'

He shook his head. I shook mine. 'What do they teach you in college these days?'

'Economic History, in my case . . . I'm thinking of dropping out.'

'Most people do at one time or another. But most people don't in the end.'

Maya enchanted Peter, but when Jimmy Baldwin came to visit with his new companion he was on his guard.

Jimmy had not long finished *Just Above My Head,* the semi-auto-biographical novel that he had talked about as an idea in Sonoma and read from as a work in progress in Malibu. It was obviously not an easy book to write and he was weary and disoriented most of the time. His conversation had become more elliptical than ever, a word here, a phrase there, a punchline without the rest of the joke, a truncated aphorism . . . Peter found him hard going. I could sympathise, I recalled my own college days listening to William Empson, a poet who led the field in ambiguity, give the same answer to twelve successive questions at a seminar. His single response to everyone was, 'Bunny rabbits, it's all about bunny rabbits. Hippity, hippity, hop!'

We had hired him to speak to the Sceptics Society and after the twelfth answer we got very sceptical about paying him his honorarium. Our mistake had been to take him to the pub before the meeting.

I explained to Peter that Baldwin had been writing and talking steadily for forty years so it was not surprising that in middle age he was tired of listening to himself and omitted connective phrases. Shakespeare, after all, got elliptical in his forties and fifties and wrote 'difficult' plays like *Measure for Measure* that are open to widely different interpretations.

'Is that what happens in middle age?' he asked with a twinkle in his eye.

221

IN GOOD COMPANY

'Sometimes. Sometimes we get long-winded and over-expository.'
'What about a deadly combination of the two?'
'Are you being personal?'
'If the cap fits wear it. Or . . . "th'cap . . .", as Shakespeare might
have written in a late play.'

Jimmy's companion was about Peter's age and both of them were
opinionated. Dinner conversation got fiery sometimes. My son had
not learned the trick of turning out polemics that proved their point
with the final line, 'You're not Black so you can't understand'. He was
young enough to *demand* to understand. Baldwin was anciently amused
when sparks flew between the youngsters. At one point during a family
dinner Peter bunched up his large fists and set them in clear view on
the table.

'If I can't understand anything of your experience . . . or of my own
because I am not, as you've observed, Black, then there is no further
point to this conversation. Let's conclude it.'

Maya started to giggle. I knew my cue. 'We have a level piece of
ground in the back yard if you two want to settle this man to man.'

'The fruit doesn't fall too far from the tree,' laughed Maya. 'You
may not know it, Peter dear, but your father once challenged a
journalist in a Fleet Street pub to a fist fight in the car park to establish
the precise meaning of "Conscience doth make cowards of us all".'

'The meaning's perfectly obvious,' said Peter.

'No, it's ambiguous. But then of course you read Economic History.'

'And that means I can't understand Shakespeare? Want to step
outside and settle this, Paul?'

Our distintegrating marriage became a subtheme to Peter's visit. In
our quirky way we were 'staying together for the sake of the child'.
Something neither of us had ever done before with any other partners.
Neither of us was any good at it. One evening when I got in late from
enjoying adultery, Maya saw through my feeble alibi and threw me out
of the house. It had been a long time since I had enjoyed adultery. In
fact the last time had been *with* Maya years before in London.

Next morning I went back to see her. She intercepted me on the
driveway and thumped me with a roundhouse right. It had been a long
time since she laid a glove on me. In fact the last time had been years
before on our first date in London. She still hit well.

Peter collected my personal belongings and a couple of pieces of
furniture and we moved into a half-remodelled house in the Oakland
flatlands. A few days later Maya and I met up in Bob Treuhaft's

222

office and settled divorce terms in twenty minutes. Then we went to the corner bar for a farewell drink. She decided she was hungry.

'What about a chicken sandwich?' I teased.

'Chicken would be *good*!' The words were out of her mouth before she realised I was joshing. We started to laugh. I remembered a story she told about another marital break-up. She was in West Africa, her husband was gone and she had just put her beloved son on a plane back to the States. Her life was in tatters and she was all alone. At that poignant moment, her only thought was at last I get to eat the breast of chicken all to myself.

Not long after she accepted a professorship in North Carolina and it was time for Peter to return to England. He helped her pack up the house then on his way home drove a pantechnicon with her furniture cross country to Winston Salem. He turned out to be a dismal failure as a college drop-out and graduated with a first-class degree instead.